ISBN 0-634-05409-0

7777 W. Bluemound Rd. P.O. Box 13819 Milwaukee, WI 53213

Visit Hal Leonard Online at
www.halleonard.com

ABOUT THIS BOOK

When playing through the transcriptions in this book, it is important to consider the following:

1. The primary keyboard part always appears directly below the vocal line.
2. Any secondary keyboard parts appear below the primary keyboard part. The instrument sound is always indicated in the measure in which the part is first played. (Sound changes are also indicated where appropriate.) In some instances, background keyboard parts, such as those involving "comping," or "playing the chords," are omitted.
3. Other prominent instrumental parts, such as string and horn lines, are also included. It is important to note that these parts are arranged so that they may be played as secondary keyboard parts. The pitches are accurate; however, the voicings of the chords may be modified to be more indicative of a keyboard approach.
4. If there is no keyboard part on the recording for an extended time, other instrumental parts are often arranged to be played by the primary keyboard part. These sections are optional and are intended to be played only if the actual instruments (such as guitar) are not available.
5. "Fill" boxes are sometimes included when a particular fill, or figure, is played on the repeat or D.S. only. A typical indication would be "Play Fill 1 (2nd time)." In some instances, minor differences on a repeat or D.S. are not notated.

The transcriptions in this book are useful in a variety of situations: with a band, with a sequencer, with a CD, or solo playing. Whatever your purpose, you can now play your favorite songs just as the artists recorded them.

CONTENTS

Against the Wind

Words and Music by
Bob Seger

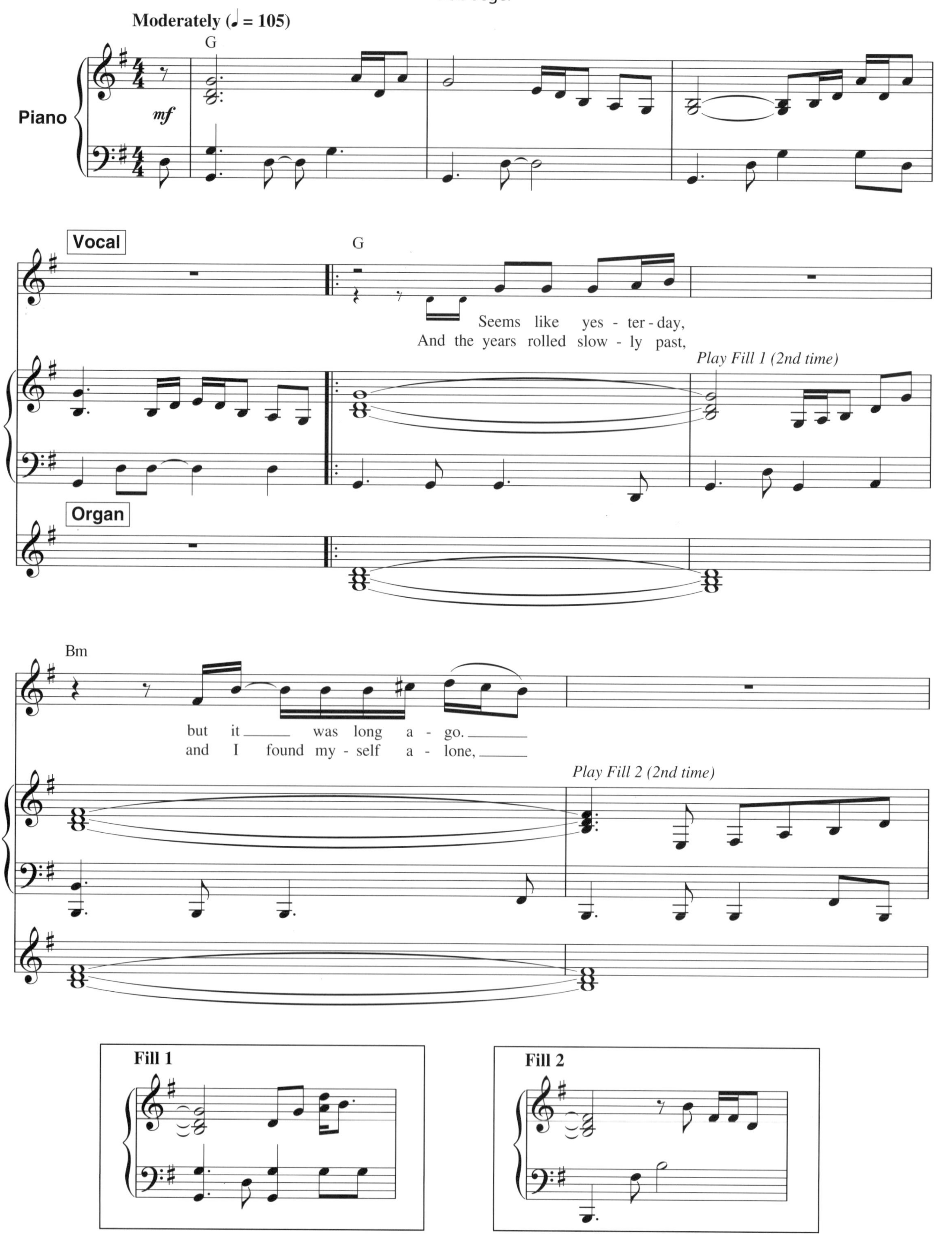

C
G
Jan - ey was love - ly, she was the queen of my nights,
sur-round - ed by stran - gers I thought were my friends.
D
C
there in the dark - ness with a ra - di - o play - in' low, and,
I found my - self fur - ther and fur - ther from my home, and I
G
and the se - crets that we shared,
guess I lost my way.
Play Fill 3 (2nd time)
Fill 3

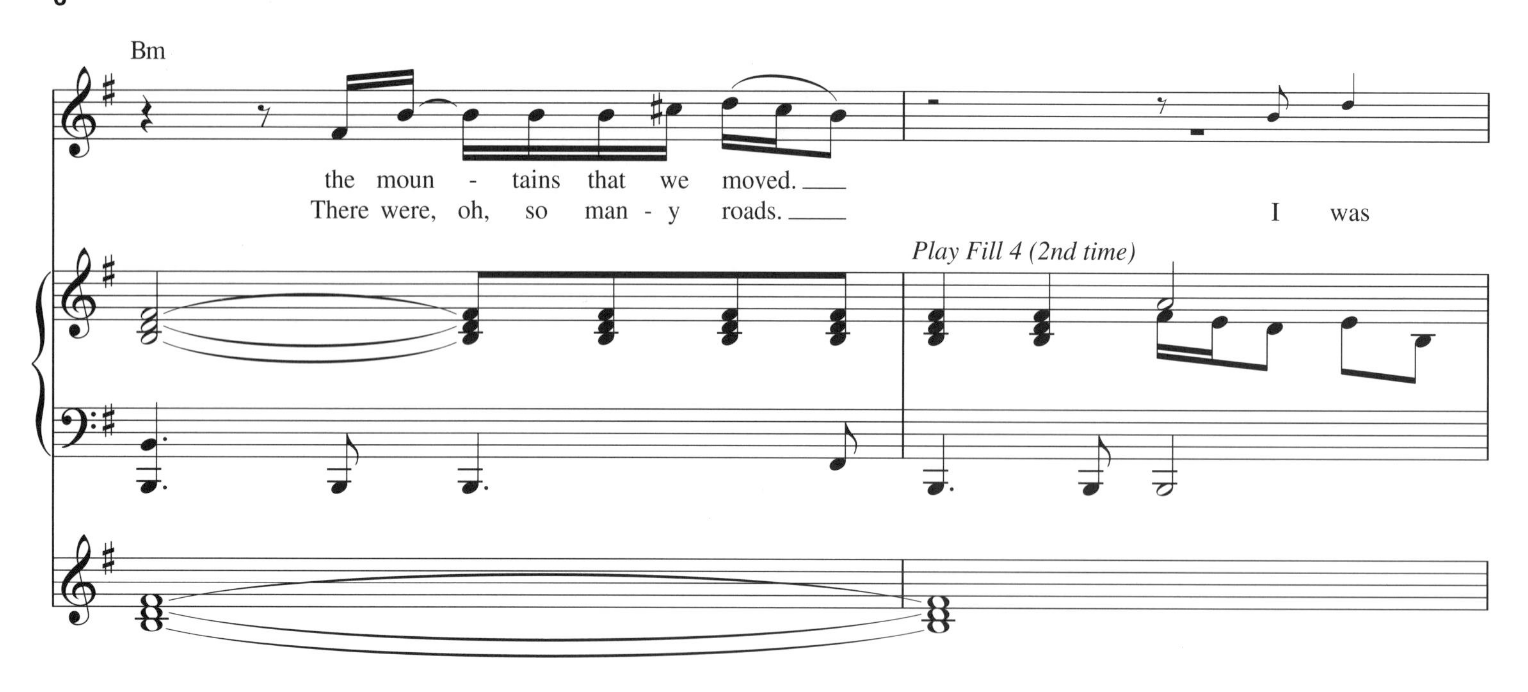
Bm
the moun - tains that we moved.
There were, oh, so man - y roads.
I was
Play Fill 4 (2nd time)

C
G
Caught like a wild - fire out of con - trol till there was
liv - in' to run and run - nin' to live, nev - er wor -

Fill 4

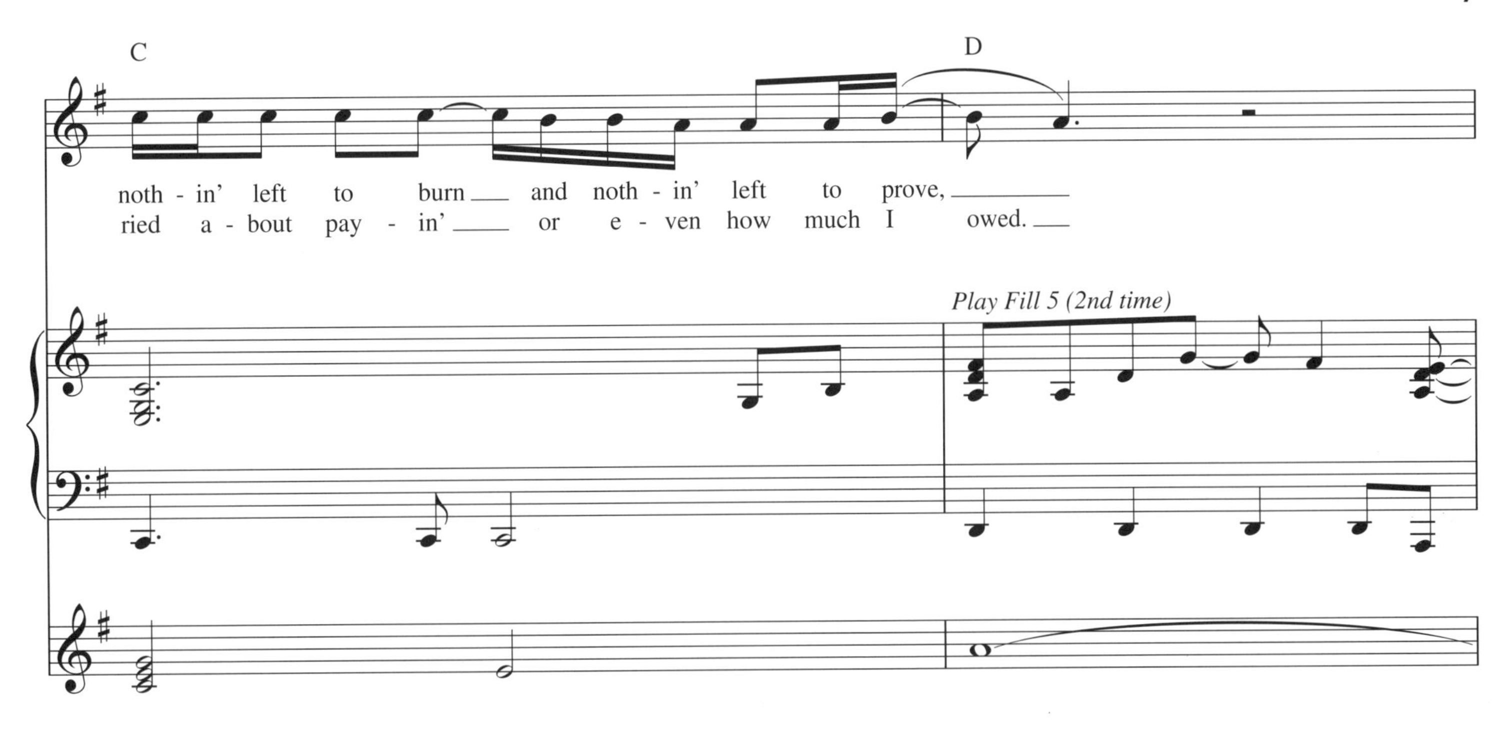
C
D
noth - in' left to burn and noth - in' left to prove,
ried a - bout pay - in' or e - ven how much I owed.
Play Fill 5 (2nd time)

Em
D
3
and I re - mem - ber what she said to
Mov - in' eight miles, a min - ute for months at a
drift - er's days are past me

Fill 5
D

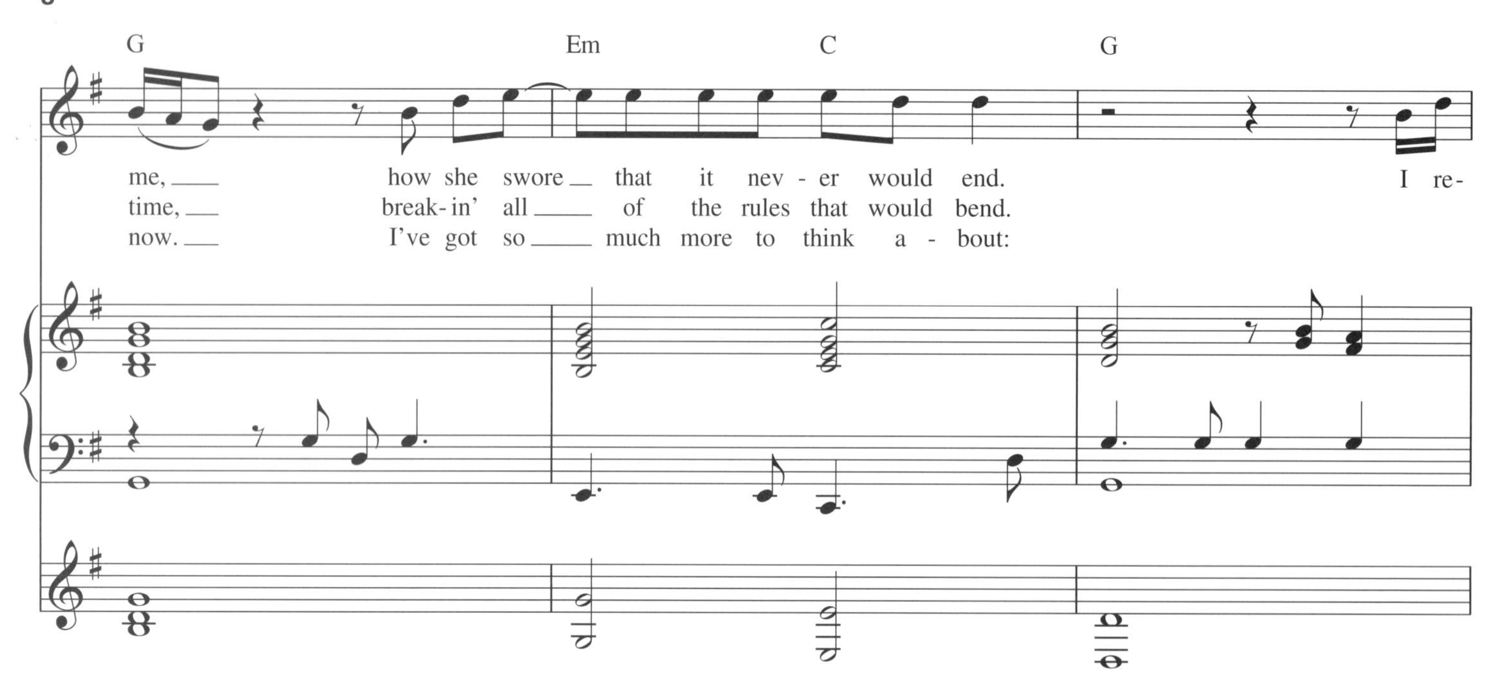
G
Em
C
G
me, how she swore that it nev - er would end. I re-
time, break-in' all of the rules that would bend.
now. I've got so much more to think a - bout:

Em
D
C
mem-ber how she held me, oh, so tight. Wish I did-n't know now what I
I be-gan to find my-self search-in', search - in' for shel-ter a-gain
dead - lines and com - mit - ments. What to leave in?
Play Fill 6 (2nd time)

Fill 6

D
G
did - n't know then.
and a - gain.
What to leave out?
A - gainst the wind.
A - gainst the wind.
A - gainst the wind.

Bm
C
G
3
We were run - nin' a - gainst the wind.
Lit - tle some - thin' a - gainst the wind.
I'm still run - nin' a - gainst the wind.
We were
I
I'm
Play Fill 7 (2nd time)

Fill 7
G

To Coda
1
C
Bm
Am
C
G
young and strong we were run - ning a - gainst the wind.
found my - self seek - ing shel - ter a - gainst the
old - er now, but still run - ning a - gainst the
2
G
Piano Solo
wind.

3
3
Bm
3
3
C
3
G
3
D
C
3
3
G
3
3
Bm
3
3

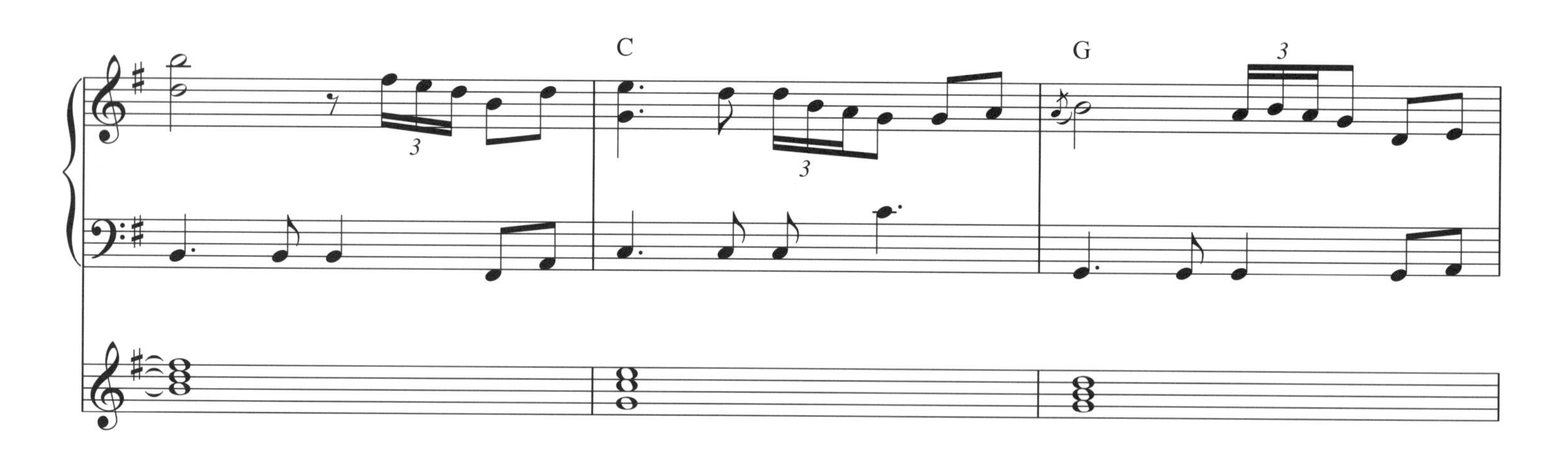
C
G

Vocal
C
D
D.S. al Coda
Solo ends
Well, those

CODA
G
wind.
Well, I'm old -

C
Bm
D
- er now and still run - nin' a - gainst the
Repeat and Fade
C
G
wind, a - gainst the wind,
Optional Ending
G
a - gainst the wind.

Beth

Words and Music by Peter Criss,
Bob Ezrin and Stan Penridge

F
G/F
C/E
Me and the boys are play - in', and we just can't find the sound.

Esus
E
Am
G
Just a few more hours and I'll
mf
Piano
Flute
mf

F
Em
D7
be right home to you. I think I hear them call -

F6
Gsus
G
Am
Gsus
- ing.
Oh,
Beth,
what
can
I
do?
F
G7sus
C
C(add2)
Beth,
what
can
I
do?
You
say
you
feel
so
emp -
Strings
8va
French Horn
F/C
G/C
Am
G
- ty,
that
our
house
just
ain't
a
home,
that
(8va)

F
G/F
C/E
3
I'm al - ways some-where else,
and you're al - ways there a - lone.

Esus
E
Am
G
Just a few more hours
and I'll
Strings

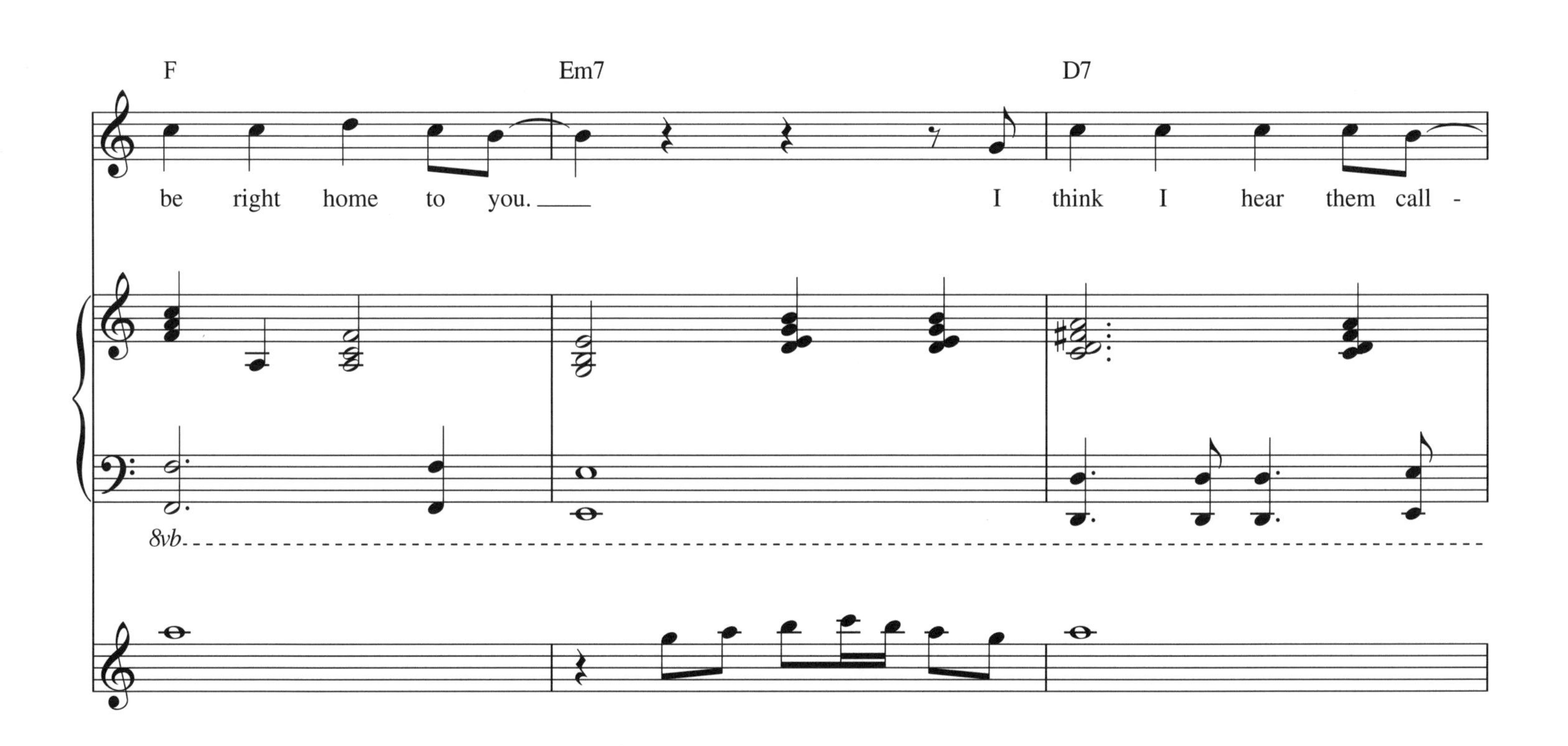
F
Em7
D7
be right home to you.
I think I hear them call -
8vb

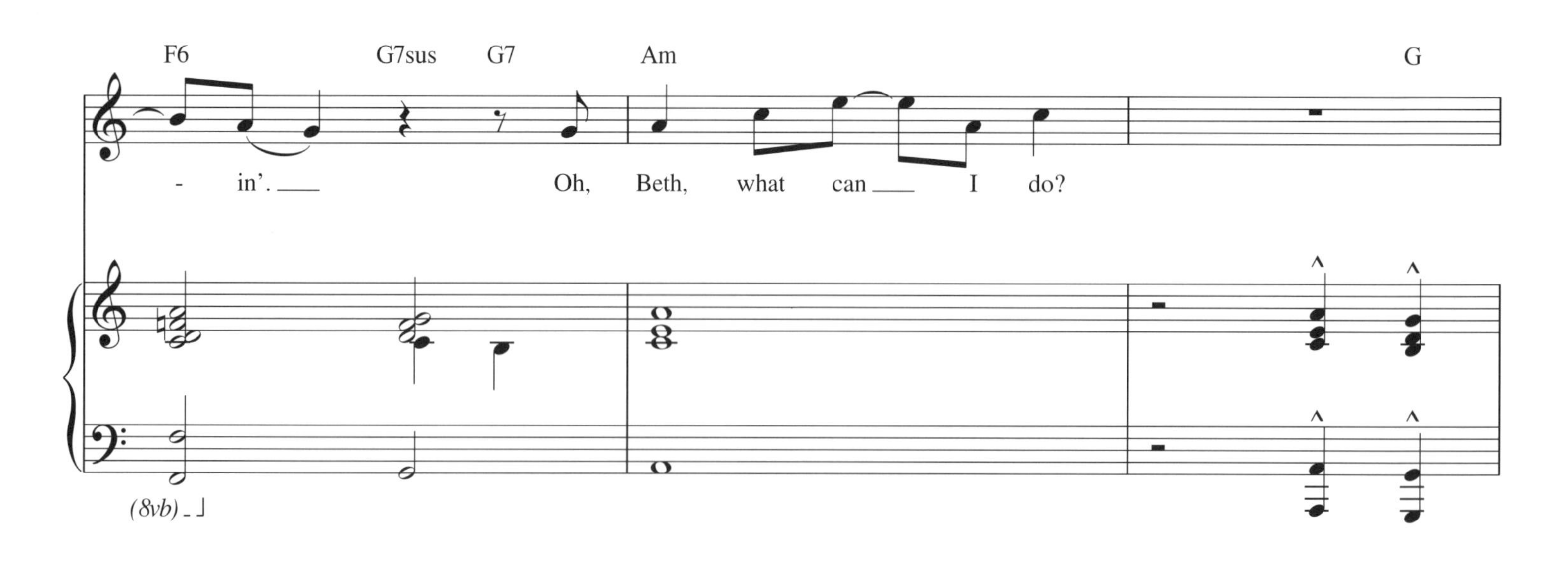
F6
G7sus
G7
Am
G
- in'. ___
Oh, Beth, what can ___ I do?
(8vb)

F
F/G
C(add2)
Beth, what can ___ I do? ___
Strings

Csus
G/C
C(add2)

Csus
Esus
3
E
Strings
Am
G
F
Em7
D7
F6
G7

Am
G
F
G7sus
C
Brass
Brass
Vocal
C(add2)
F6/C
Beth, I know you're lone - ly, and I
mp
Strings
8va
mp
Cmaj9
Am
G
F
hope you'll be al - right. 'cause me and the boys will be play -

G7
C
in'
all
night.
poco rit.
a tempo
Strings
Csus
G/C
C(add2)
Ah.
Csus
G
G7
C
poco rit.
poco rit.
Oboe & French Horn
Strings
poco rit.

Bloody Well Right

Words and Music by Rick Davies
and Roger Hodgson

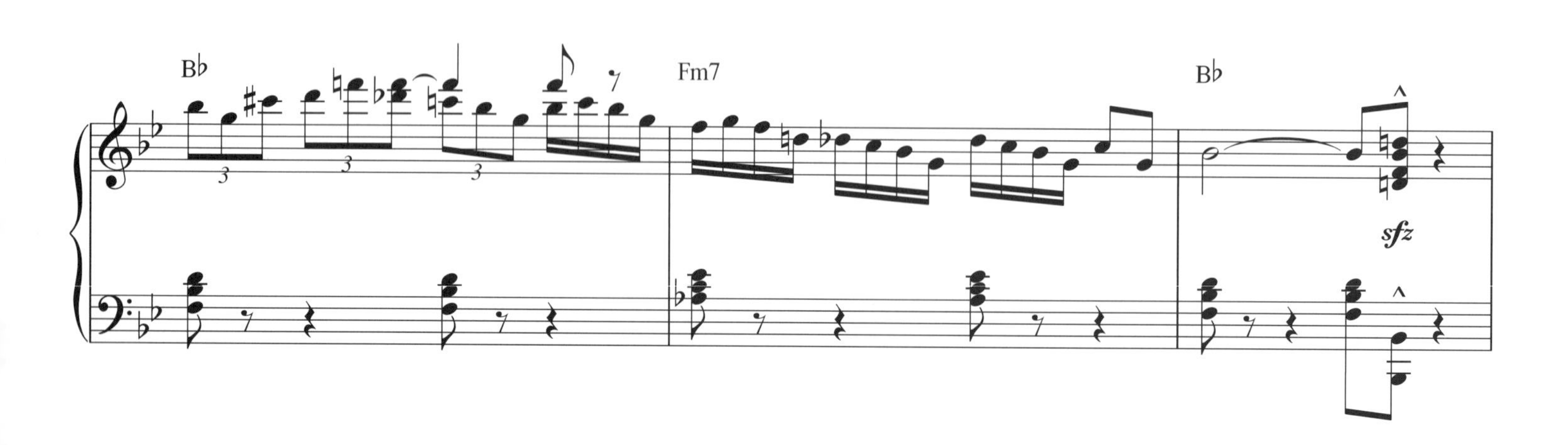

Fm7
B♭
Fm7

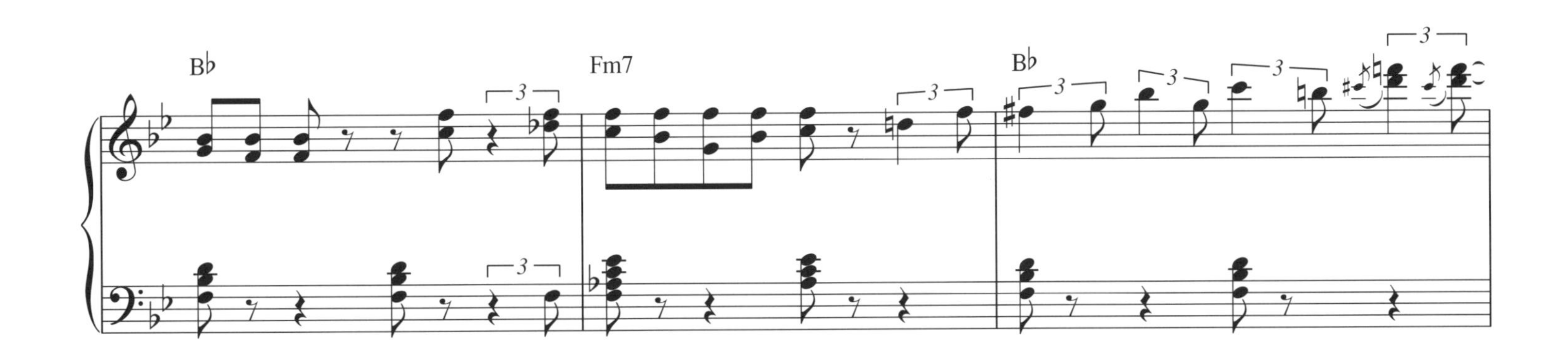
B♭
Fm7
B♭
3

Fm7
B♭
A♭maj7
Fm7
sfz
sfz
3

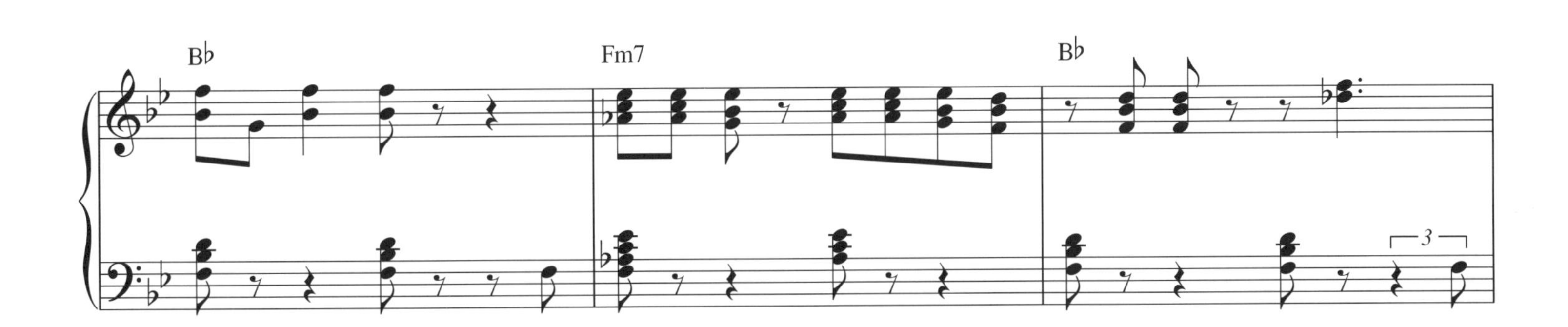
B♭
Fm7
B♭
3

Fm7
B♭
Fm7
3

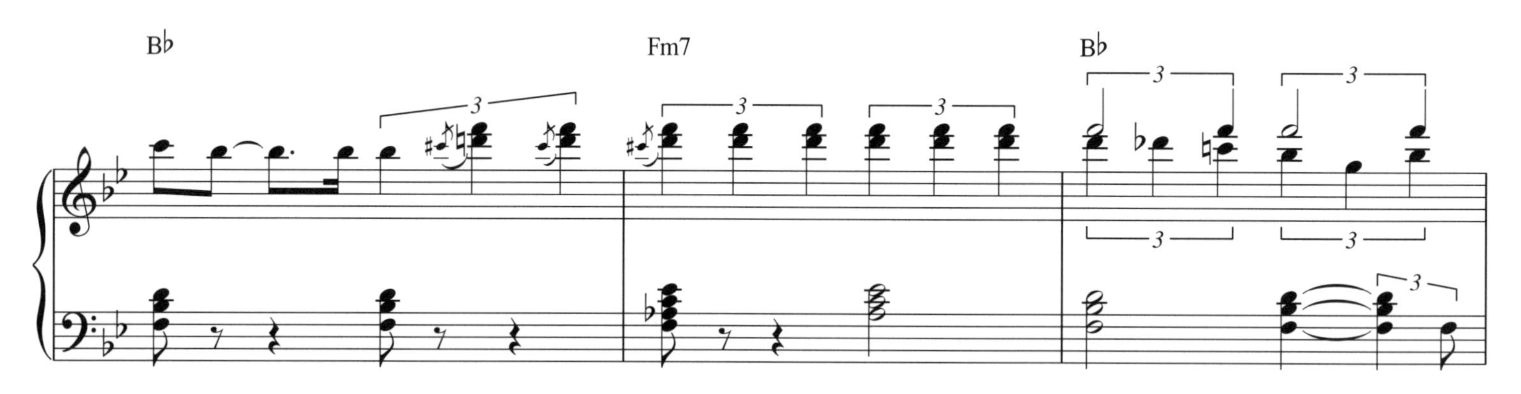
B♭
Fm7
B♭
3

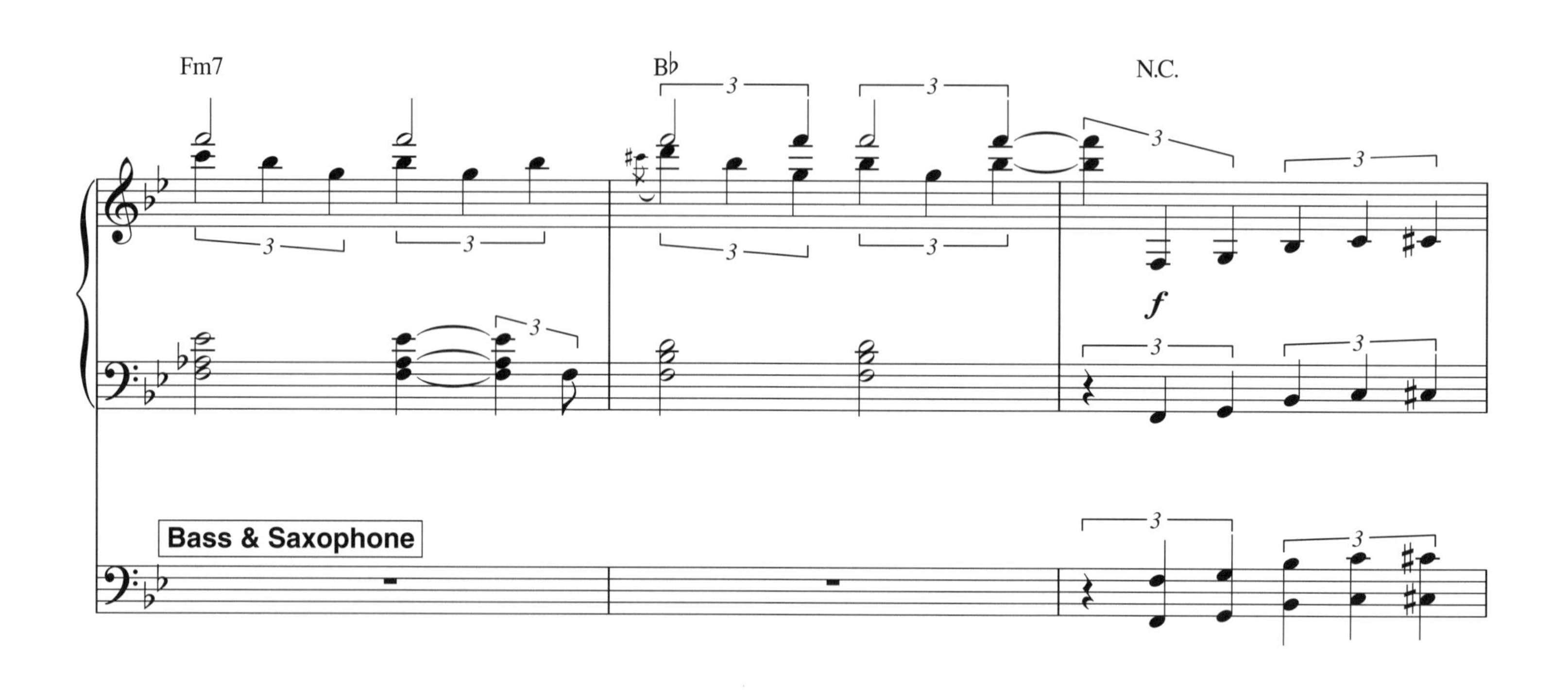
Fm7
B♭
N.C.
3
f
Bass & Saxophone

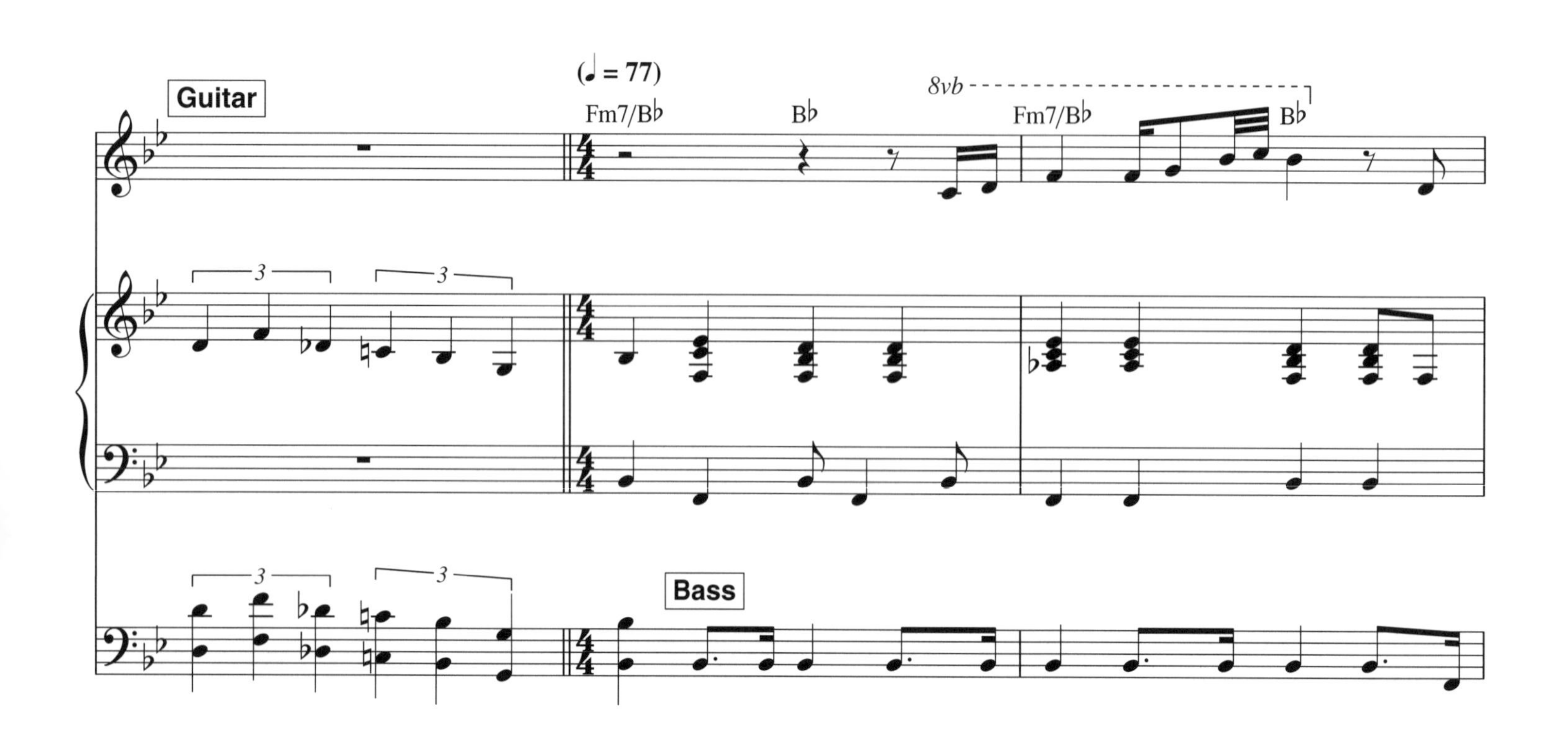
Guitar
(♩ = 77)
Fm7/B♭
B♭
8vb
Fm7/B♭
B♭
3
Bass

Fm7/B♭
B♭
Fm7/B♭
B♭
Fm7/B♭
B♭
Fm7/B♭
B♭
Fm7/B♭
B♭
Fm7/B♭
B♭
Fm7/B♭
B♭
Fm7/B♭
B♭

Fm7/B♭
B♭
Fm7/B♭
B♭
Vocal
(1st time only)
Guitar
Bass
G5
B♭5
C5
G5
B♭5
F5
So you think your school-ing's phon-y,
Write your prob - lems down in de-tail
I guess it's hard not to a - gree.
and take them to a high-er place.
You say it all de-pends on
You had your cry, no, I should-n't

G5
Bb5 F5
G5
Bb5
C5
G5
Bb5 F5
mon - ey
say wail.
and who is in your fam - 'ly tree.
In the mean - time hush your face.
Fm7/Ab
Eb(add2)/Bb
Eb/Bb
Bb
Right, (right,) you're blood-y well right, you got a blood-y right to say.
Electric Piano
mf
Electric Piano
Electric Piano
Fm7
Eb(add2)/Bb
Eb/Bb
Bb
Right, you're blood-y well right, you know you got a right to say.

Fm7
E♭(add2)/G
E♭/G
B♭/F
Ha, ha, you're blood-y well right, you know you're right to say.
Fm7
E♭(add2)
E♭/G
B♭/F
Yeah, yeah, you're blood-y well right, you know you're right to say, and
Yeah, yeah, you're blood-y well right, you know you got a right to say.
1
A♭/B♭
B♭
A
A♭
G5
B♭
C
me I don't care an-y-way.
Saxes
Guitar
Bass
f

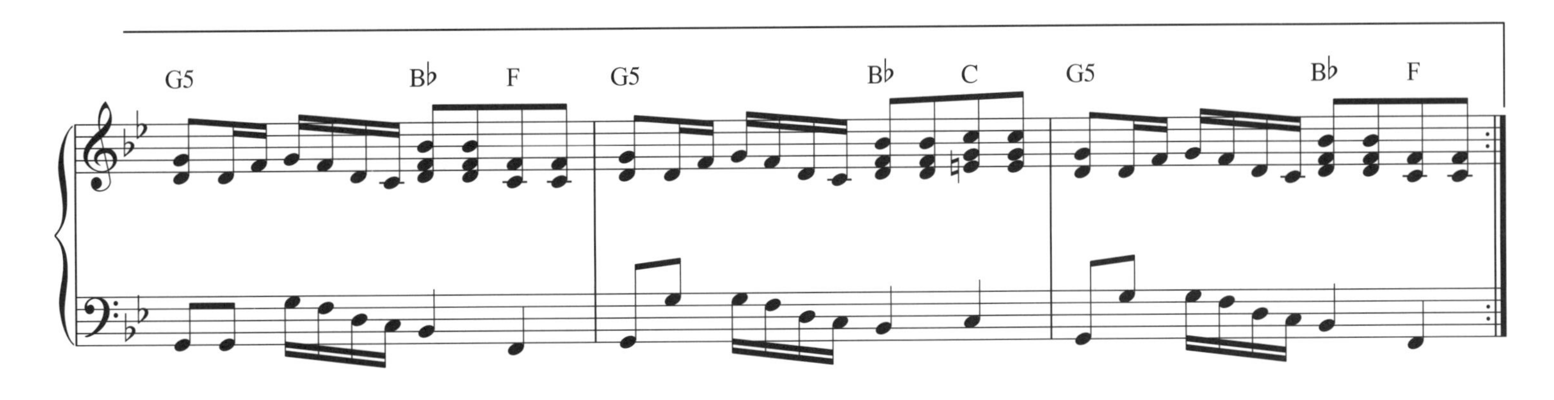
G5
B♭
F
G5
B♭
C
G5
B♭
F

2 Repeat and Fade
Fm7/B♭
B♭
Fm7/B♭
B♭
You got a blood - y right to say.
Electric Piano
Electric Piano
Bass

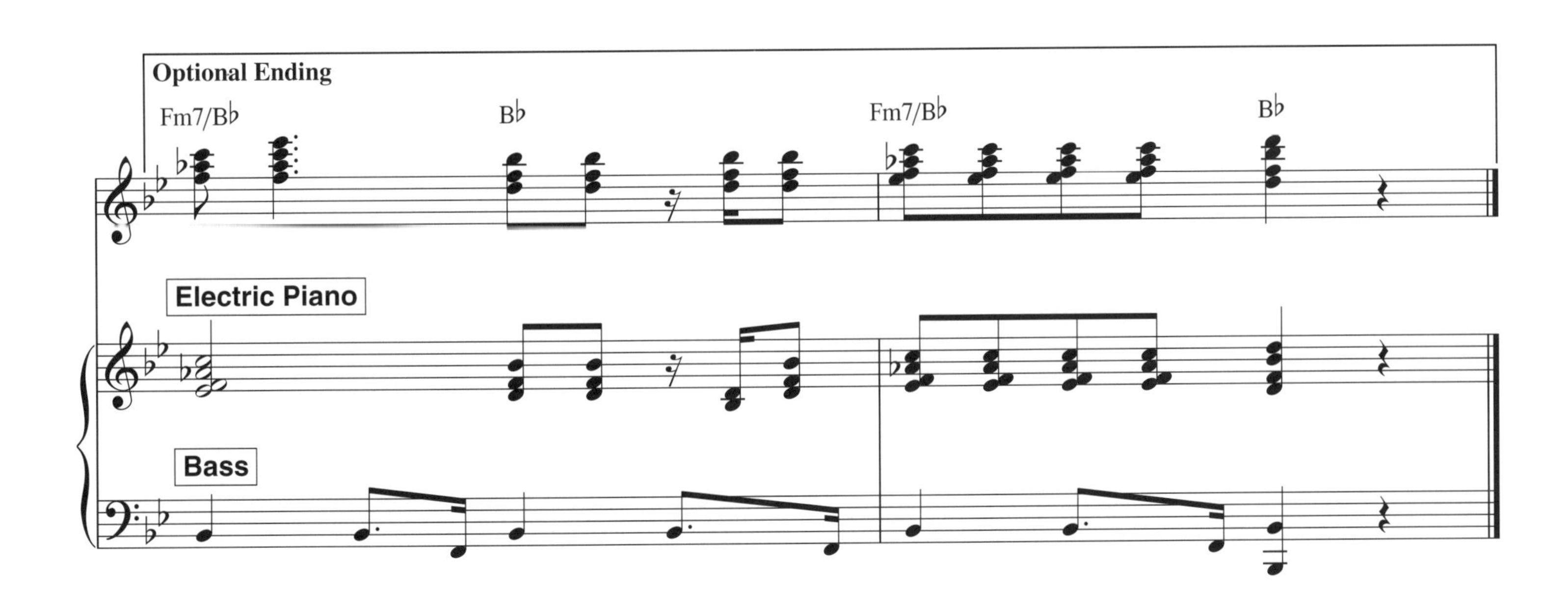
Optional Ending
Fm7/B♭
B♭
Fm7/B♭
B♭
Electric Piano
Bass

Changes

Words and Music by
David Bowie

F G F C
time was run-ning wild. A mil-lion dead - end streets and ev-'ry time I thought I'd
never leave the stream of warm im - per - ma - nence, and so the days flow
Play Fill 2 (2nd time)
Em F G
got it made it seemed the taste was not so sweet. So I
through my eyes, but still the days seem the same. And these
Play Fill 3 (2nd time)
Cmaj7 Dm7 Em7 E♭m7 Dm7
turned my - self to face me, but I've nev - er caught a glimpse
chil - dren that you spit on as they try to change their worlds
3
Fill 2
Fill 3

G7 Cmaj7 Dm7 Em7 E♭m7
how the oth - ers must see the fak - er. I'm much too
are im - mune to your con - sul - ta - tions. They're quite a -
Dm7 G F C C/B
fast to take that test.
ware what they're going through.
(Ch, ch, ch, ch, chang - es.) Turn and face the strange.
cresc.
mf
Am7 C/G F F/E D7
(Ch, ch, chang - es.)
Don't want to be a rich - er man.
Don't tell them to grow up and out of it.
G F C C/B Am7 C/G
(Ch, ch, ch, ch, chang - es.) Turn and face the strange. (Ch, ch, chang - es.)

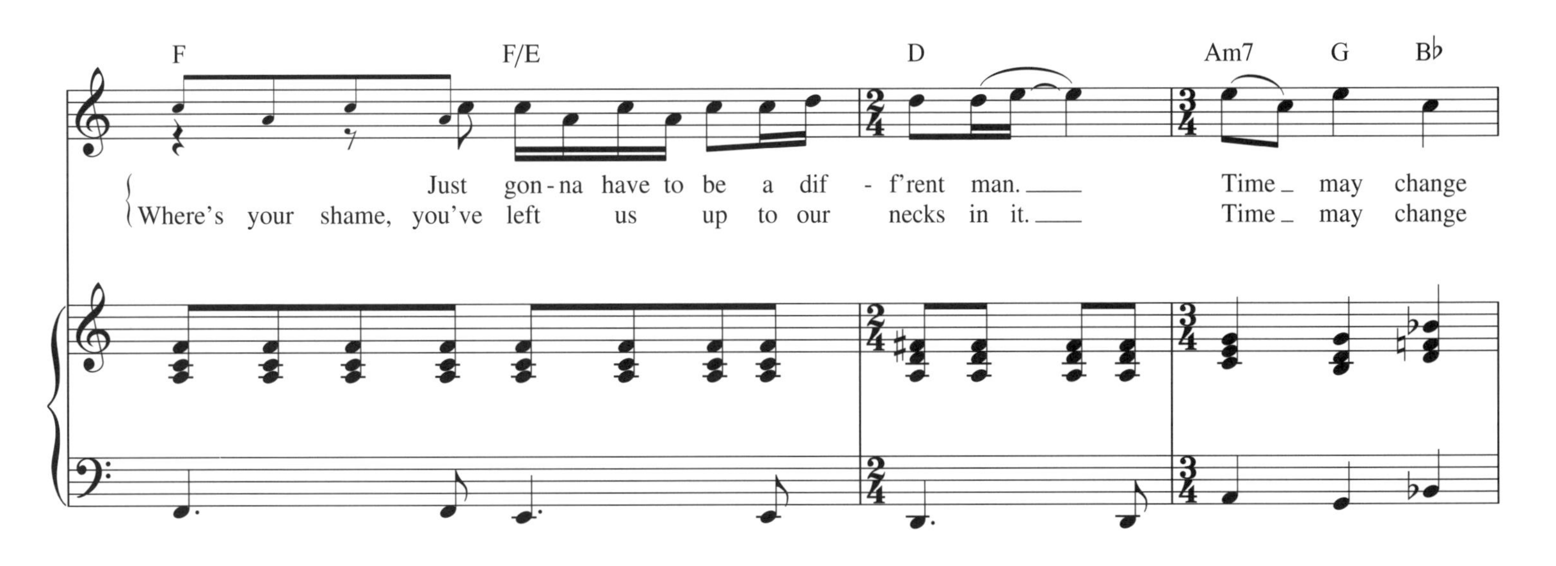
F
F/E
D
Am7
G
B♭
Just gon-na have to be a dif - f'rent man.
Time may change
Where's your shame, you've left us up to our necks in it.
Time may change

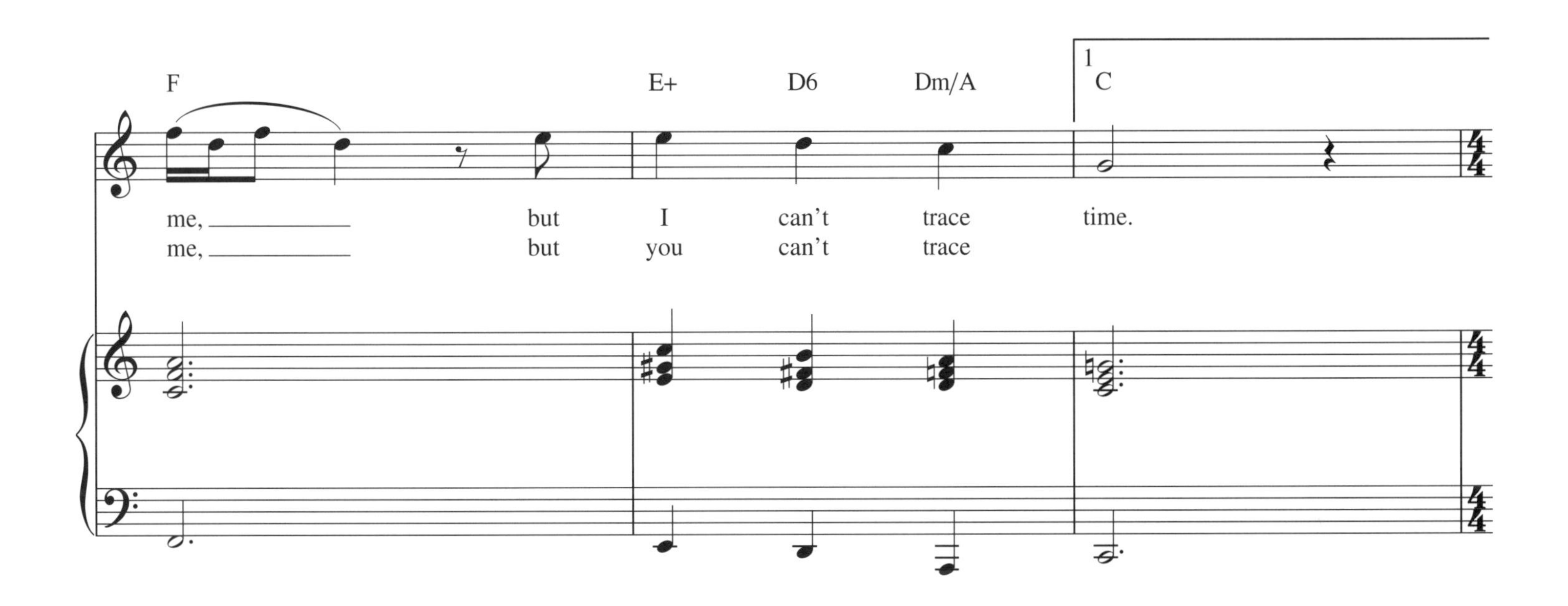
F
E+
D6
Dm/A
1
C
me, but I can't trace time.
me, but you can't trace

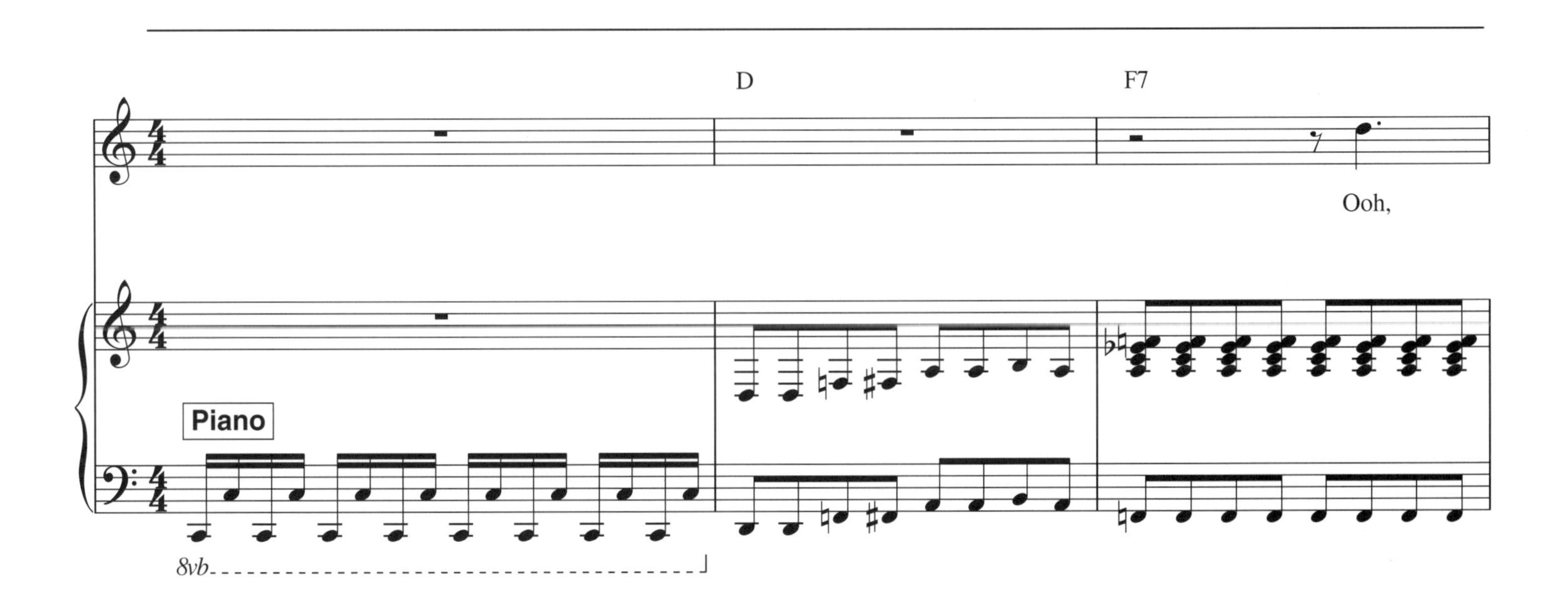
D
F7
Ooh,
Piano
8vb

2
D
F7
C
Dm7
Em7
yeah.
time.
F
C
F/C
Strange fas - ci - na - tion fas - ci - nat - ing me.
C
F
Ah, chang - es are tak - ing the
G
F
C
C/B
pace I'm go - ing through. (Ch, ch, ch, ch, chang - es.) Turn and face the strange.

Am7
C/G
F
F/E
D
(Ch, ch, chang - es.)
Oh, look out, you rock 'n' roll - ers.
G
F
C
C/B
Am7
C/G
(Ch, ch, ch, ch, chang - es.) Turn and face the strange. (Ch, ch, chang - es.)
F
F/E
D
Am
G
B♭
Pret - ty soon now you're gon - na get old - er.
Time may change
F
E+
D6
Dm/A
C
me, but I can't trace time.
I said that

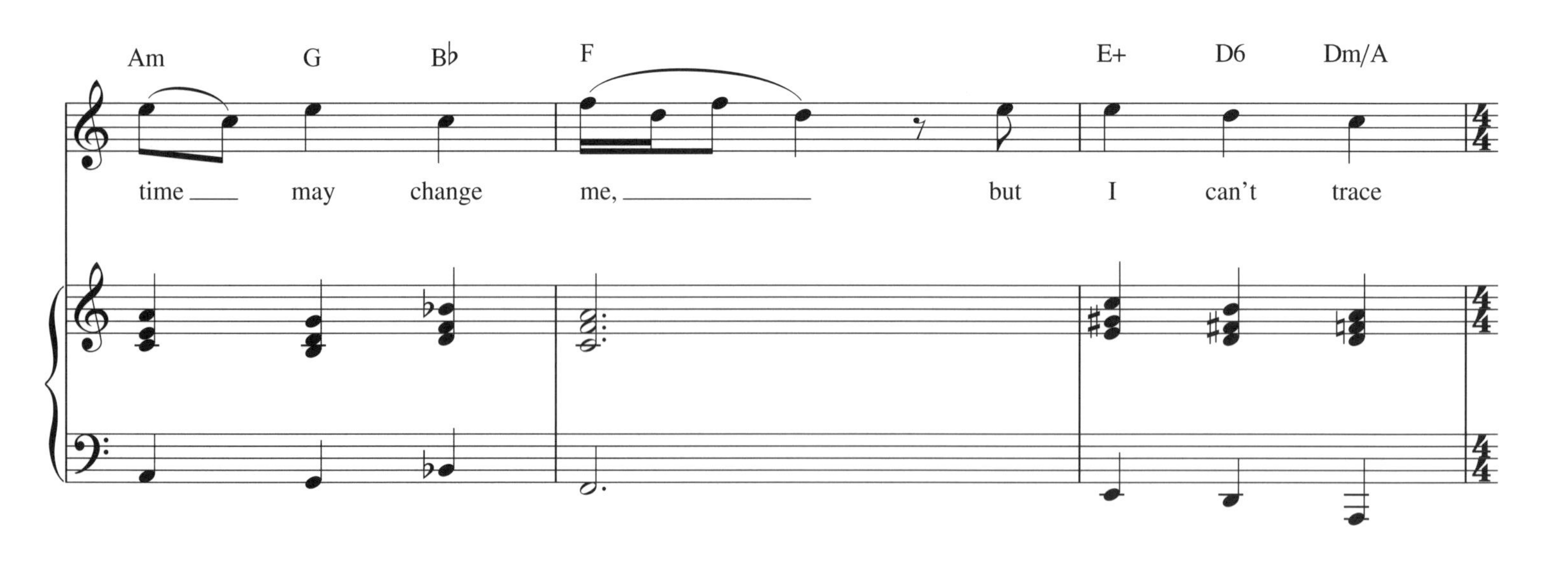
Am G B♭ F E+ D6 Dm/A
time may change me, but I can't trace

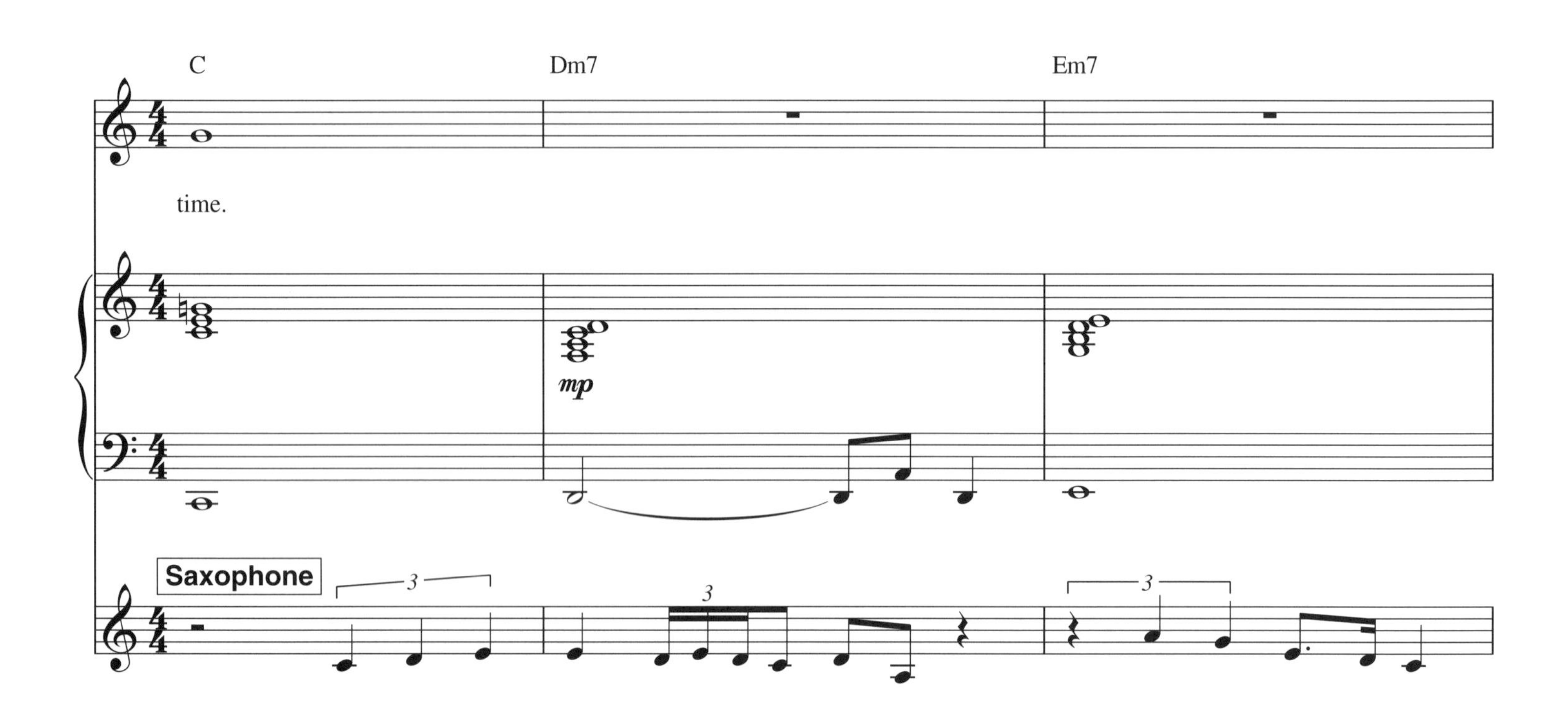
C Dm7 Em7
time.
mp
Saxophone

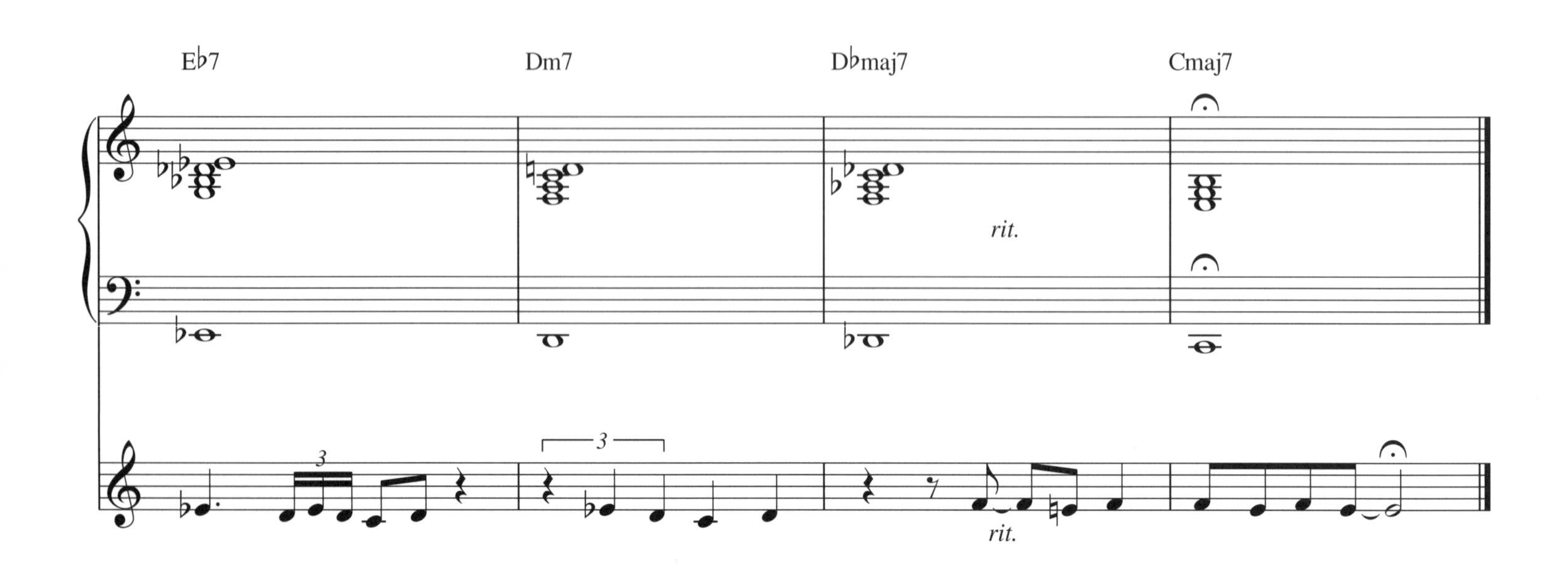
E♭7 Dm7 D♭maj7 Cmaj7
rit.
rit.

Come Sail Away

Words and Music by
Dennis DeYoung

G
C
vir - gin sea,
'cause I've
Em/B
Am
G
got to be free,
F
G
3
free to face the life that's a - head of me.
Am
On board I'm the cap - tain,

G
Am
so climb a - board.
We'll search for to-
8va
mor - row
G
on ev - 'ry shore.
And I'll
3
C
Em/B
Am
try,
oh, Lord,
I'll
try
G
F
G
to car - ry

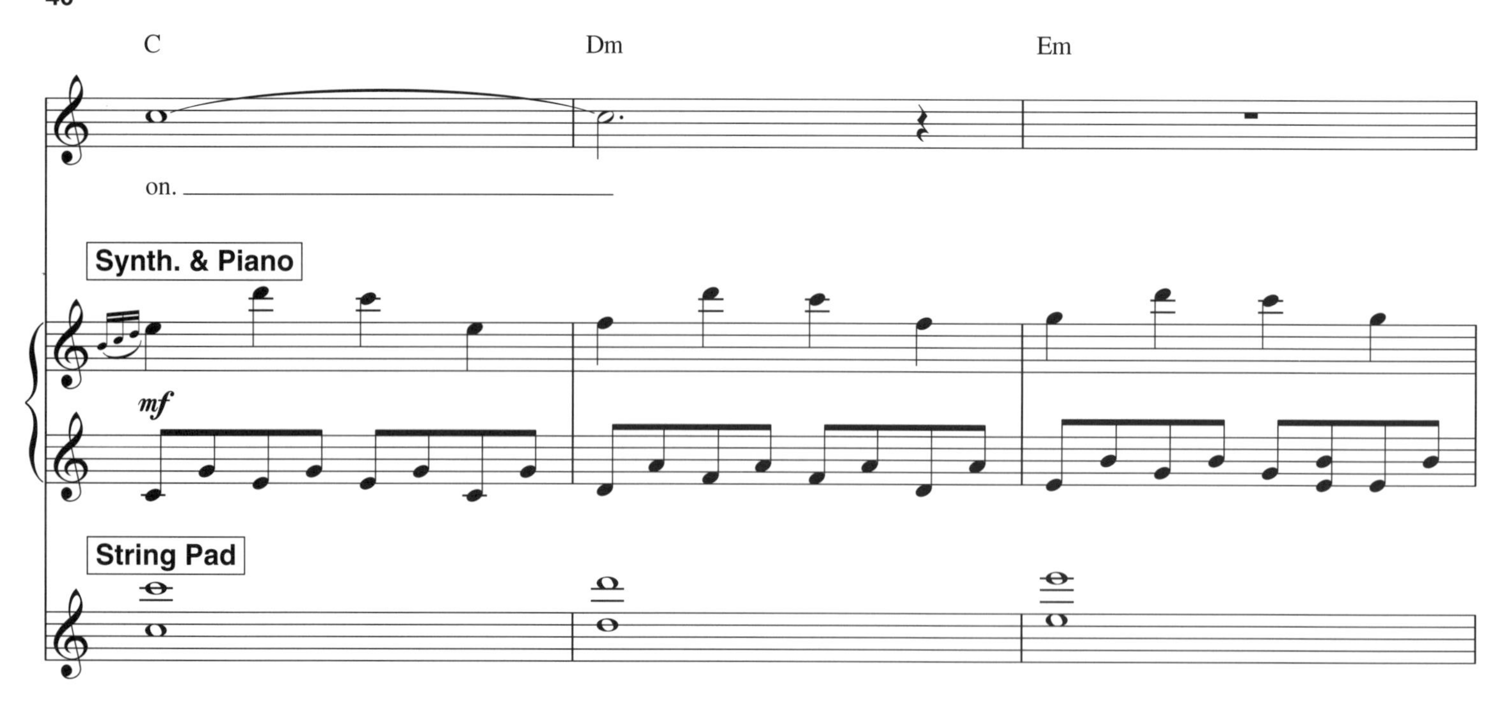

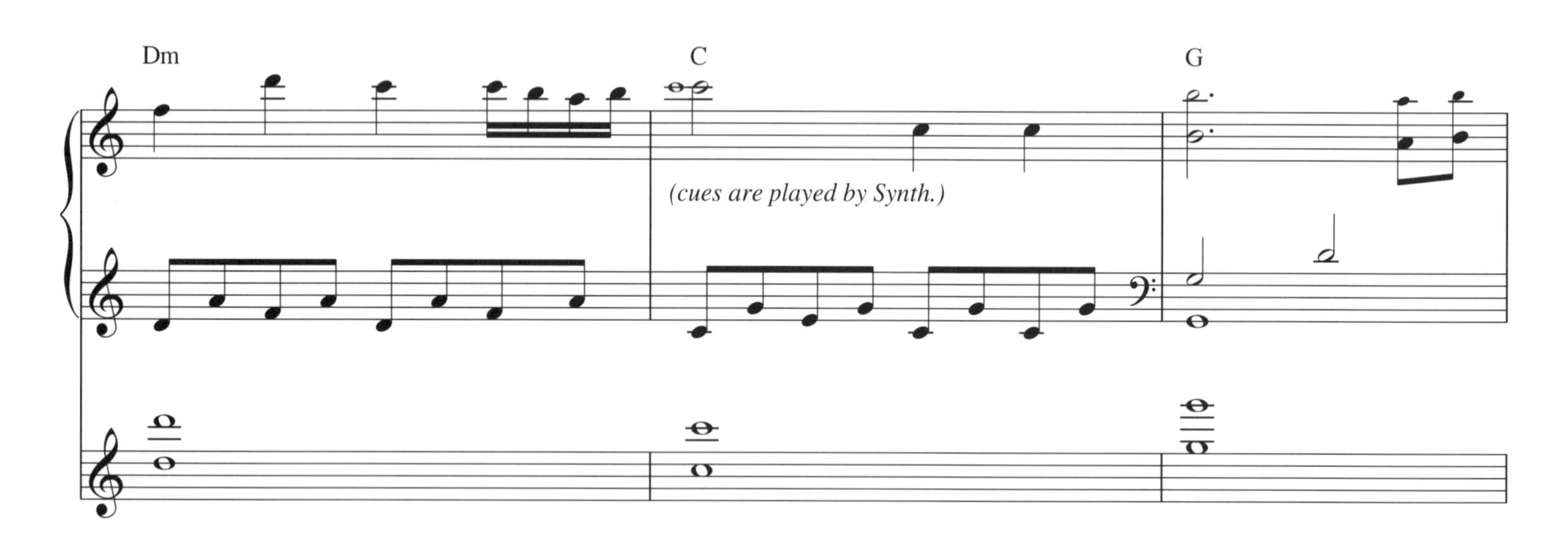

* Organ sustains throughout this verse.

G
Fmaj7
Re - flec - tions in the waves
spark my
G
mem - o - ries.
C
Some
Em/B
hap - py,
some
Am
sad;
G

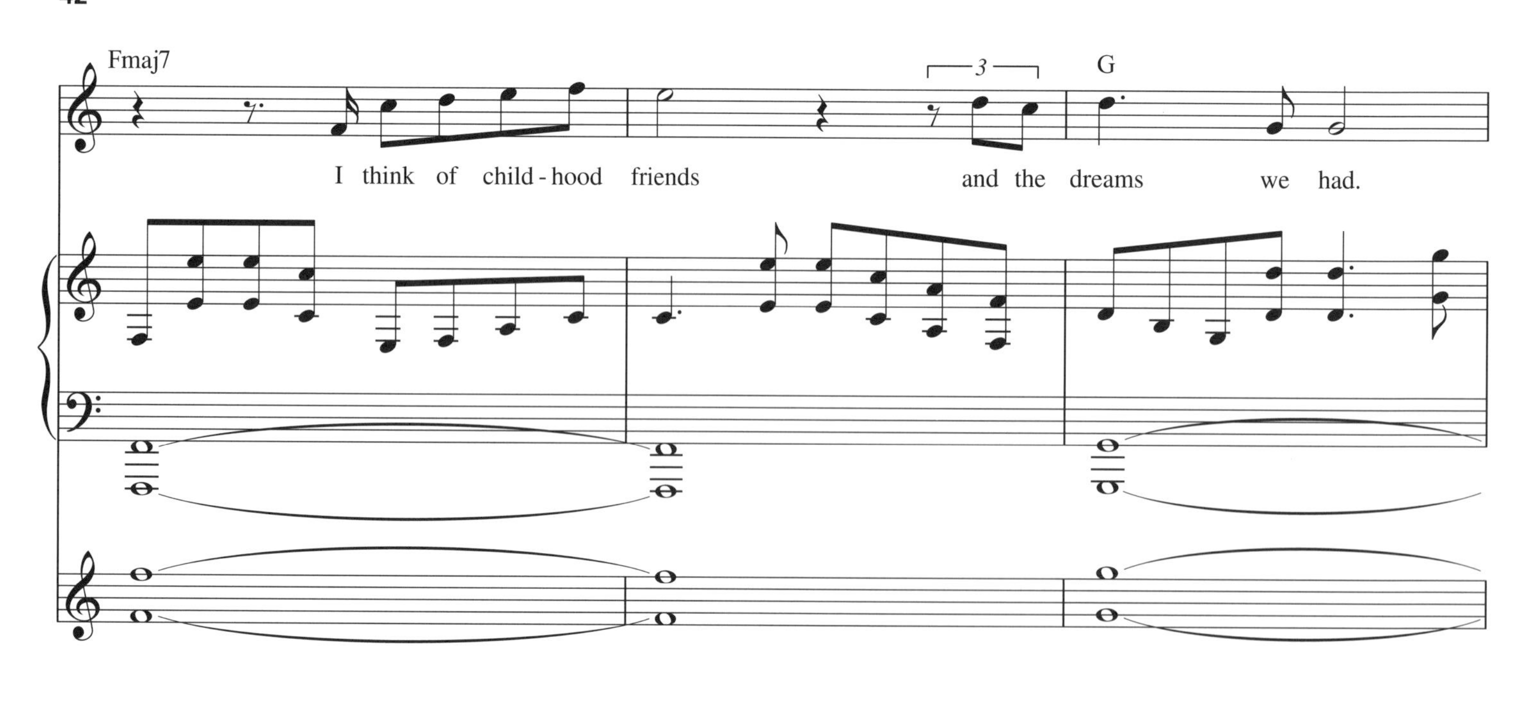
Fmaj7
G
3
I think of child - hood friends
and the dreams we had.

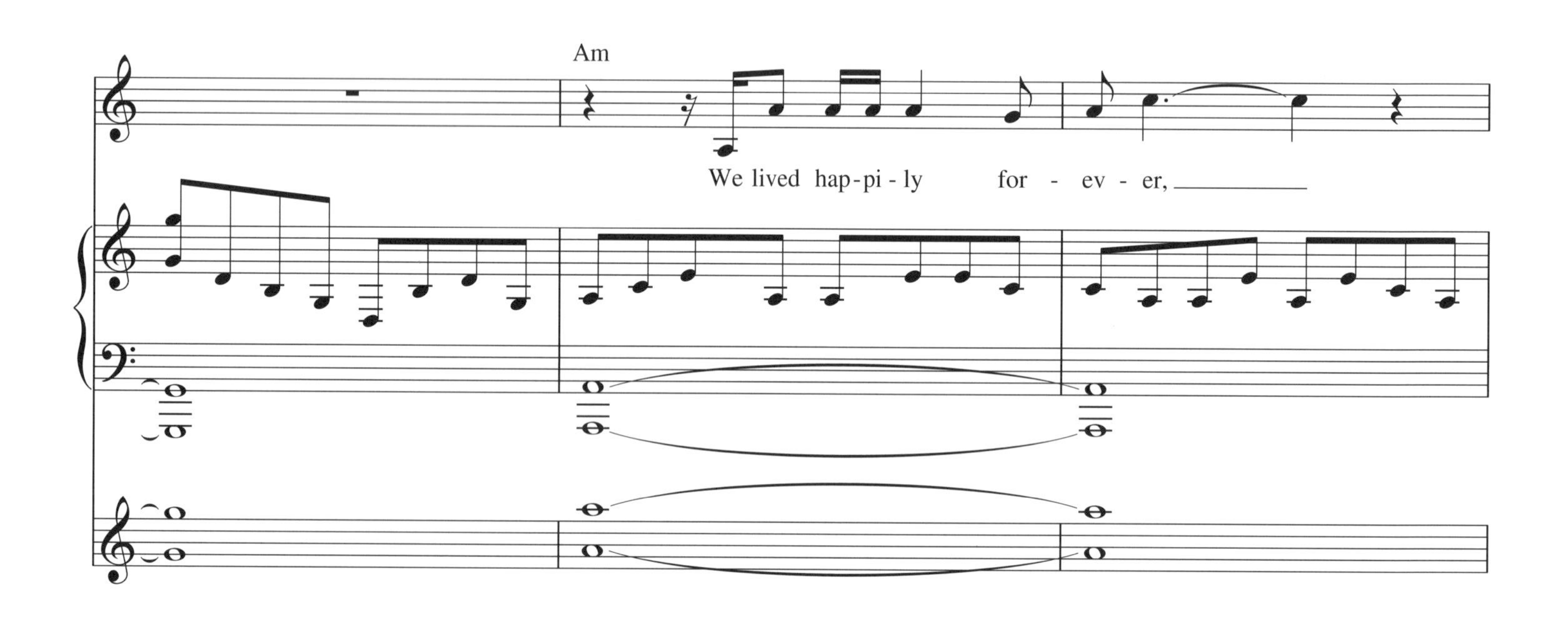
Am
We lived hap-pi - ly for - ev - er,

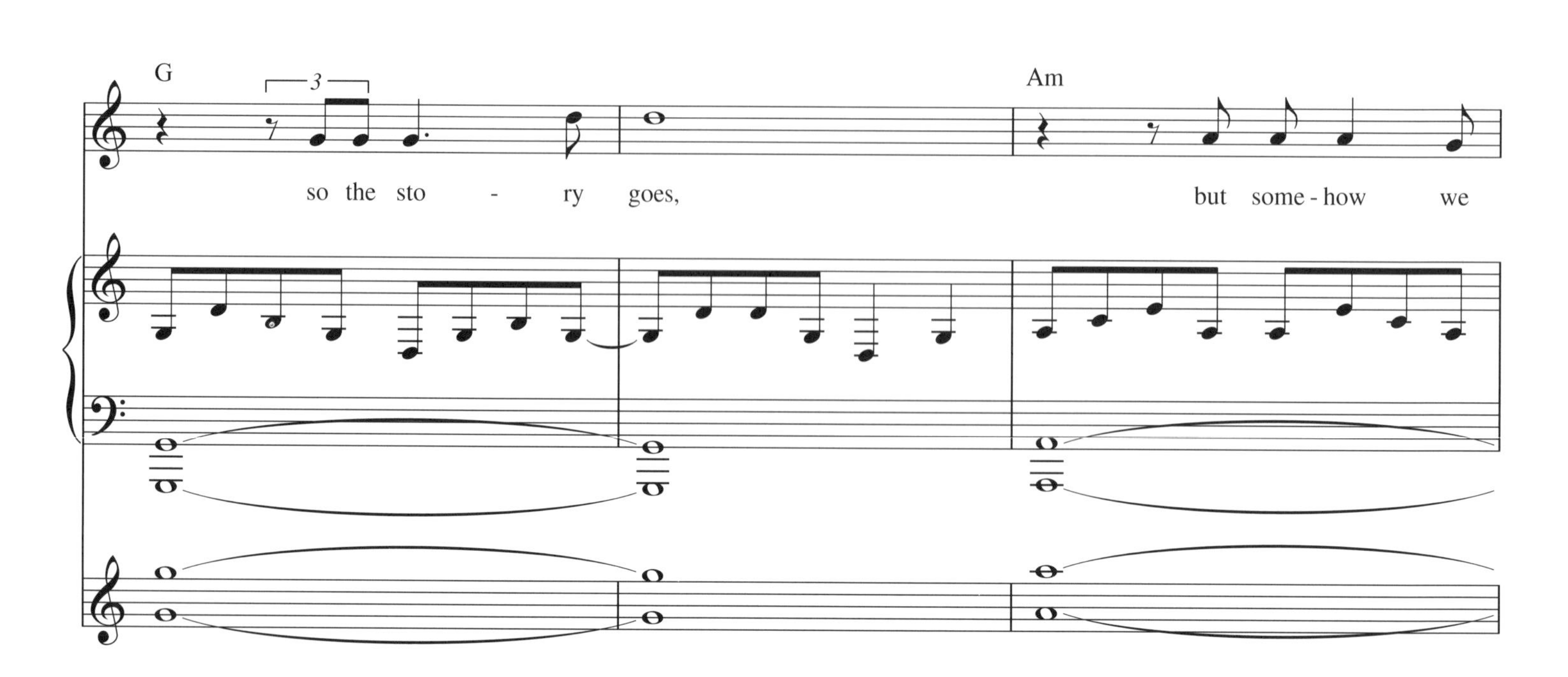
G
3
Am
so the sto - ry goes,
but some - how we

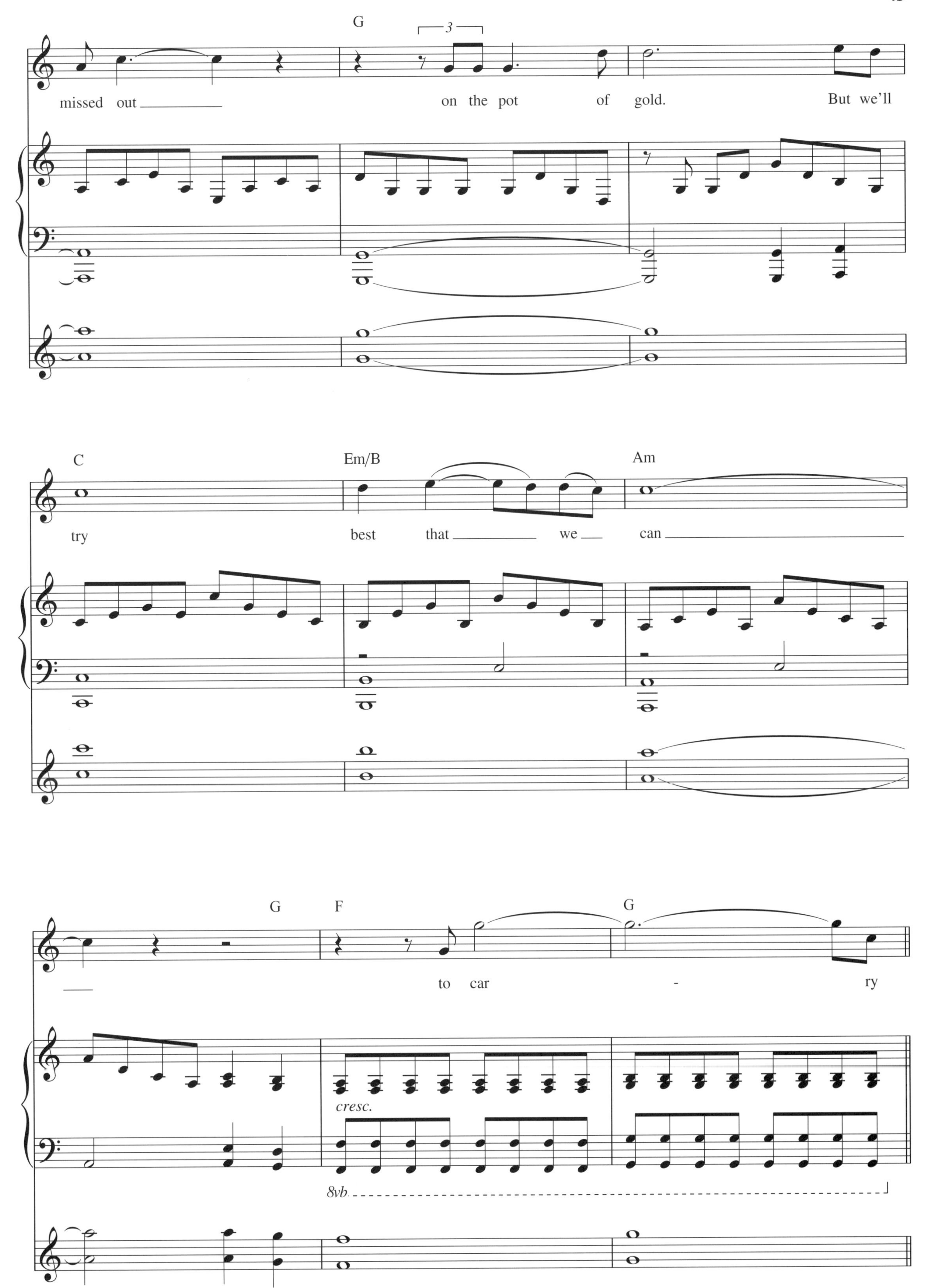
G
3
missed out
on the pot of gold.
But we'll
C
Em/B
Am
try
best that we can
G
F
G
to car - ry
cresc.
8vb

C5
F5/C
G5/C
on. (Vocal 1st time only)
Guitar
Bass & Guitar
1
F5/C
2
F5/C
C
A gath - er - ing of
Bass
F5/C
G5/C
F5/C
an - gels ap - peared a - bove my head.
They
C
F5/C
G5/C
sang to me this song of hope and this is what they said,

F5/C
C
F5/C
they said,
"Come sail a - way,
come sail a - way, come
1-3
G5/C
F5/C
sail a - way with me."
4
G5/C
sail a - way with me."
A♭5
Analog Synth.
Synth. Bass
Filter Sweep Pad
G♭/A♭
mf
A♭5
G♭5/A♭

Echo Synth.
Ab5
Gb5/Ab
Ab5
Gb5/Ab
Ab5
Gb5/Ab
Analog Synth.
Ab5
Gb5/Ab
Ab5
Guitar & Synth. Bass
1
Gb5/Ab
2
Gb5/Ab
Ab5
Synth. Flute
Synth. Brass

Gb5/Ab
Ab5
Gb5/Ab

Ab5
Gb5/Ab
Ab5
Echo Synth. & Synth. Brass

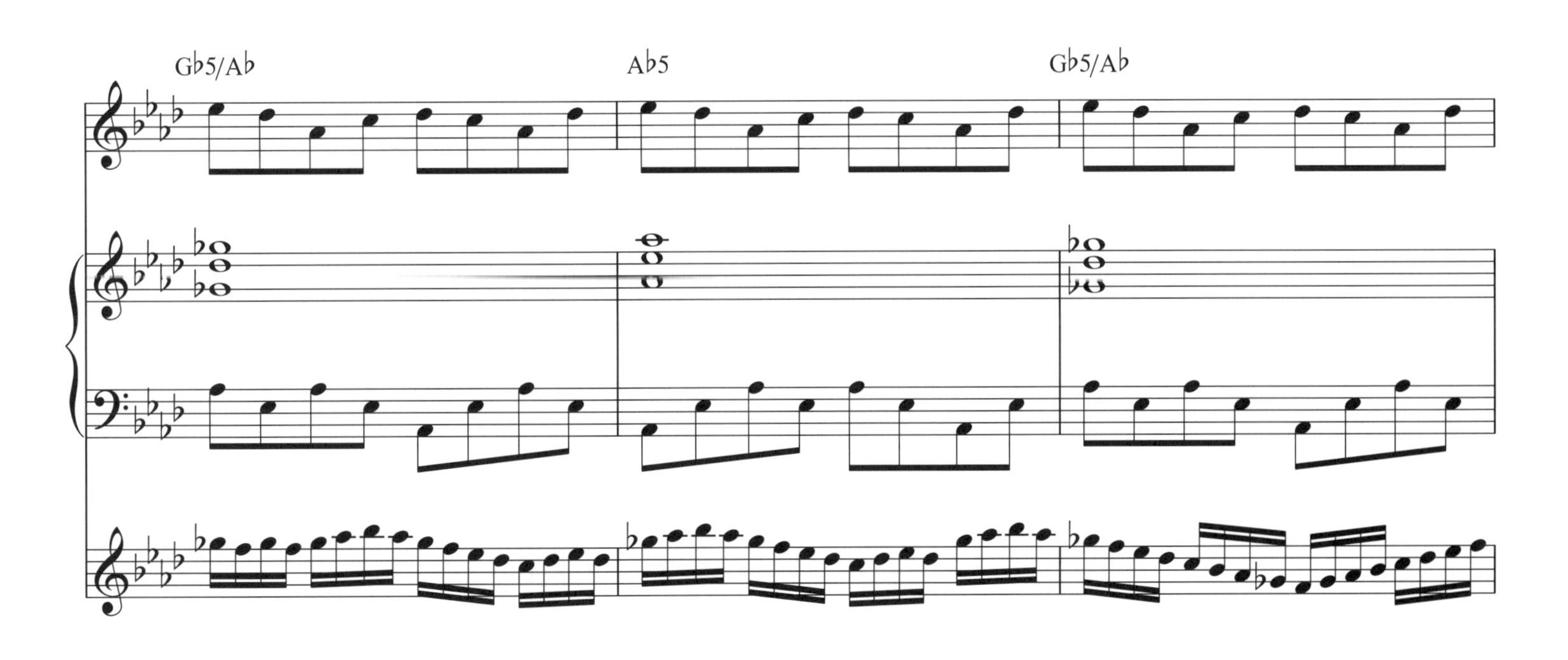
Gb5/Ab
Ab5
Gb5/Ab

A♭5
N.C.
Echo Synth.
Guitar
C
Bass & Guitar
F5/C
G5/C
1, 2
3
Vocal
C5
I thought that they were an - gels,
Bass

G5/C
F5/C
C5
but to my sur - prise, we climbed a - board their
F5/C
G5/C
F5/C
star - ship, we head - ed for the skies, sing - ing,
C
F5/C
"Come sail a - way, come sail a - way, come
G5/C
F5/C
Repeat and Fade
Optional Ending
C
sail a - way with me."

Cold as Ice

Words and Music by Mick Jones
and Lou Gramm

E♭sus
E♭m
Vocal
E♭sus
E♭m
C♭6
C♭
3
You nev - er take ad - vice, some - day you'll

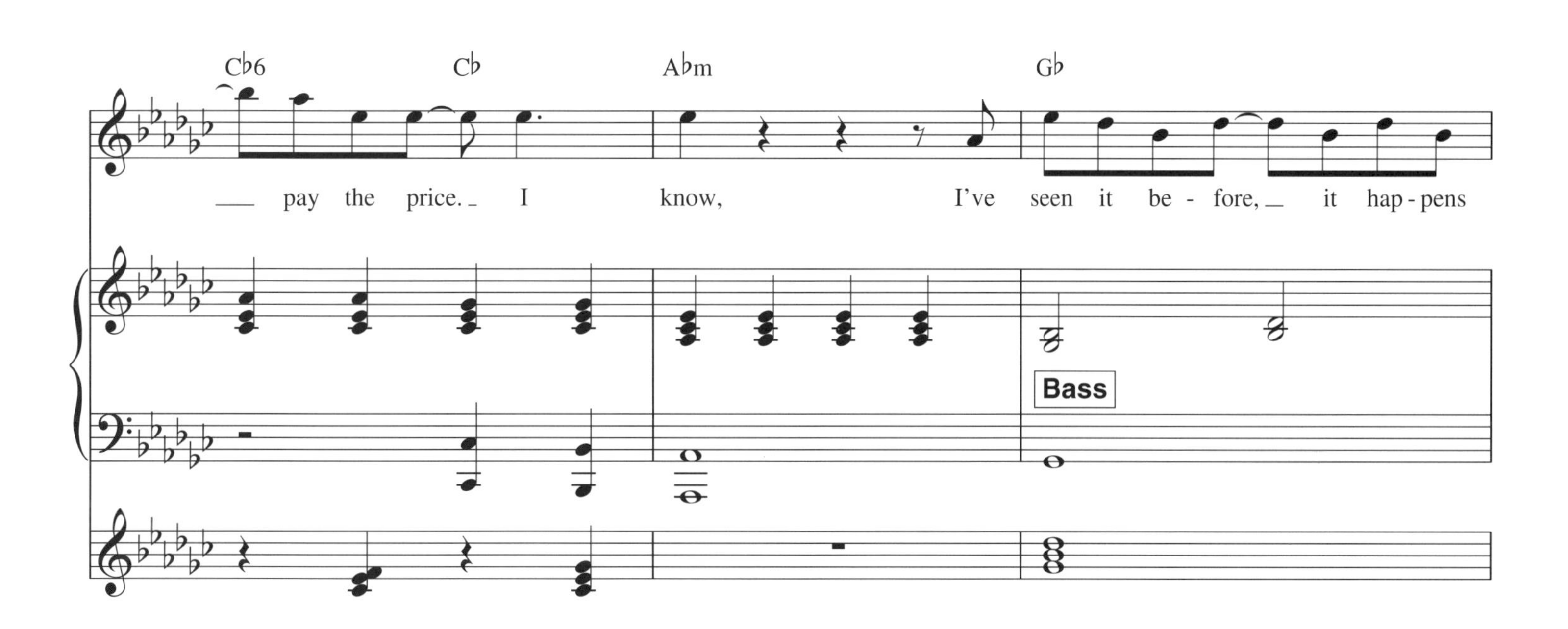
C♭6
C♭
A♭m
G♭
pay the price. I know, I've seen it be - fore, it hap - pens
Bass

F+
A♭m
C♭
D♭sus
all the time. You're clos - ing the door, you leave the world be - hind. You're

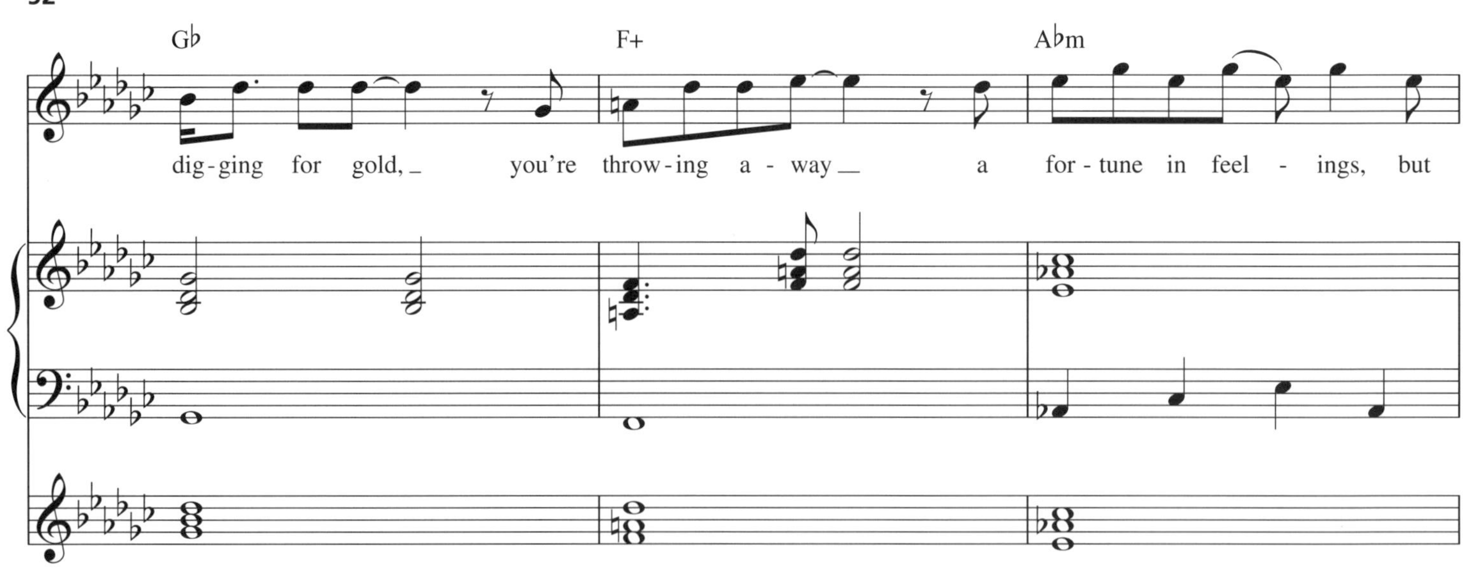
G♭
F+
A♭m
dig-ging for gold, you're throw-ing a-way a for-tune in feel-ings, but

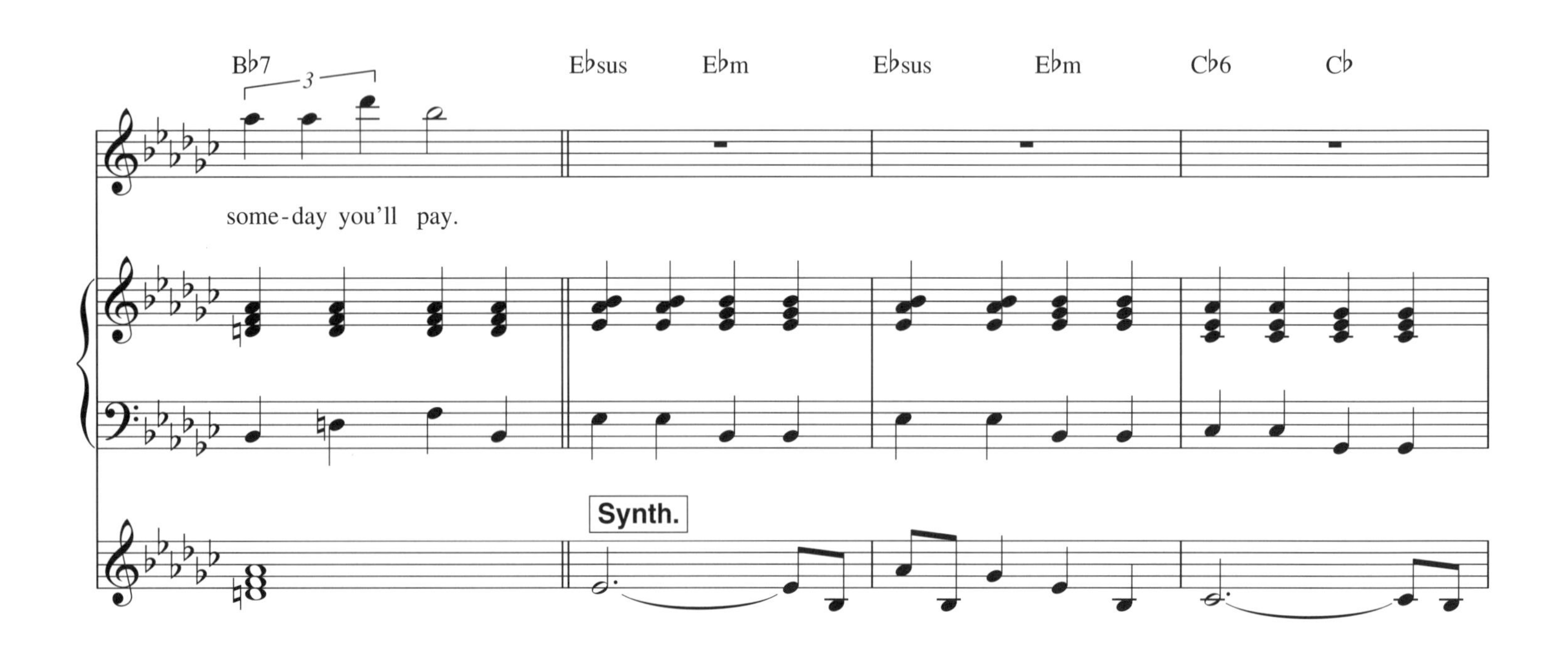
B♭7
E♭sus
E♭m
E♭sus
E♭m
C♭6
C♭
3
some-day you'll pay.
Synth.

C♭6
C♭
E♭sus
E♭m
E♭sus
E♭m
You're as cold as ice,

C♭6 C♭ C♭6 C♭ E♭sus E♭m
you're will - ing to sac - ri - fice __ our __ love. ____
E♭sus E♭m C♭6 C♭ C♭6 C♭
Synth.
E♭sus E♭m E♭sus E♭m C♭6 C♭
Vocal
3
You want par - a - dise, but some - day you'll __
C♭6 C♭ A♭m G♭
__ pay the price. _ I know, I've seen it be - fore, _ it hap - pens

F+
Abm
Cb
Dbsus
all the time. You're clos-ing the door, you leave the world be - hind. You're
Gb
F+
Abm
dig-ging for gold, you're throw-ing a - way a for - tune in feel - ings must
Bb7
Cb
some - day you'll pay.
Synth. & Bass
Guitar Solo
8vb
Ebm/Bb
Cb
Cb/Bb
8vb

A♭m
G♭
B♭7
Vocal
E♭m
B♭7/F
B♭7/A♭
(Cold as ice,) you know
that you are (cold, cold as, as
Piano
B♭7/A♭
E♭m
ice,) as cold as ice to me.
(Cold
Vocal
(cold, cold

B♭7/F
B♭7/A♭
as
ice.)
as,
as
ice.)
C♭
E♭sus
E♭m
(Ooh.)
(Lead vocal ad lib.)
Organ
E♭sus
E♭m
C♭6
C♭
C♭6
C♭
(Cold
as,
cold
as

Repeat ad lib. and Fade
Ebsus Ebm Ebsus Ebm Cb6 Cb
ice.)
Cb6 Cb
(Cold as, cold as
Optional Ending
Ebsus Ebm Ebsus Ebm
ice.)
Cb6 Cb Cb6 Cb Ebm

Don't Do Me Like That

Words and Music by
Tom Petty

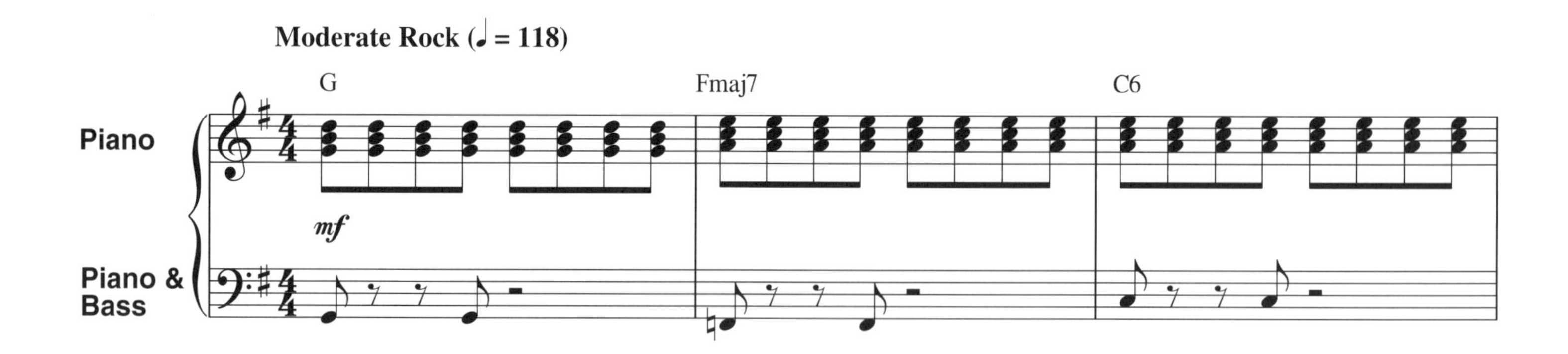

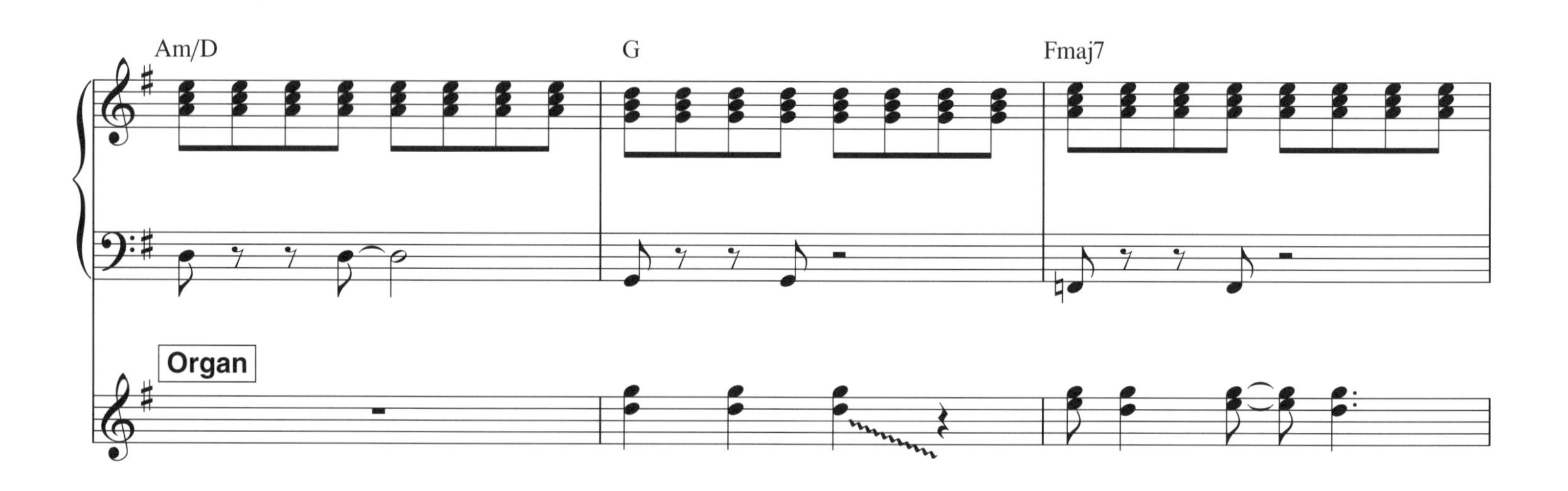

Fmaj7
C6
said a wom-an had hurt his pride,
Ba-by, it would bur-y me
told him that she loved him so and
if you were in the pub-lic eye,

Am/D
G
turned a-round and let him go.
giv-in' some-one else a try.
Then he said, "You bet-ter watch your step
And you know you bet-ter watch your step

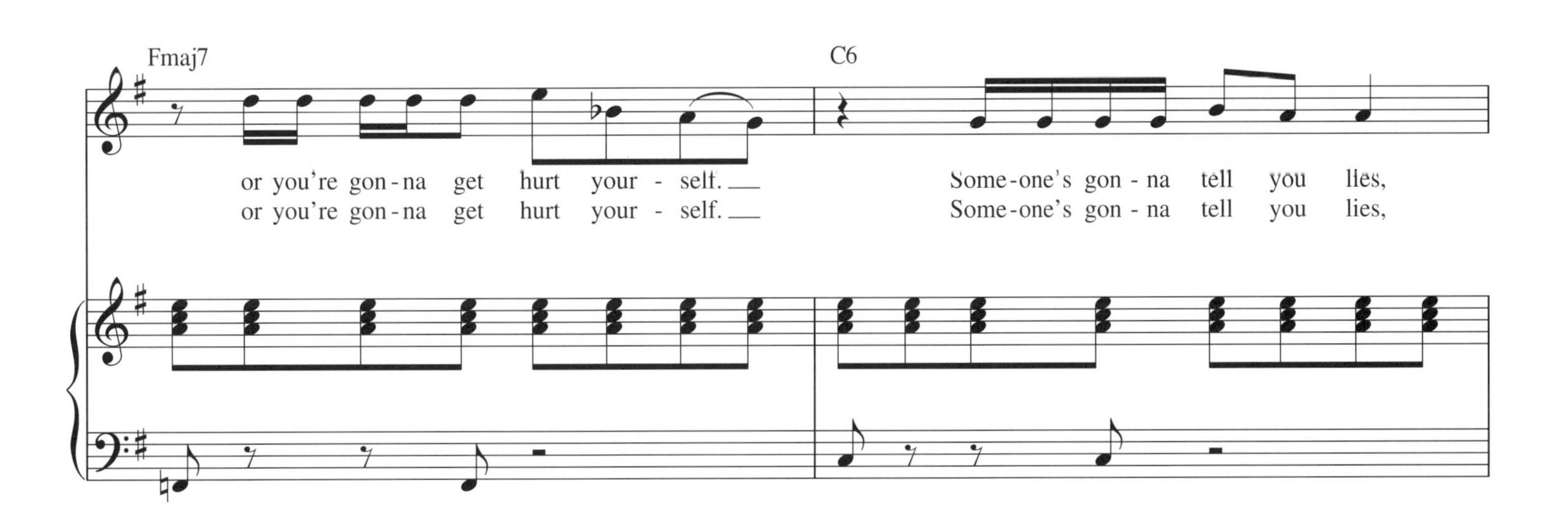
Fmaj7
C6
or you're gon-na get hurt your-self.
or you're gon-na get hurt your-self.
Some-one's gon-na tell you lies,
Some-one's gon-na tell you lies,

Am/D
G
Fmaj7
cut you down to size."
cut you down to size.
Don't do me like that,
don't do me like that.
Em
C6
D
G
(1.) Girl, I love you, ba - by,
(2.,D.S.) Boy, do I love you, ba - by.
don't do me like that.
Don't, don't, don't, don't.
Don't do me like that,
8va
To Coda
1
Fmaj7
Em
C6
D
don't do me like that.
Some-day I might need you, ba - by,
don't do me like that.

2
Em
C6
G7
What if I need you, ba - by? Don't do me like that. 'Cause some-where deep down in-side,
8va
Saxes

C7
G7
C7
some-one is say - in', "Love does-n't last that long."

G7
C7
Cm
I've had this feel-in' in - side night out and day in, and now I can't take it no more.
Guitar
Saxes
Guitar

D
D.S. al Coda
CODA
Em
I just_ might need you, hon - ey.
Piano
8va
3
C6
D
Don't do me like that.
G
Don't do me like that,
Fmaj7
don't do me like that.
Guitar
loco on repeat
Repeat and Fade
Optional Ending
Em
Ba - by, ba - by, ba - by,
C6
D
don't, don't, don't, don't.
G

Don't Know What You Got
(Till It's Gone)

Words and Music by
Tom Keifer

* Acoustic and Electric Guitar parts have been combined to be playable by one piano.

Bm
F♯m
E
Take some time. Let me know if you real - ly want to go.
D/E
A
E
D
Bm
Don't know what you got till it's gone.
f
f
A
E
F♯m
E
D(add2)
Don't know what it is I did so wrong, oh.

A
E
F♯m
E
D
Now I know what I've got, it's just this song, and
A
E
F♯m
E
it ain't eas - y to get back. Takes so long, oh.
D(add2)
1
A(add2)
Piano

2
C♯m
A
Do you want to see me beg - ging, ba - by?
Can't you give me just one more day?
Synth. Brass
C♯m
E
Can't you see my heart's been drag - ging late - ly?
I've been look - ing for the words to say.
D/E
Bm
F♯m
Guitar Solo
Play 3 times
Ooh.
Guitar
Synth. Strings

Bm
F♯m
E
D/E
Solo ends
Vocal
A
E
D
Bm
Don't know what you got till it's gone.
A
E
F♯m
E
D(add2)
Don't know what it is I did so wrong, oh.

A
E
F♯m
E
D
Now I know what I've got, it's just this song, and
A
E
F♯m
E
it ain't eas - y to get back. Takes so long, oh.
D
Repeat and Fade
Optional Ending
D(add2)
A
Piano
rall.

Dream On

Words and Music by
Steven Tyler

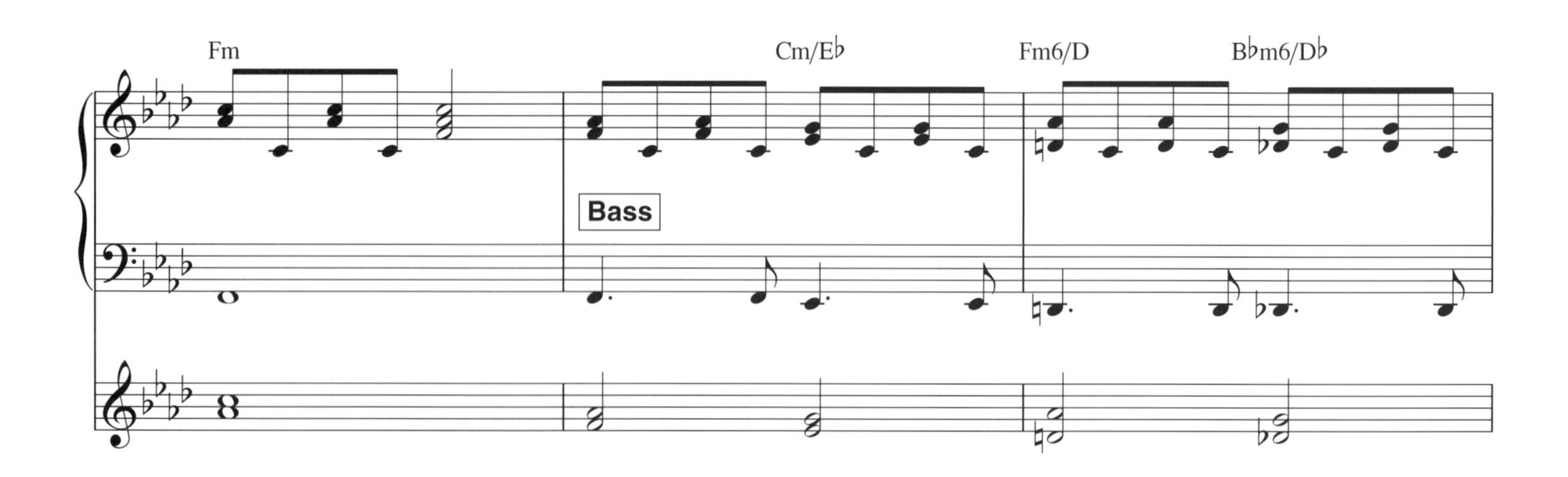

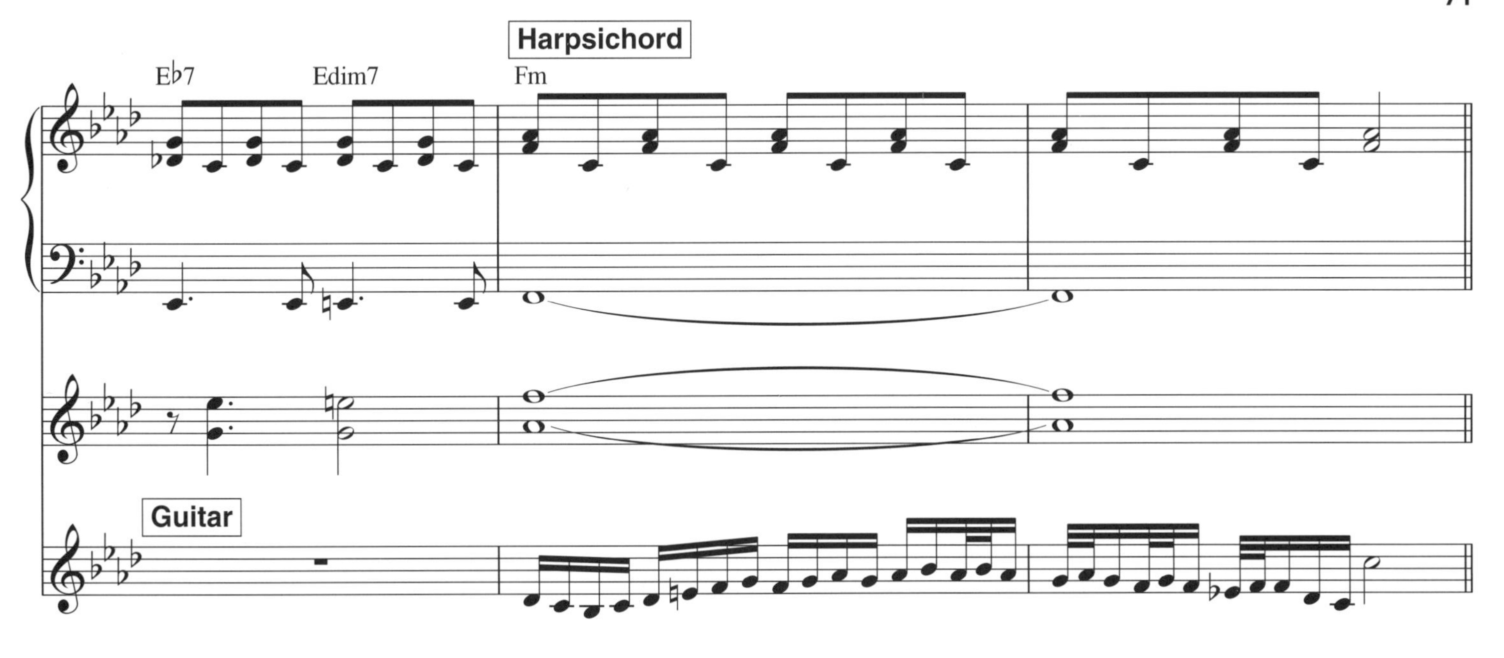
Harpsichord
E♭7
Edim7
Fm
Guitar

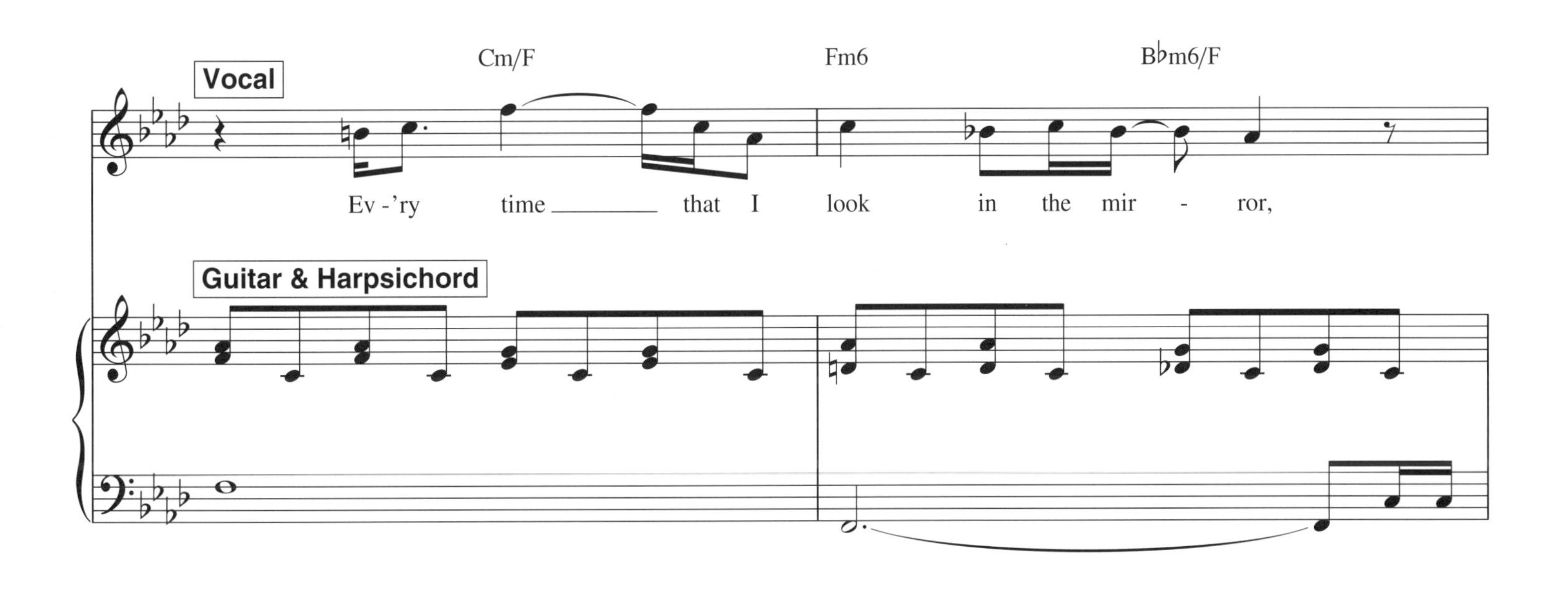
Vocal
Cm/F
Fm6
B♭m6/F
Ev - 'ry time that I look in the mir - ror,
Guitar & Harpsichord

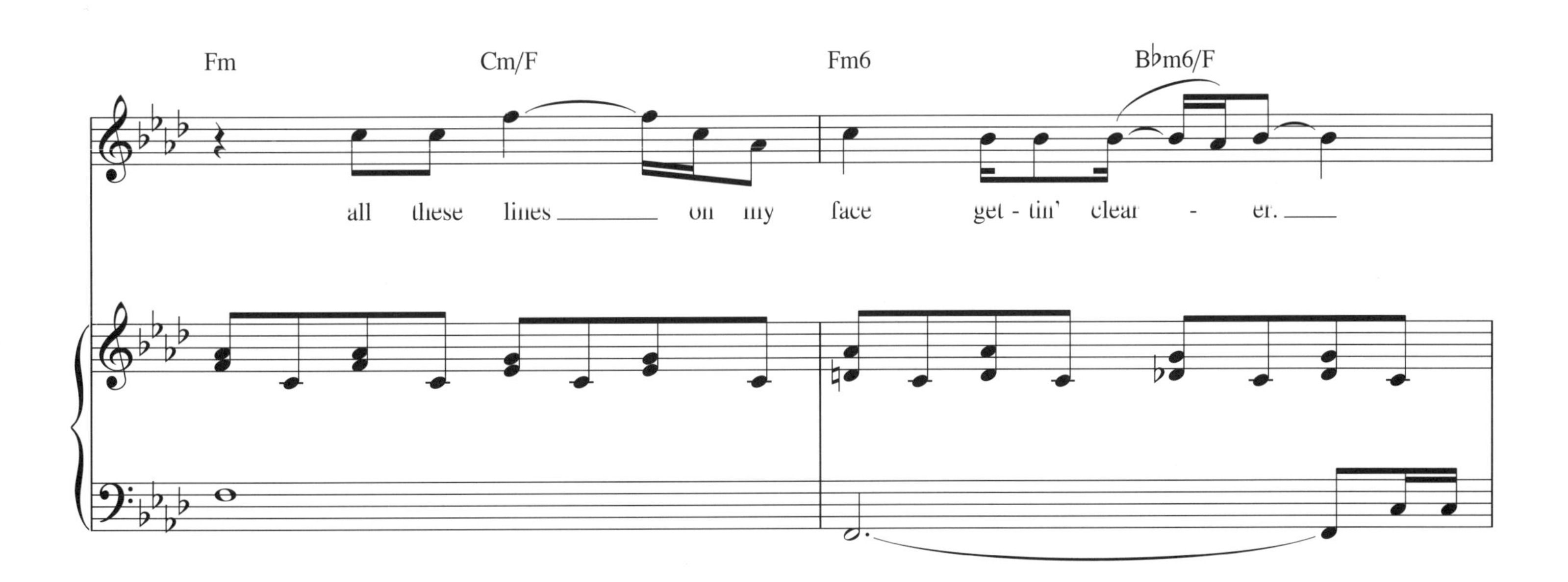
Fm
Cm/F
Fm6
B♭m6/F
all these lines on my face get - tin' clear - er.

Fm
Cm/F
Fm6
B♭m6/F
The past is gone.
Fm
Cm/F
Fm6
B♭m6/F
It went by like dusk to dawn.
Dm7♭5
Csus
C
Dm7♭5
B♭m6/D♭
Is-n't that the way? Ev - 'ry-bod-y's got their dues in life to pay.
C
D♭/C
D/C
C7
Yeah,
cresc.

F5
Eb5
Db5
Eb5
I know no - bod - y knows where it comes _ and where _ it goes. _
Guitar
mf
F5
Eb5
Db5
Eb5
I know ev - 'ry - bod - y's sin; you got to lose to know how to win. _
F
Cm/F
Fm6
Bbm6/F
Guitar & Harpsichord
decresc.
mp
Guitar
Fm
Fsus(add2)
Fm
Cm/F
Half _ my life's in
Bass & Harpsichord

Fm6
B♭m6/F
Fm
Cm/F
books' writ - ten pag - es, lived and learned from
Fm6
B♭m6/F
Fm
Cm/F
fools and from sag - es. You know it's
Fm6
B♭m6/F
Fm
Cm/F
true, whoa, all these things
Fm6
B♭m6/F
F5
E♭5
come back to you. Sing with me, sing for the years,
Guitar
mf
Bass

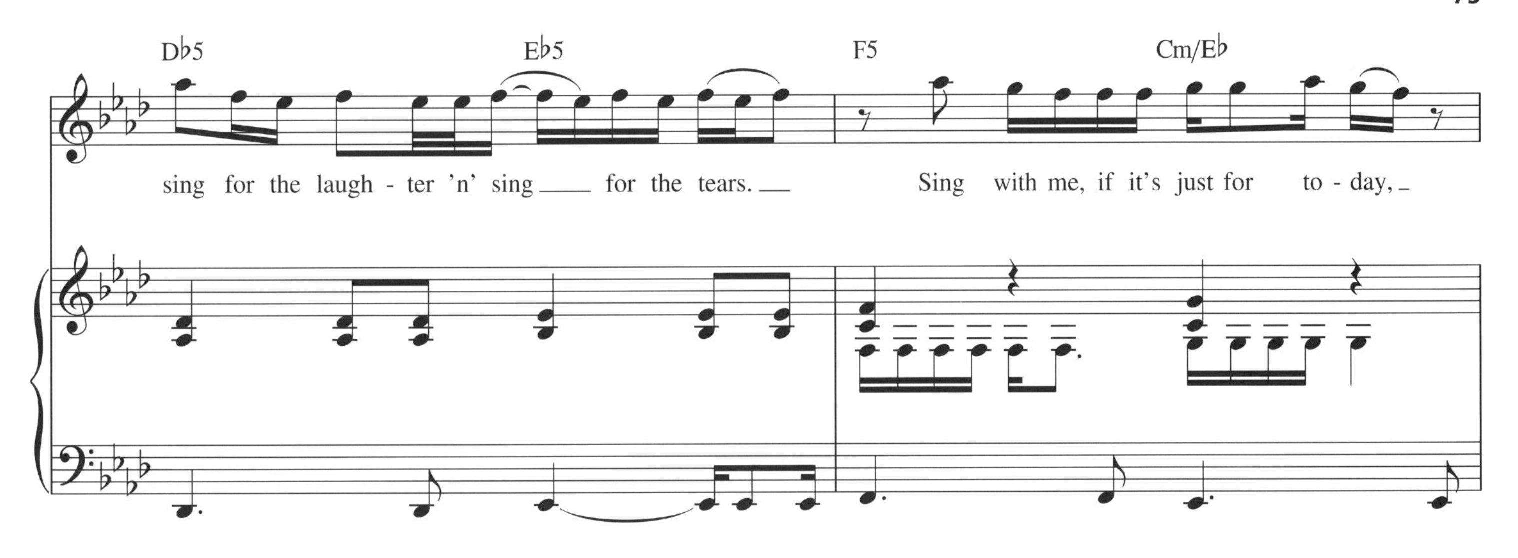
Db5
Eb5
F5
Cm/Eb
sing for the laugh - ter 'n' sing for the tears.
Sing with me, if it's just for to - day,

Dm7b5
Db
C5
may-be to-mor - row the good Lord will take you a - way.
Guitar & Harpsichord

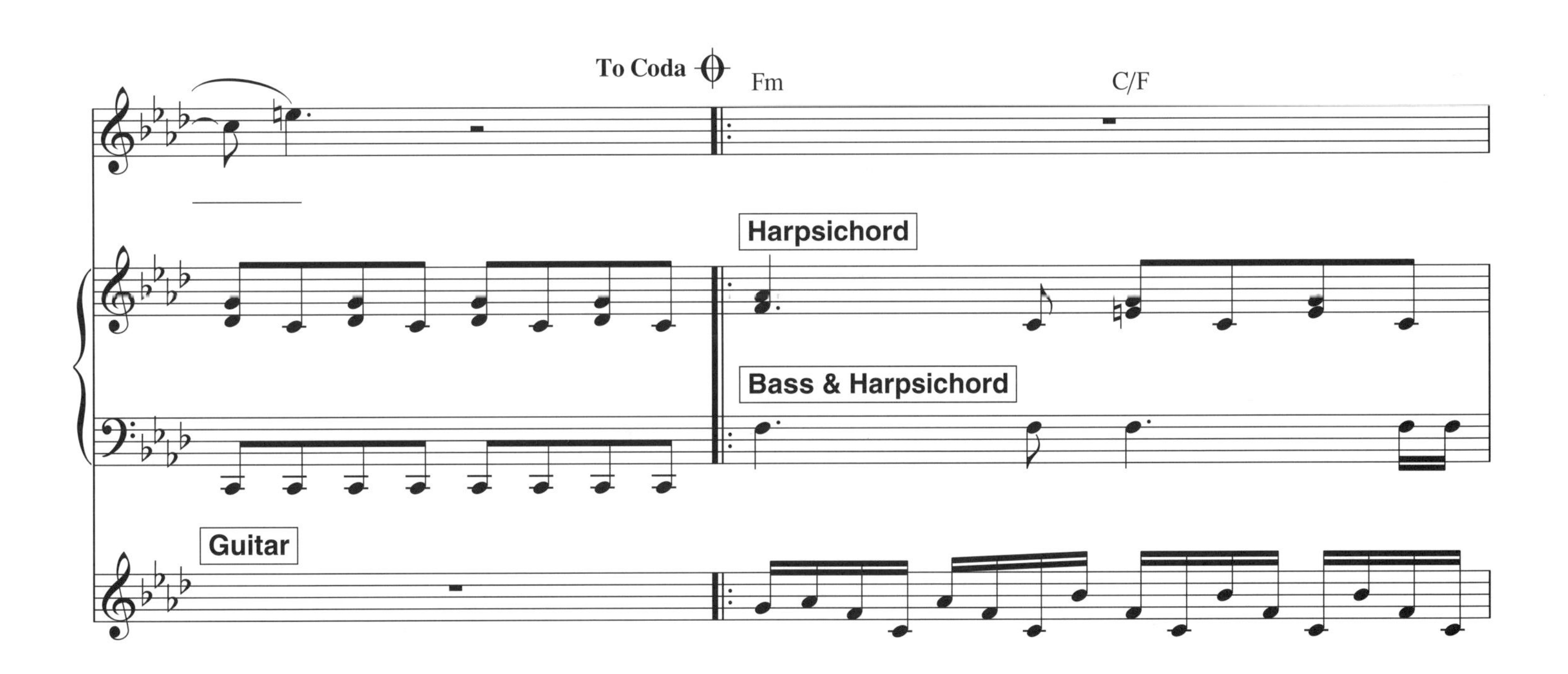
To Coda
Fm
C/F
Harpsichord
Bass & Harpsichord
Guitar

1
Cm/F
B♭(add2)
E♭7
Edim7
Fm

2
Vocal
E♭7
Edim7
D.S. al Coda
Yeah,
CODA
B♭5
C5
Dream on,
dream on,
Guitar

D♭5
E♭5
F5
dream on, dream your-self a dream come true.

B♭5
C5
D♭5
E♭5
Dream on, dream on, dream on, and dream un - til your dreams come
F5
8vb
true.
B♭5
C5
D♭5
E♭5
F5
8va
G5
Dream on, dream on, dream on, dream on, dream on, dream on,
A♭5
B♭5
C5
(8va)
dream on, ah. Ah.
Harpsichord & Guitar

Fm
Cm/E♭
D♭
E♭5
Sing with me, sing for the years, sing for the laugh - ter 'n' sing for the tears.
Fm
E♭5
1
D♭
E♭5
Sing with me if it's just for to - day, may - be to - mor - row the good Lord will take you a - way.
2
Dm7♭5
D♭
C5
may - be to - mor - row the good Lord will take you a - way.
Repeat and Fade
Optional Ending

Evil Woman

Words and Music by
Jeff Lynne

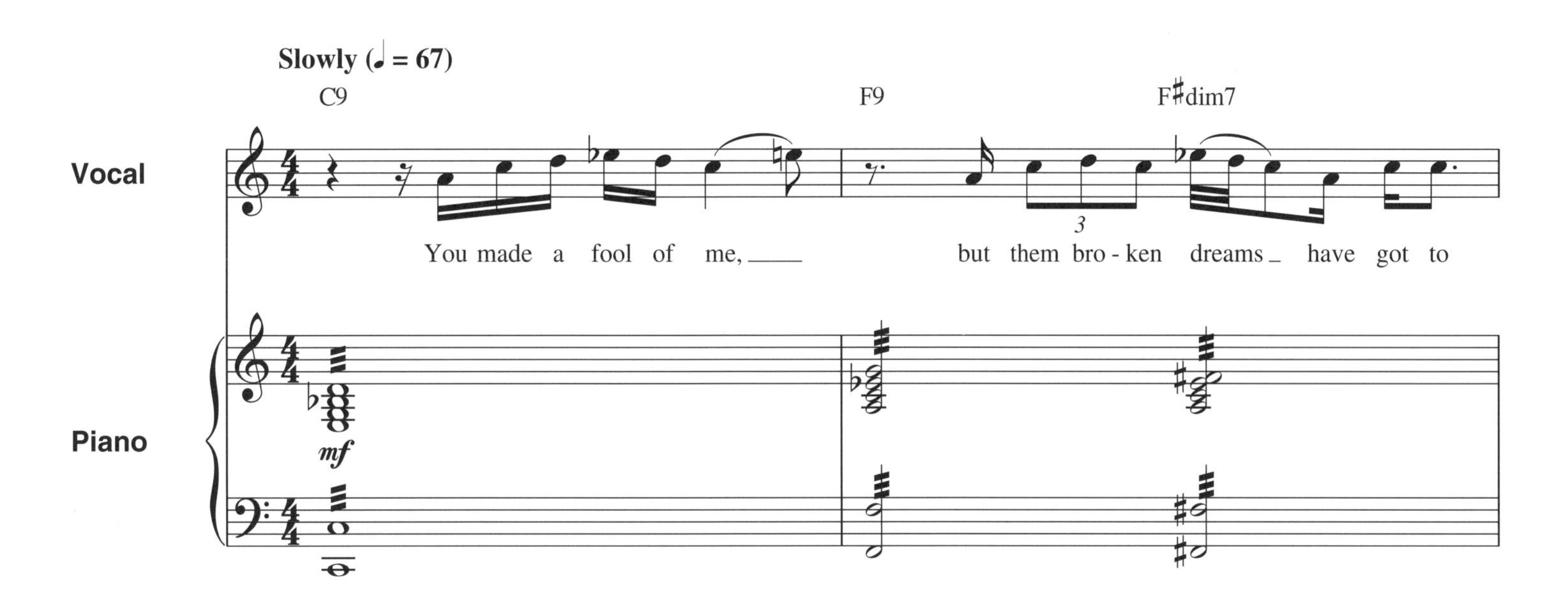

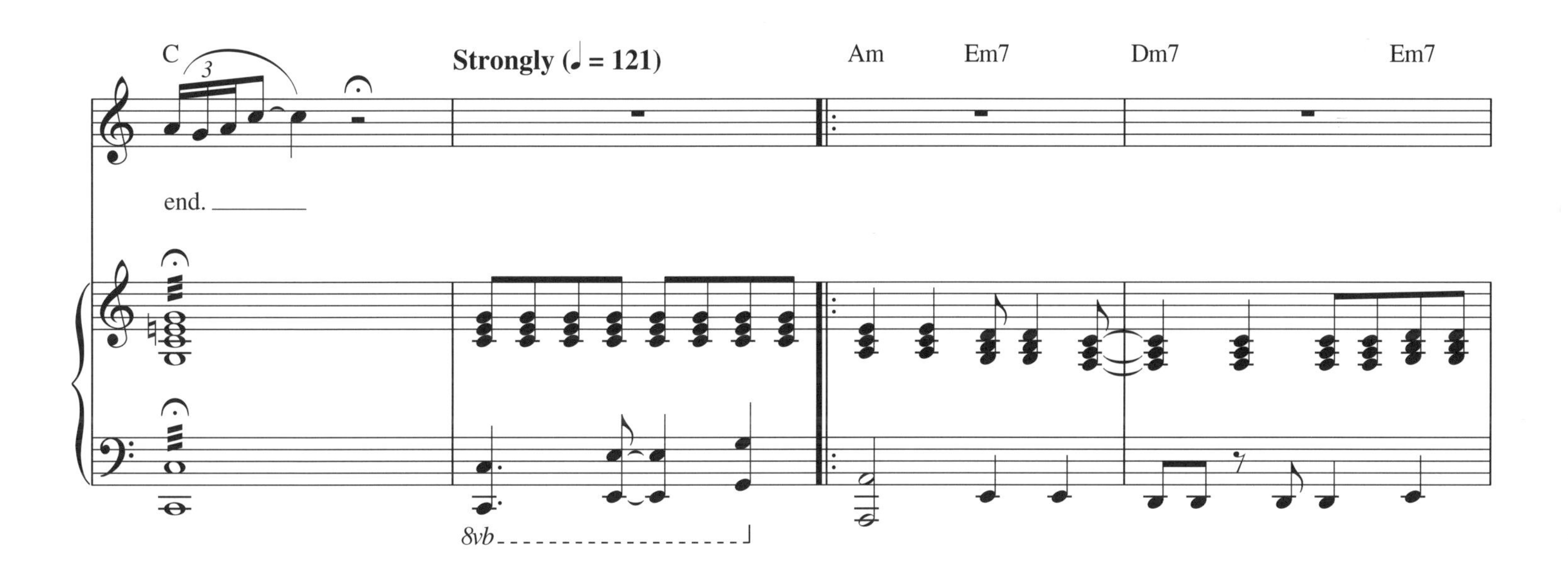

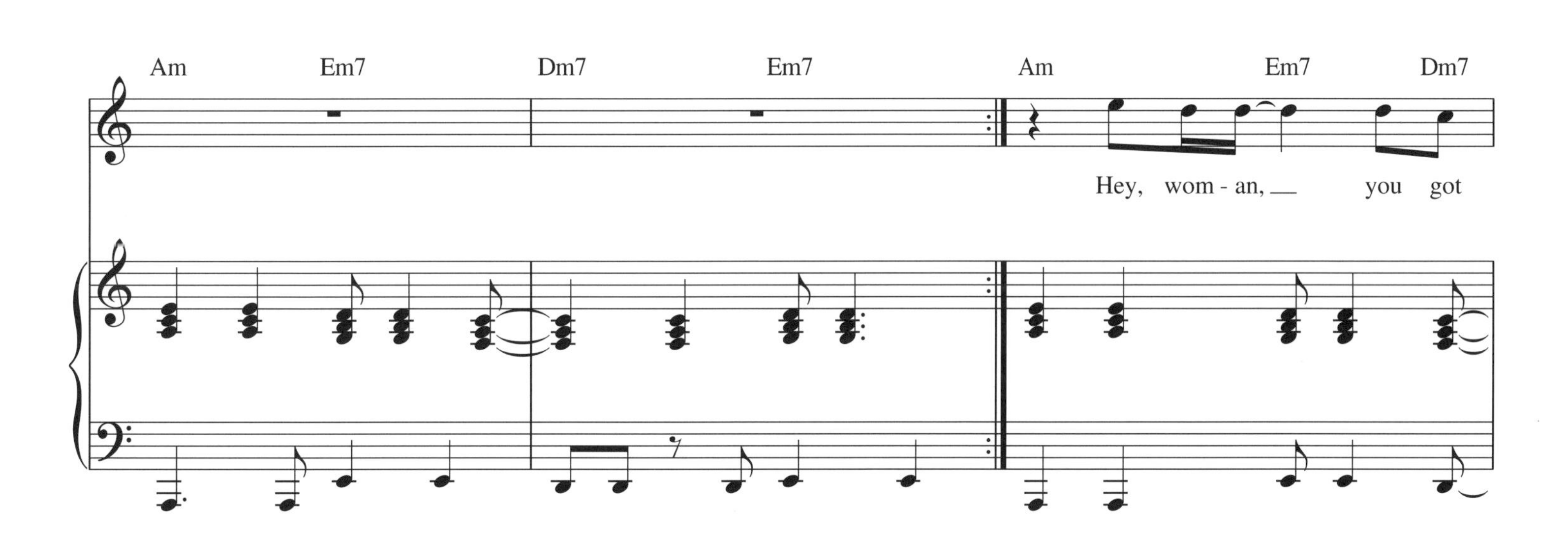

Em7 Am Em7 Dm7 Em7
the blues 'cause you ain't got no one else to use. There's an
Am Em7 Dm7 Em7 Am Em7 Dm7
o - pen road that leads no - where, so just make some miles be - tween here
Em7 Am Em7 Dm7 Em7
and there. There's a hole in my head where the rain comes in.
Am Em7 Dm7 Em7 Am Em7 Dm7
You took my bod - y and played to win. Ha ha, wom - an, it's a

Em7
Fmaj7
G
C
cry - in' shame, but you ain't got no - bod - y else to blame.
Am
Em7
Dm7
Em7
E - vil wom - an.
8vb
Strings
Clavichord
Am
Em7
Dm7
Em7
Am
Em7
Dm7
E - vil wom - an.
E - vil wom -

To Coda
Em7
Am
Em7
Dm7
Em7
- an.
E - vil wom - an
E - vil wom-an.

Am
Em7
Dm7
Em7
Am
Em7
Dm7
Rolled in from an - oth - er town,
hit some gold too hard to set -
3

Em7
Am
Em7
Dm7
Em7
-tle down._ But a fool and his mon - ey soon go___ sep-'rate ways,___

Am
Em7
Dm7
Em7
Am
Em7
Dm7
and you found a fool ly-in' in a daze. Ha ha, wom-an, what you

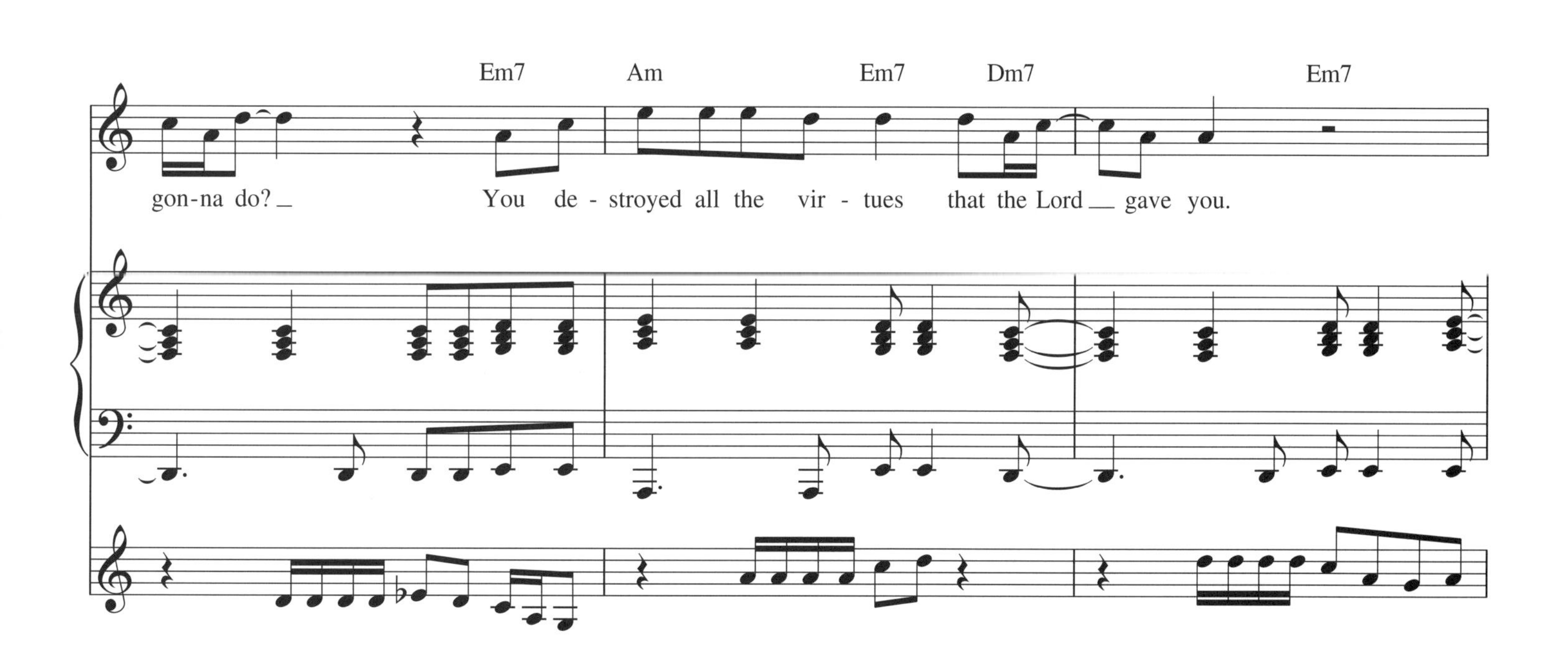
Em7
Am
Em7
Dm7
Em7
gon-na do?_ You de-stroyed all the vir-tues that the Lord_ gave you.

Am
Em7
Dm7
Em7
Fmaj7
G
It's so good that you're feel-in' pain, but you bet-ter get your face on board the
C
D.S. al Coda
ver - y next train. (Hey, hey.)
8vb
CODA
Em7
Am
Em7
Dm7
Em7
Solo Piano
8va
Clavichord

Am
Em7
Dm7
Em7
Am
Em7
Dm7
Vocal
Em7
Am
Em7
Dm7
Em7
(Hey, hey, hey, hey.)
Am
Em7
Dm7
Em7
Am
Em7
Dm7
8va
8va

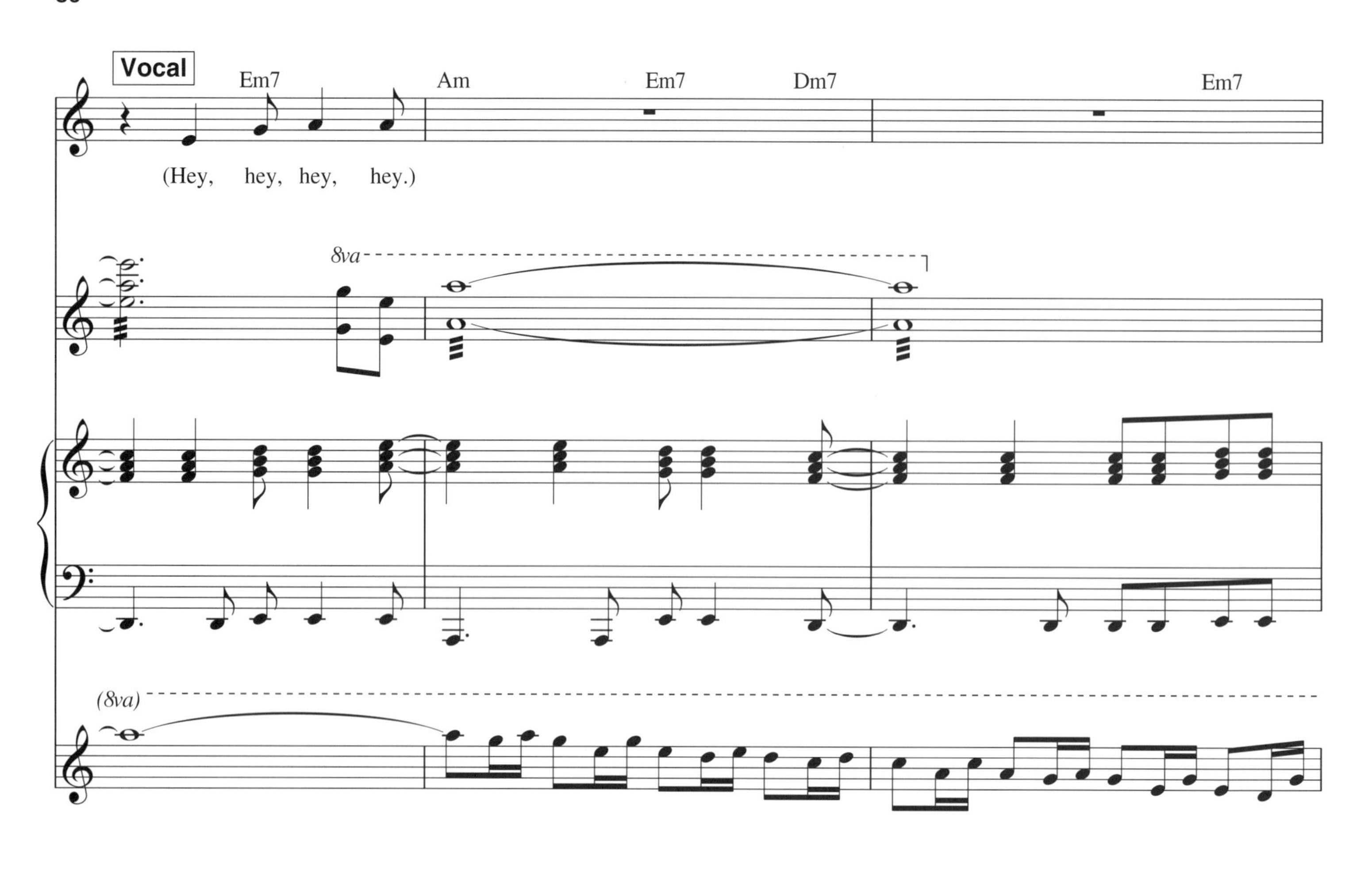
Vocal
Em7
Am
Em7
Dm7
Em7
(Hey, hey, hey, hey.)
8va
(8va)

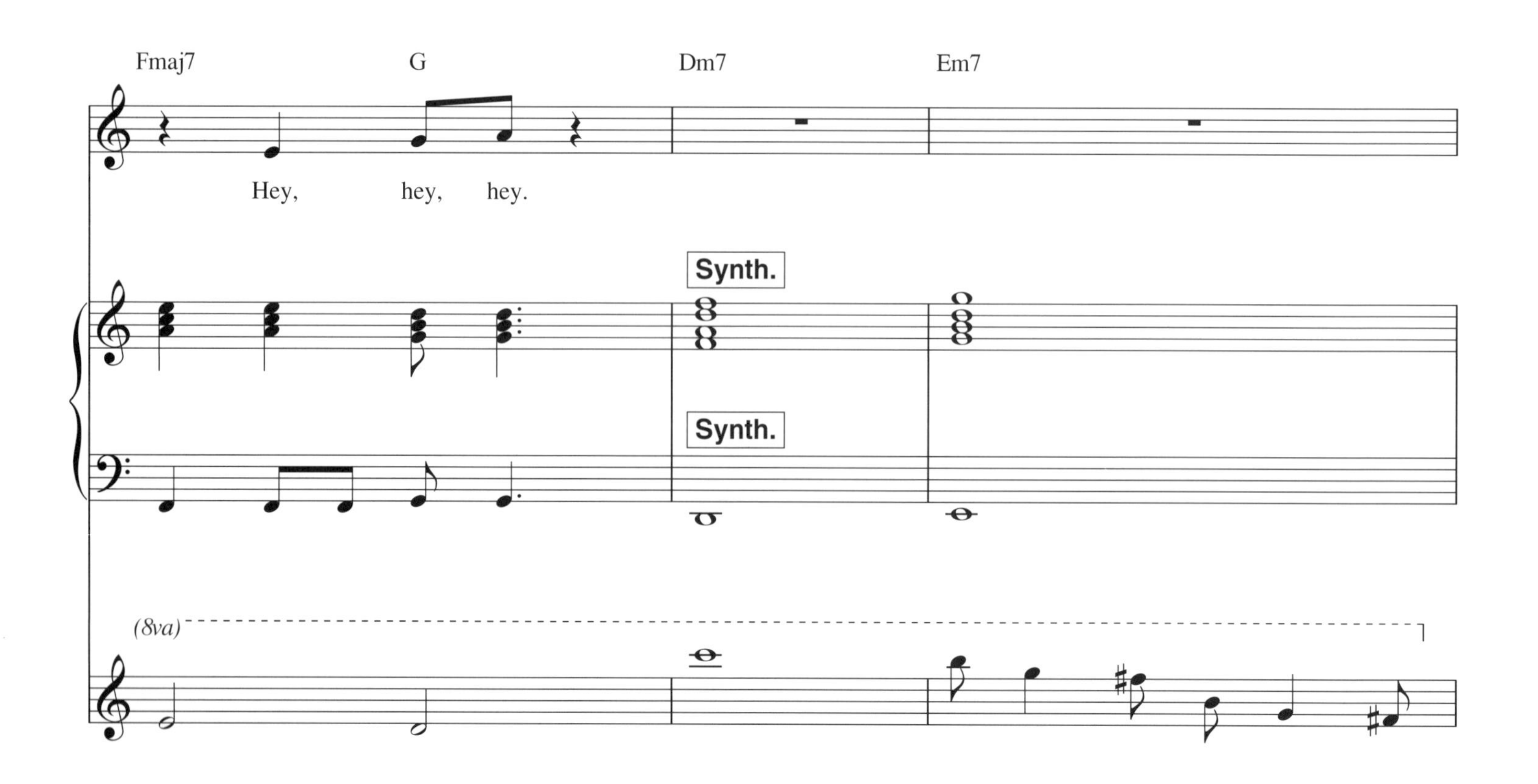
Fmaj7
G
Dm7
Em7
Hey, hey, hey.
Synth.
Synth.
(8va)

Am
Em7
Dm7
Em7
Am
Em7
Dm7
E - vil wom - an.
E - vil wom -
Piano
Piano
Strings
Clavichord

Em7
Am
Em7
Dm7
Em7
an.
E - vil wom - an.
(You're an e - vil wom -

Am Em7 Dm7 Em7 Am Em7 Dm7
E - vil wom - an. E - vil wom - an, how you
an.)
Em7 Am Em7 Dm7 Em7
done me wrong. Now you're try - in' to wail a dif - f'rent song.
Am Em7 Dm7 Em7 Am Em7 Dm7
Ha ha fun - ny, how you broke me up. You made the wine, now you drink

Em7 Am Em7 Dm7 Em7
a cup. I came a run - nin' ev - 'ry time you cried,
Am Em7 Dm7 Em7 Am Em7 Dm7
thought I saw love smil-in' in your eyes. Ha ha, ver - y
Em7 Fmaj7 G C
nice to know that you ain't got no place a - left to go.

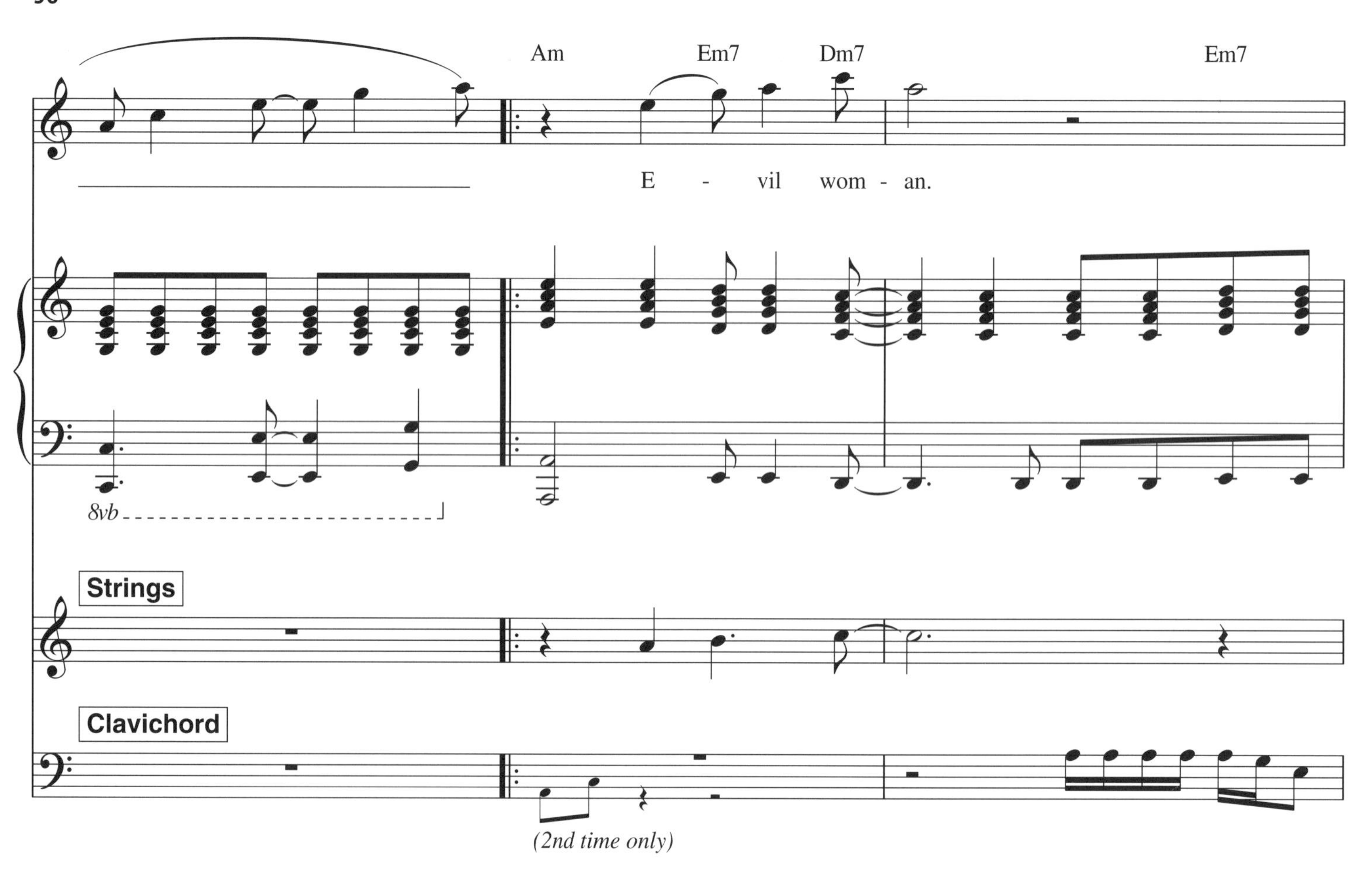
Am
Em7
Dm7
Em7
E - vil wom - an.
8vb
Strings
Clavichord
(2nd time only)

Am
Em7
Dm7
Em7
Am
Em7
Dm7
E - vil wom - an.
E - vil wom -

Em7
Am
Em7
Dm7
Em7
Repeat and Fade
an.
E - vil wom - an.
(You're an e - vil wom - an.)

Optional Ending
Am
Em7
Dm7
G
Am

Final Countdown

Words and Music by
Joey Tempest

* *The Synth. and Organ parts have been combined to be playable by one keyboard.*

F♯m
D
Bm
Synth. Brass 2
3
E
C♯7/E♯
F♯m
D
Bm
E
C♯7/E♯
F♯m
E/G♯

A
D
C♯sus
C♯
3
Organ
F♯m
D
Bm
Bass
E
F♯m
D
Bm
E
F♯m
E/G♯

A
D
C♯sus
C♯
F♯5
Synth. Vocal Pad
Vocal
F♯m
We're leav - ing to - geth - er,
we're head - ing for Ve - nus,
Synth. Pad
Synth. Brass 1
(2nd time only)
Bm
F♯m
but still it's fare - well,
and still we stand tall
and may - be we'll
'cause may - be they've

E/G♯
A
come back to Earth. Who can tell?
seen us and wel - come us all, yeah.
D
E
A
E/G♯
I guess there is no one to blame; we're leav - ing
With so man - y light - years to go and things to be
Synth.
F♯m
A/E
D
C♯m
ground (leav - ing ground). Will things ev - er be the same a - gain?
found, (to be found,) I'm sure that we all miss her so.
E
N.C.
F♯m
It's the fi - nal count - down.
Organ
Synth. Brass 1

D
Bm
E
The fi - nal
F♯m
D
Bm
count - down.
1
2
E
E
F♯m
E/G♯
Oh,
The fi - nal
count - down.

A
D
C♯sus
C♯
Oh,
oh.
F♯m
Bm
Guitar Solo
Organ & Synth.
Drum Solo
Bass
Synth. Brass
A
D
G
D/F♯
Em
A
Bm

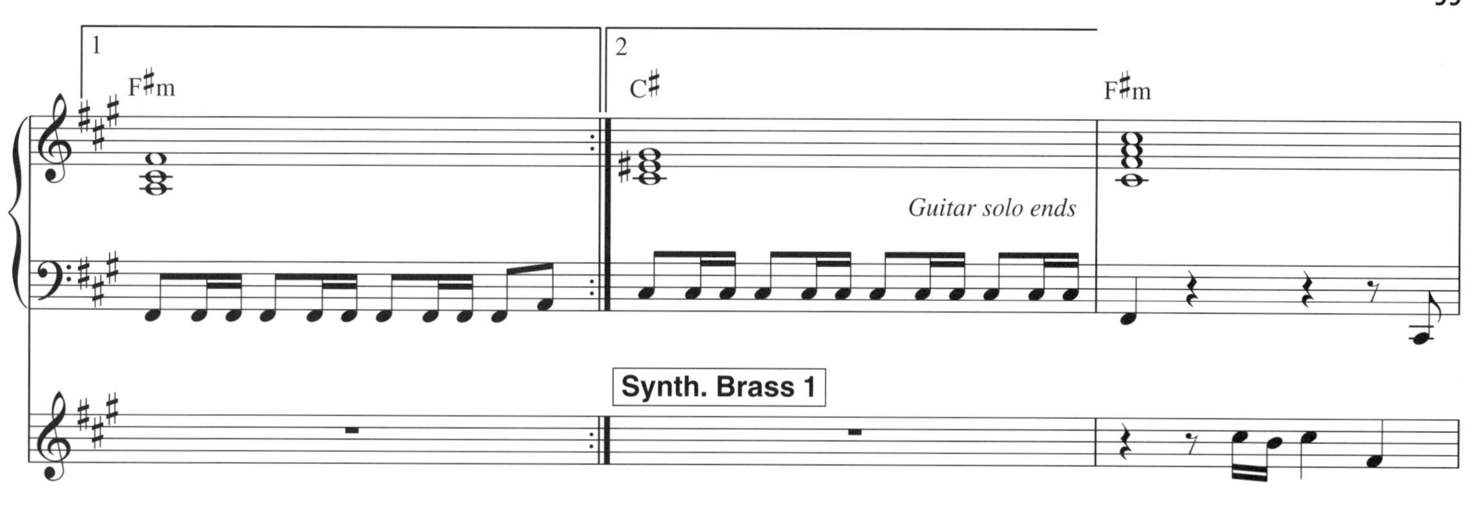
1
F#m
2
C#
F#m
Guitar solo ends
Synth. Brass 1

D
Bm
E
F#m
Synth. Brass 2
3

Vocal
D
Bm
E
F#m
E/G#
The fi - nal count - down.
3

A
D
C#sus
C#
Oh,
it's the fi - nal
F#m
D
Bm
count - down.
count - down.
We're leav - ing to - geth - er.
Organ
E
F#m
D
The fi - nal count - down.
The fi - nal count - down.
We'll all miss her

Bm
E
F♯m
E/G♯
The fin - al count - down. (Fi - nal
so. It's the fi - nal count - down. (Fi - nal
A
D
Repeat and Fade
C♯sus
C♯
count - down.) Oh, it's the fi - nal
count - down.)
Optional Ending
C♯sus
C♯
F♯m

Green-Eyed Lady

Words and Music by Jerry Corbetta,
J.C. Phillips and David Riordan

Vocal
Em7
A7
Green-eyed la-dy, love-ly la - dy stroll - ing
Organ
(Clavinet)
C6
Em7
slow - ly towards the sun.
A7
Green-eyed la - dy, o-cean la - dy sooth - ing

C6
Em7
ev - 'ry rag-ing wave that comes.
A7
Green-eyed la - dy, pas - sion's la - dy dressed in
C6
Em7
love. She lives for life to be.

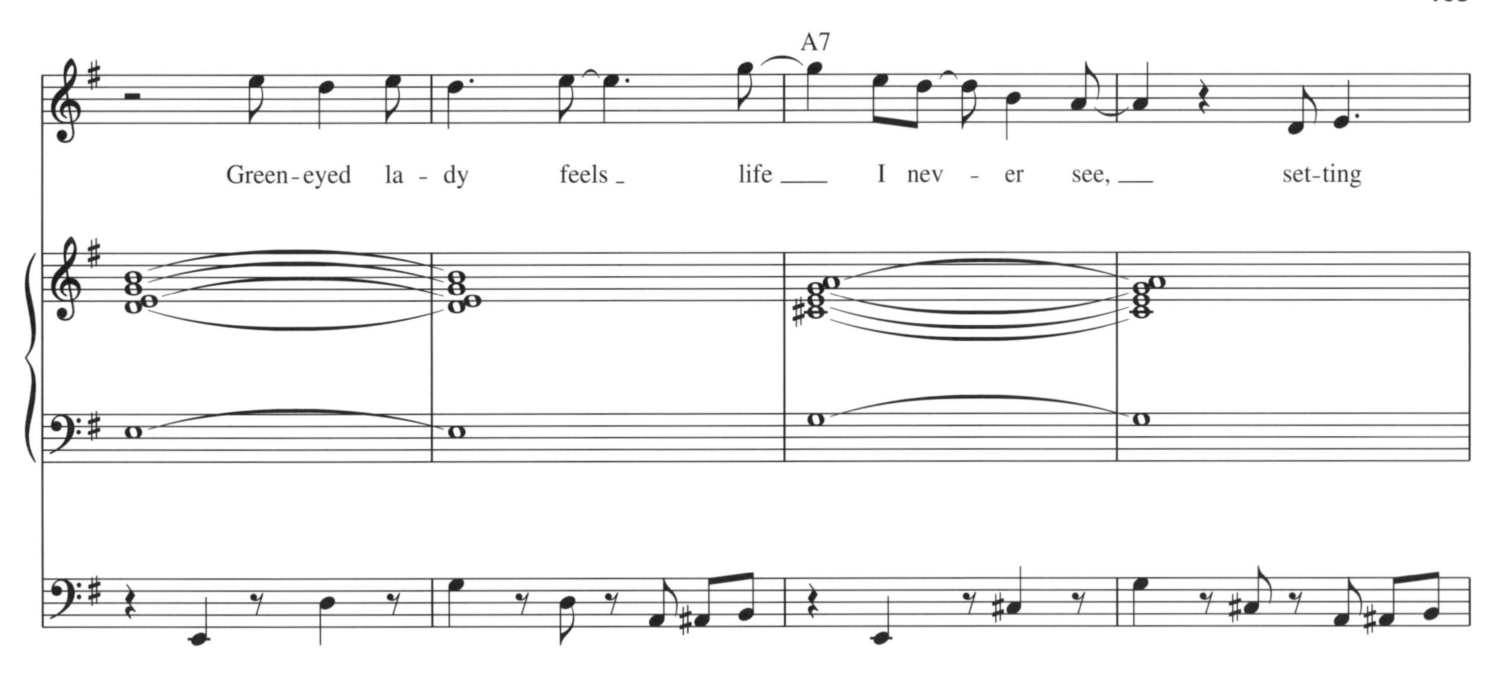
A7
Green-eyed la - dy feels life I nev - er see, set-ting

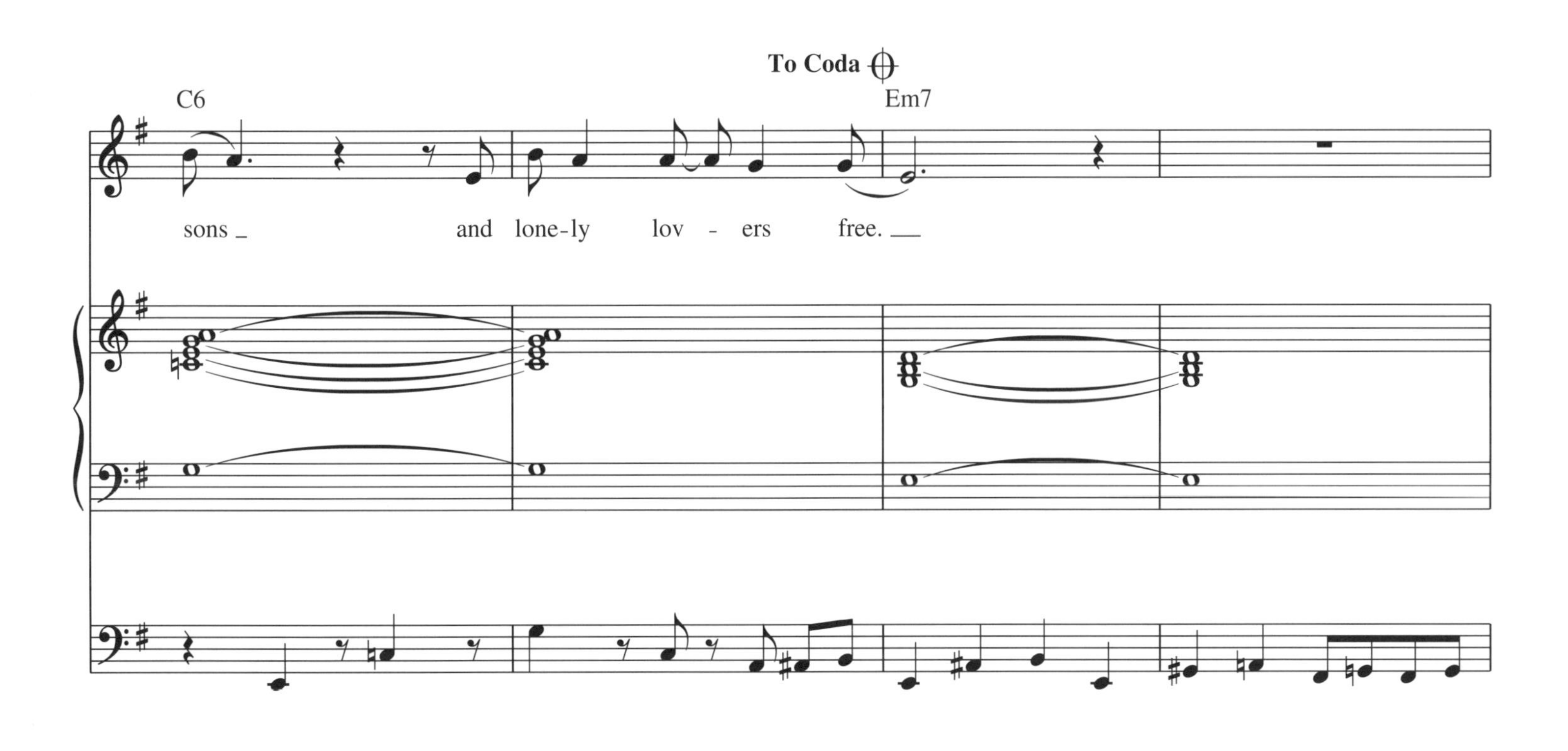
To Coda
C6
Em7
sons and lone-ly lov - ers free.

Em(maj9)
Em
A

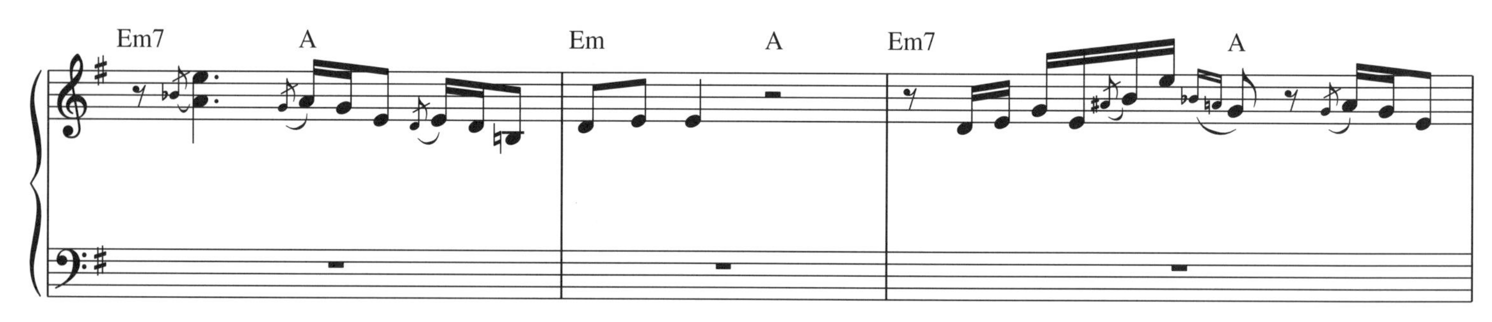
Em7
A
Em
A
Em7
A

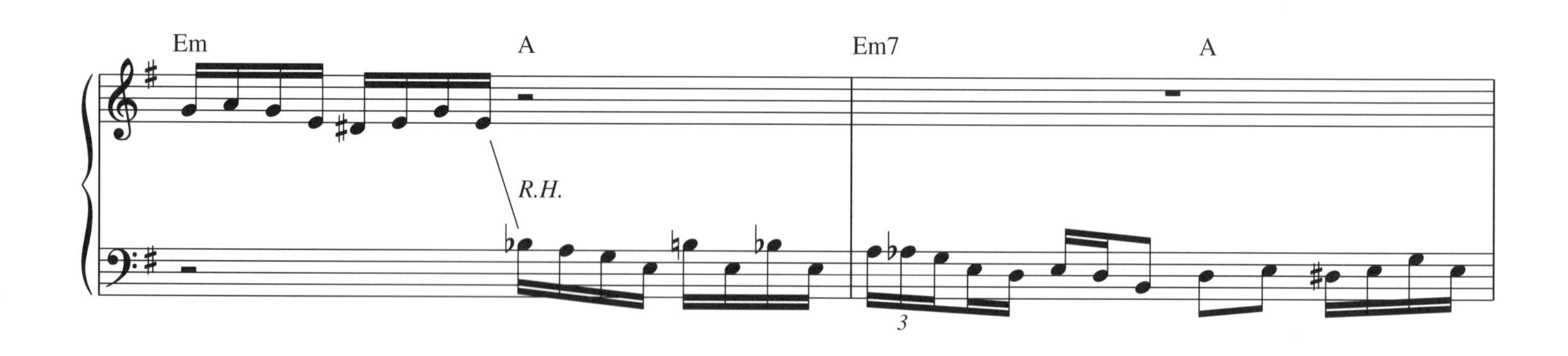
Em
A
Em7
A
R.H.
3

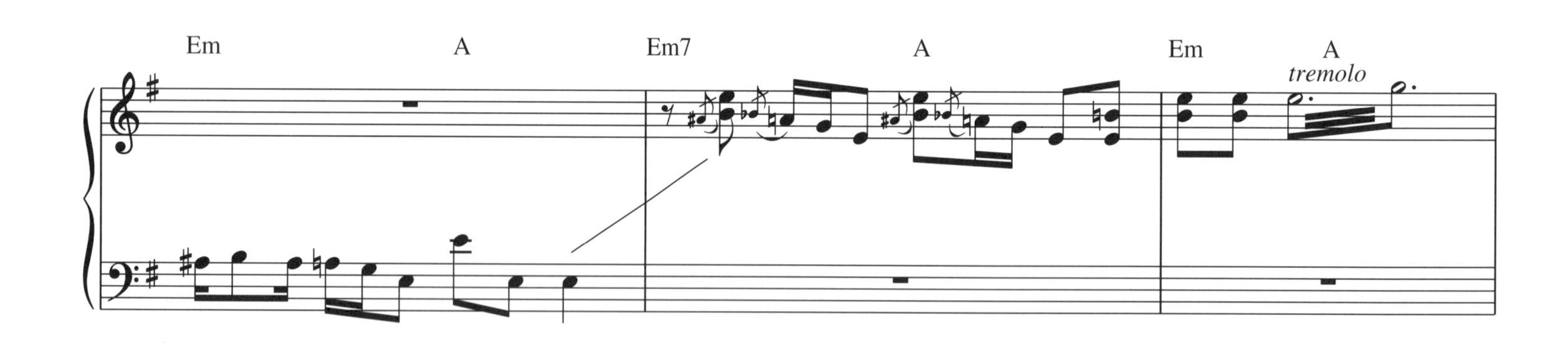
Em
A
Em7
A
Em
A
tremolo

Em7
A
Em
3
A

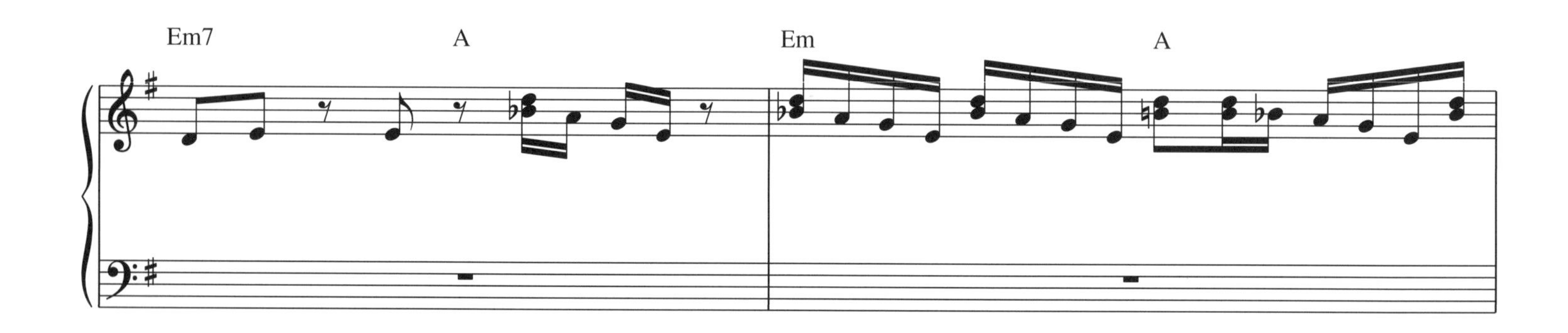
Em7
A
Em
A

Em7
A
Em
A

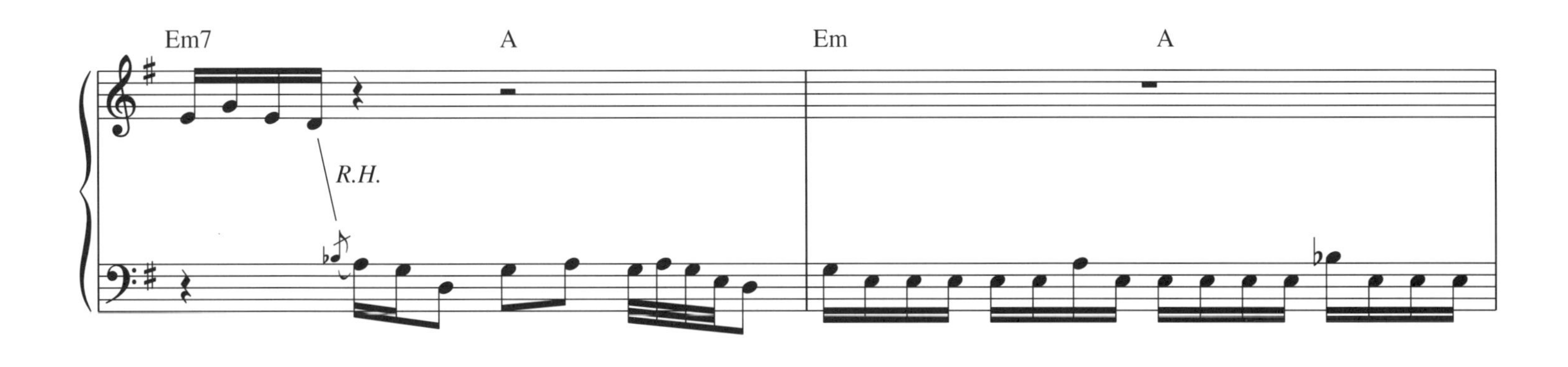
Em7
A
Em
A
R.H.

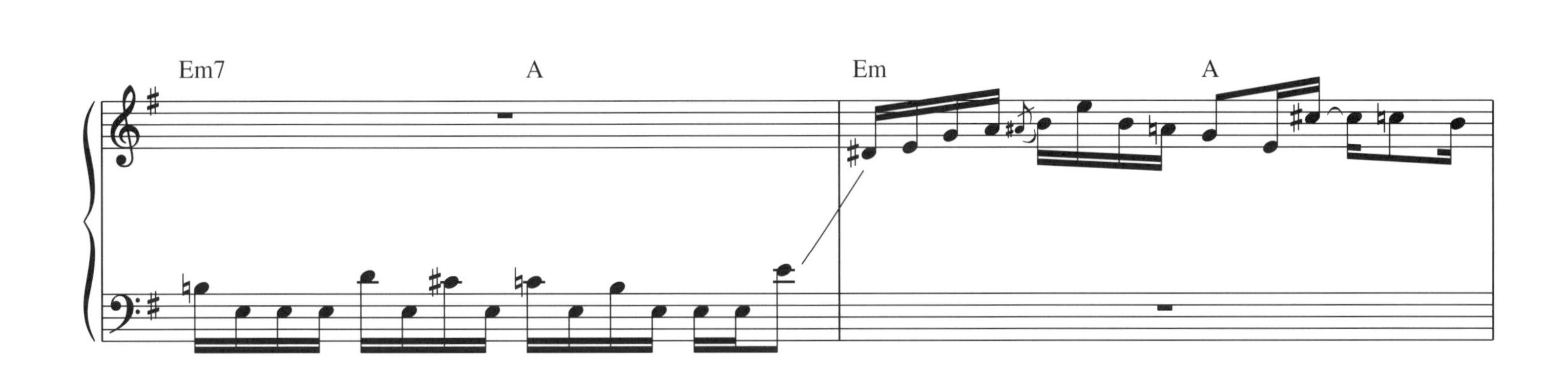
Em7
A
Em
A

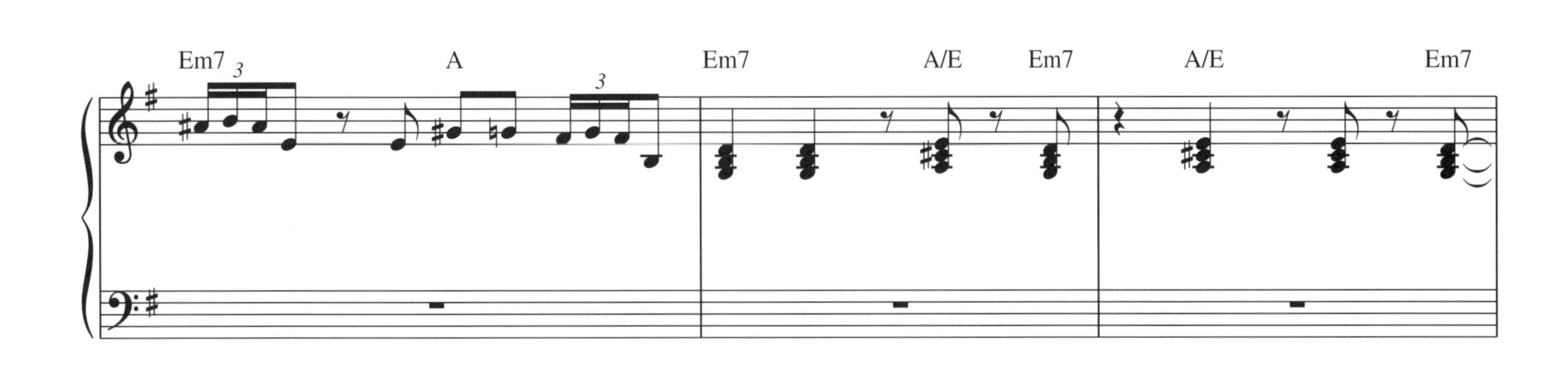
Em7
3
A
3
Em7
A/E
Em7
A/E
Em7

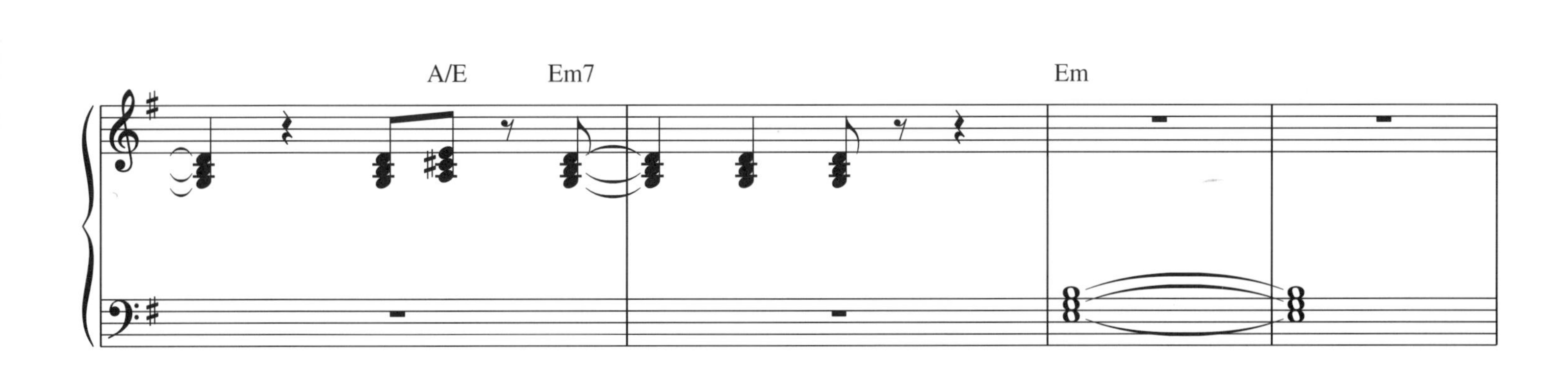
A/E
Em7
Em

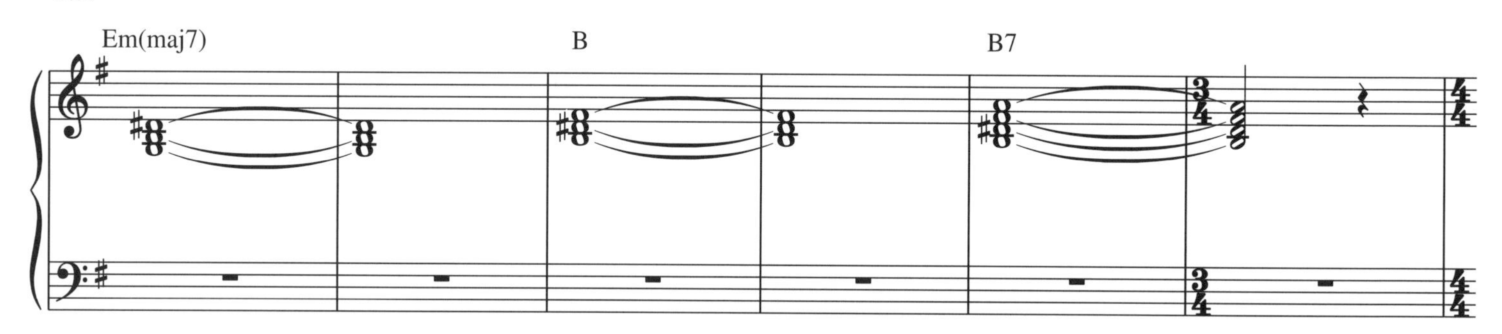
Em(maj7)
B
B7

N.C.

Em7
A7
Green-eyed la - dy, wind - swept la - dy rules the night,
(Clavinet)

C6
Em7
the waves, the sand.
Green-eyed la-dy, o-cean la-dy, child of na-
ture, friend of man.
D.S. al Coda

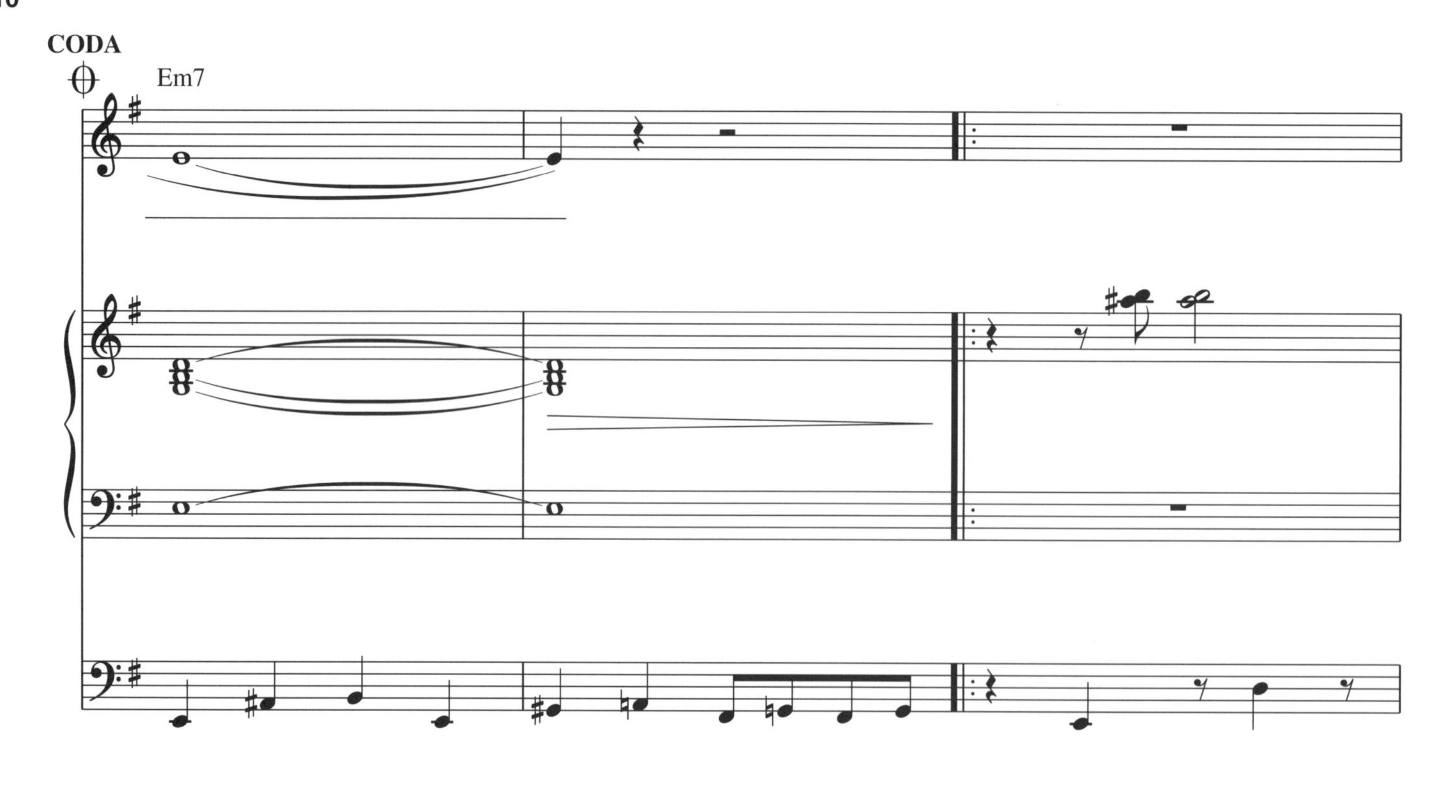
CODA
Em7

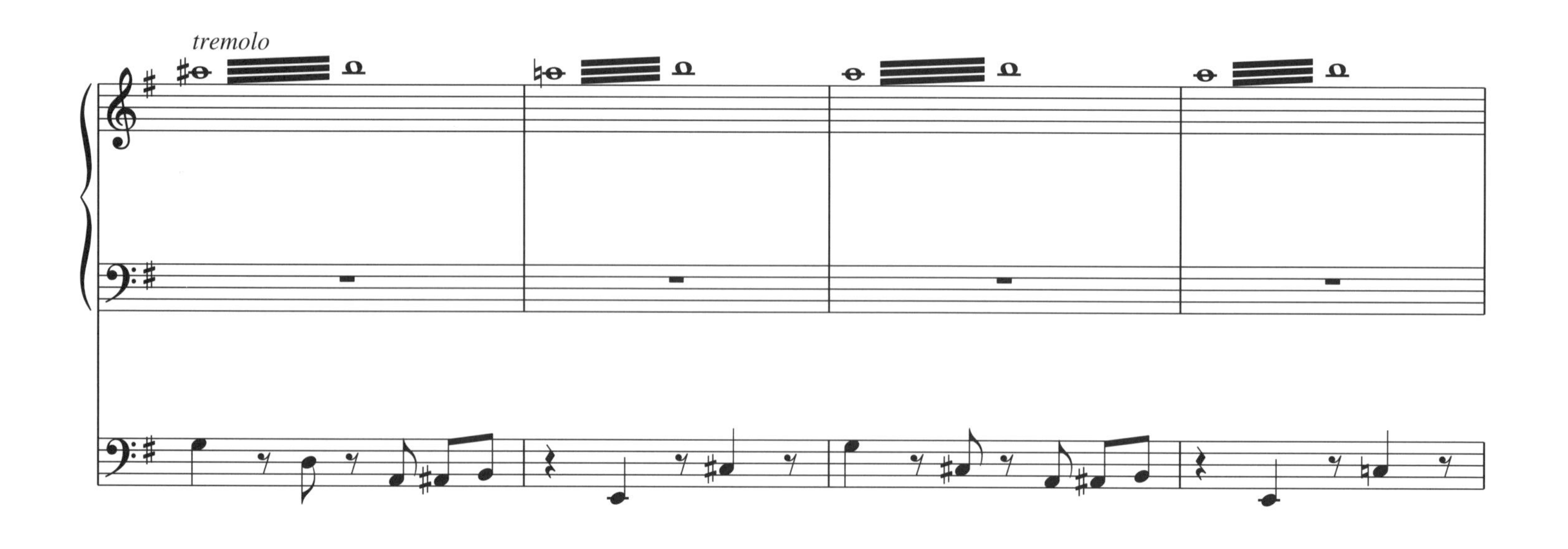
tremolo

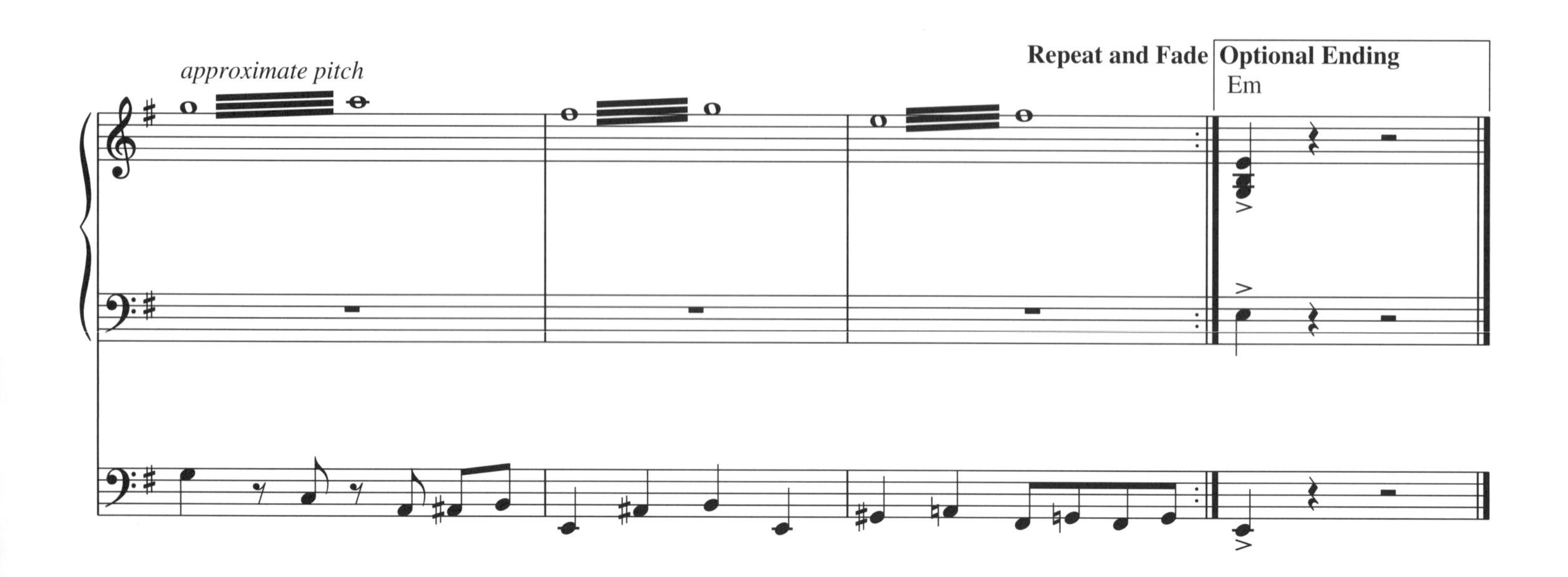
approximate pitch
Repeat and Fade
Optional Ending
Em

I'd Do Anything for Love
(But I Won't Do That)

Words and Music by
Jim Steinman

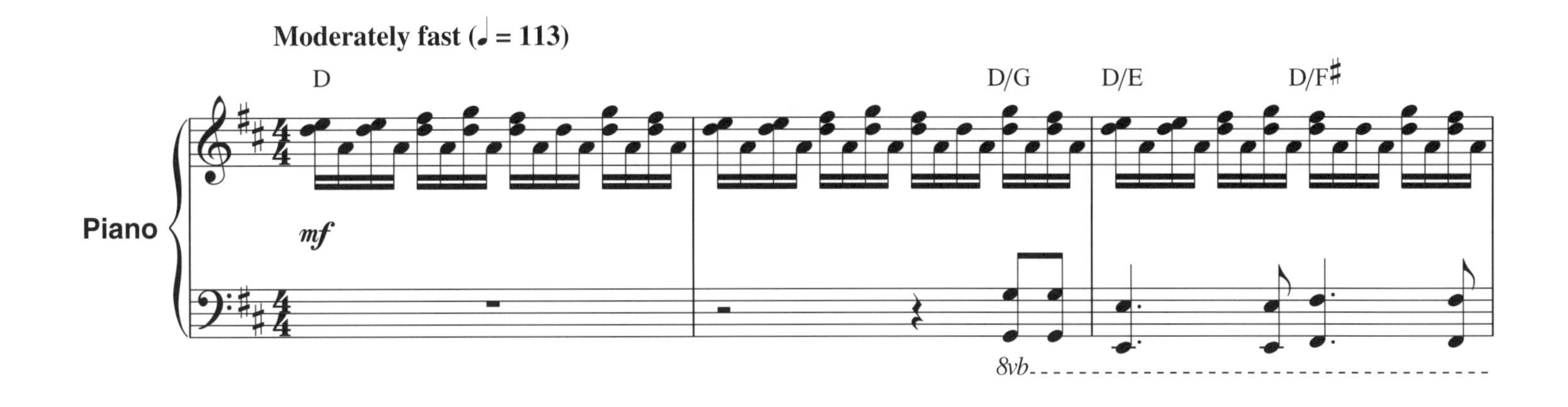

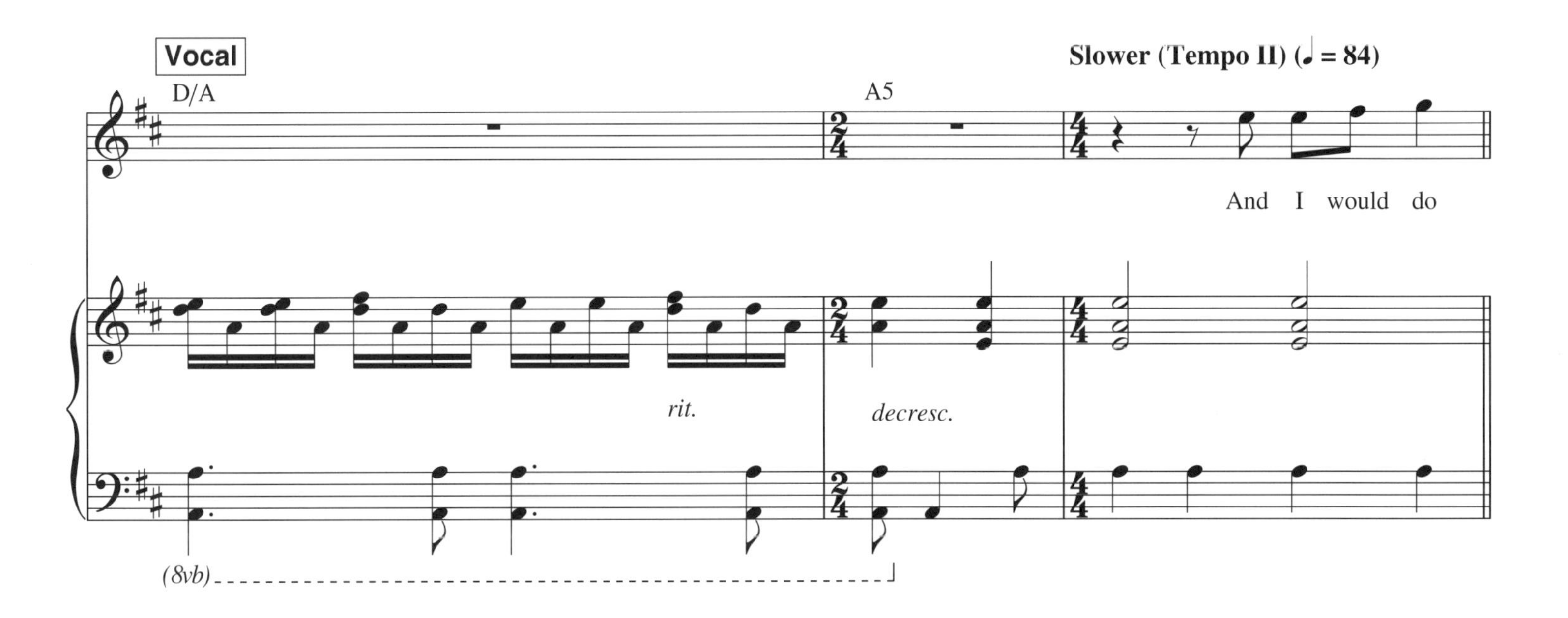

G/D D Gsus2/D Asus/E
I would do an - y - thing for love. I'll nev - er lie to you and
D A/D G(add2)/D Bm
that's a fact. But I'll nev - er for - get the way you
F♯m/A G(add2) A
feel right now, oh no, no way. And I would do
D Gsus2/D Asus/E D Gsus2/D Em7(add4)
an - y - thing for love. Oh, I would do an - y - thing for love.

D
Gsus2/D
Asus/E
D/A
A
I would do an - y - thing for love, but I won't do
G(add9)
A7sus
Tempo I
D
that.
No, I won't do that.
mf
Bass & Piano
Gmaj7
A
Bm
And some days it don't
And some nights you're breath -
that. And some days I pray
Bass

Gsus2
come eas - y, and some days it don't come hard.
- ing fire, and some nights you're carved in ice.
for si - lence, and some days I pray for soul.
Em7(add4)
D
Some days it don't come at all and these are the days that
Some nights are like noth - ing I've ev - er seen be - fore or
Some days I just pray to the god of sex and drums and
Play Fill 1 (2nd & 3rd time)
1
2, 3
D
Gsus2
nev - er end.
will a - gain. May - be I'm
rock 'n' roll. And may - be I'm
(Half-time feel)
Fill 1
D
Dsus2

D
Bm
Asus
A
cra - zy. Oh, it's cra - zy and it's true.
lone - ly, that's all I'm qual - i - fied to be.
G
D
Bm
I know you can save me. No one else can save me now but
There's just one and on - ly, one and on - ly prom - ise I can
Asus
A
Em
you. As long as the plan - ets are turn - ing,
keep. As long as the wheels are turn - ing,
(End half-time feel)
Bass & Guitar
C♯dim7
G
as long as the stars are burn - ing, as long as your dreams
as long as the fires are burn - ing, as long as your prayers

A7
___ are com - ing true, you bet - ter be - lieve ___ it, that I would do
___ are com - ing true, you bet - ter be - lieve ___ it, that I would do
Bass
molto rit.
Tempo II
D Gsus2/D Asus/E
D Gsus2/D Em7(add4)
an - y - thing _ for love. Oh, I would do an - y - thing _ for love.
an - y - thing _ for love, and you know it's true and that's a fact. _
Play Fill 2 (2nd time)
Piano
To Coda
D Gsus2/D Asus/E
Oh, I would do an - y - thing ___ for love, but I won't do ___
I would do an - y - thing ___ for love, and there'll nev - er be no
* Organ comps next eight bars.
Fill 2
D A G

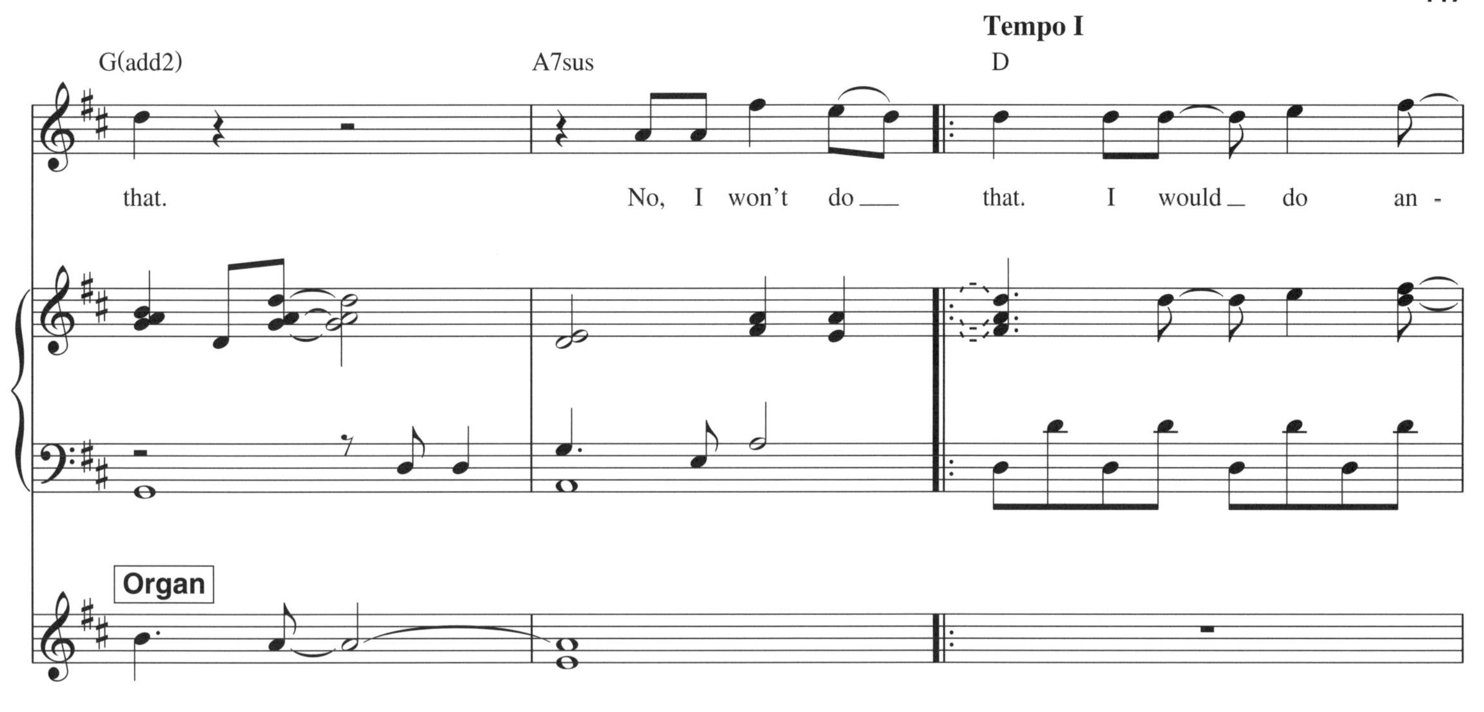
Tempo I
G(add2)
A7sus
D
that.
No, I won't do
that. I would do an -
Organ

Bm
- y - thing for love,
an - y - thing you've been dream - ing of,

Gsus2
1
A
2
A
D.S. al Coda
(take 2nd ending)
but I just
won't do
won't do...

CODA
D
A
G
Bm
turn - ing back.
But I'll nev - er do it bet - ter than I
Bass
mp

F♯m/A
G(add2)
Asus
do it with you. So long, so long. And I would do
Piano

D
Gsus2
A
D
Gsus2
Em7(add4)
an - y - thing for love. Oh, I would do an - y - thing for love.
f
Bass
8vb
Organ

D
Gsus2
A
I would do an - y - thing for love, but I won't do
(8vb)

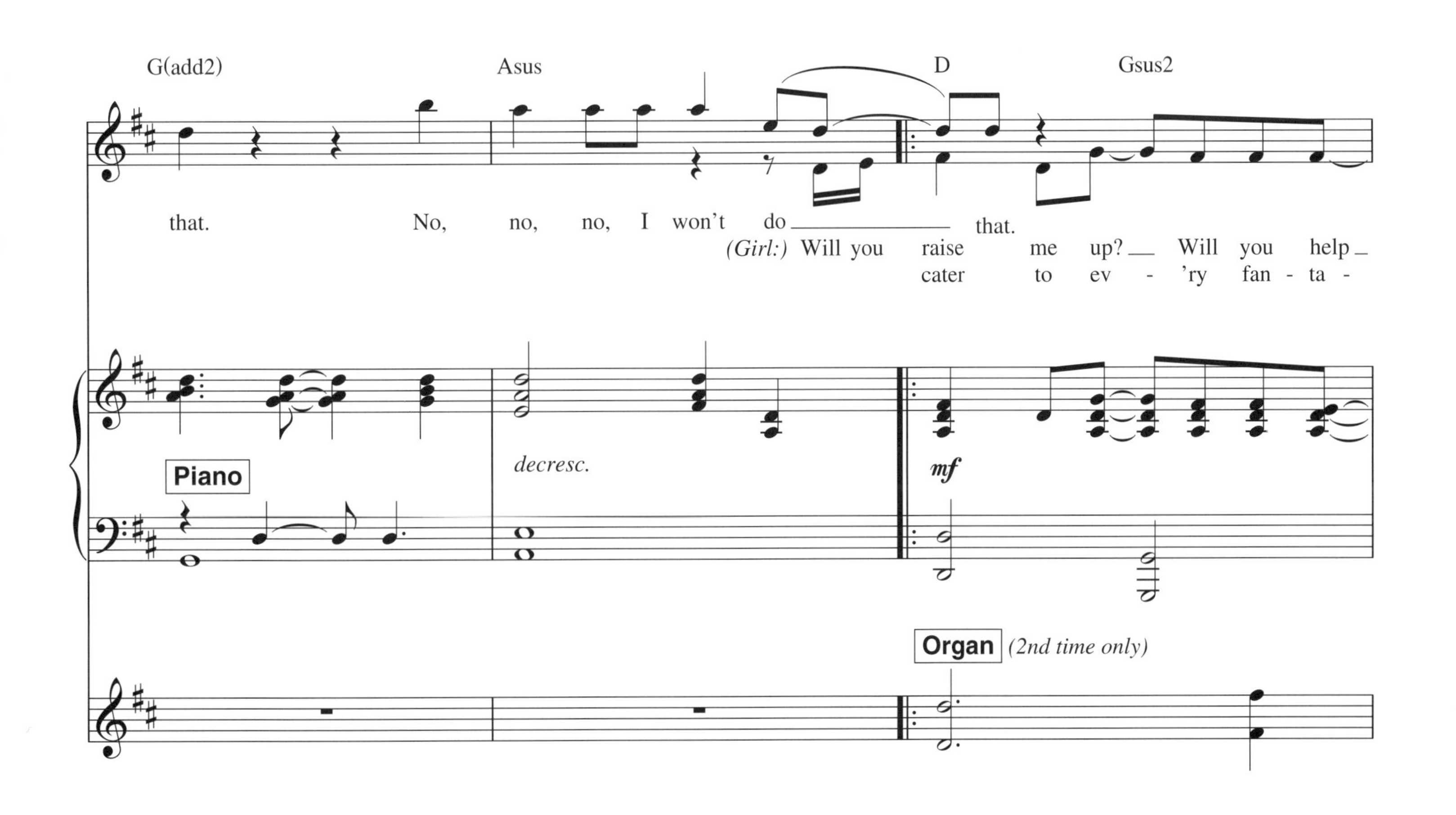
G(add2)
Asus
D
Gsus2
that. No, no, no, I won't do that.
(Girl:) Will you raise me up? Will you help
cater to ev - 'ry fan - ta -
Piano
decresc.
mf
Organ
(2nd time only)

Asus
D
Gsus2
Em7(add4)
me down? Will you get me right out of this god - for - sak - en town? Will you
sy I got? Will you hose me down with ho - ly wa - ter if I get too hot? Will you
D
Gsus2
Asus
D/A
A
Gsus2
make it all a lit - tle less cold? (Boy:) I can do that, oh,
take me plac - es I've nev - er gone? (Boy:) I can do that, oh,
1
Asus
A7
2
Asus
D
Gsus2
oh, no, I can do oh, no, I can do that.
(Girl:) Will you (Girl:) I know the ter - ri - to - ry.
Synth. & Piano
mp
Bass
Synth.

Asus
D
Gsus2
Em7(add4)
I've been a - round. It - 'll all turn to dust and we'll all fall down.
Piano
Piano
D
Gsus2
Asus
D6/A
Asus
Soon - er or lat - er you'll be screw - ing a - round.
(Boy:)
I won't do
rit.
Slower
Gsus2
Asus
D
Gsus2/D
Asus/E
that. No, I won't do that.
An - y - thing for love,
D/A
A7sus
D
but I won't do that.
8va
decresc.
pp
8vb

Heaven

Words and Music by Bryan Adams
and Jim Vallance

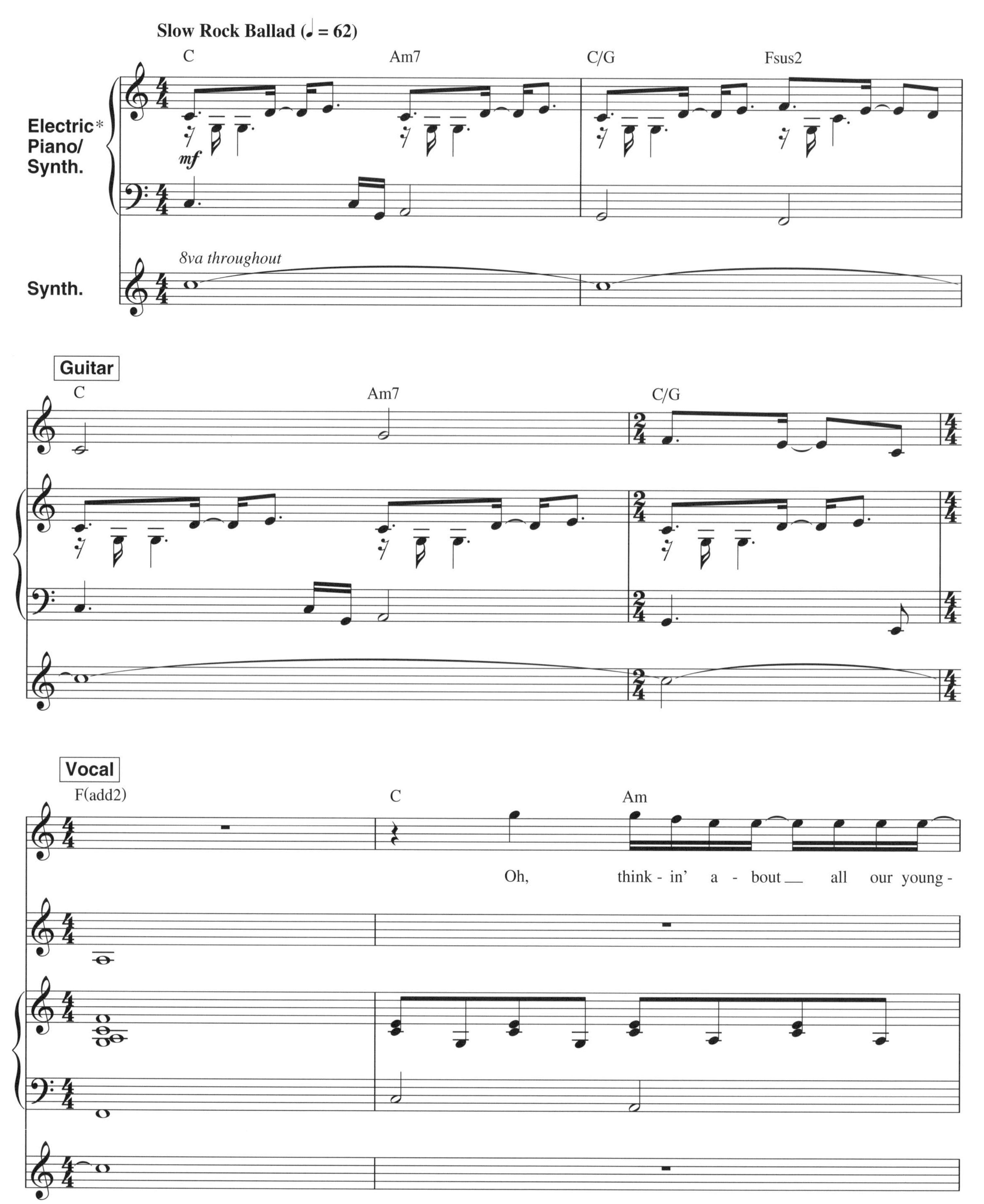

* *The Electric Piano and Synth. parts have been combined to be playable by one piano.*

G
Dm
Am
- er years. There was on - ly you and me. We were

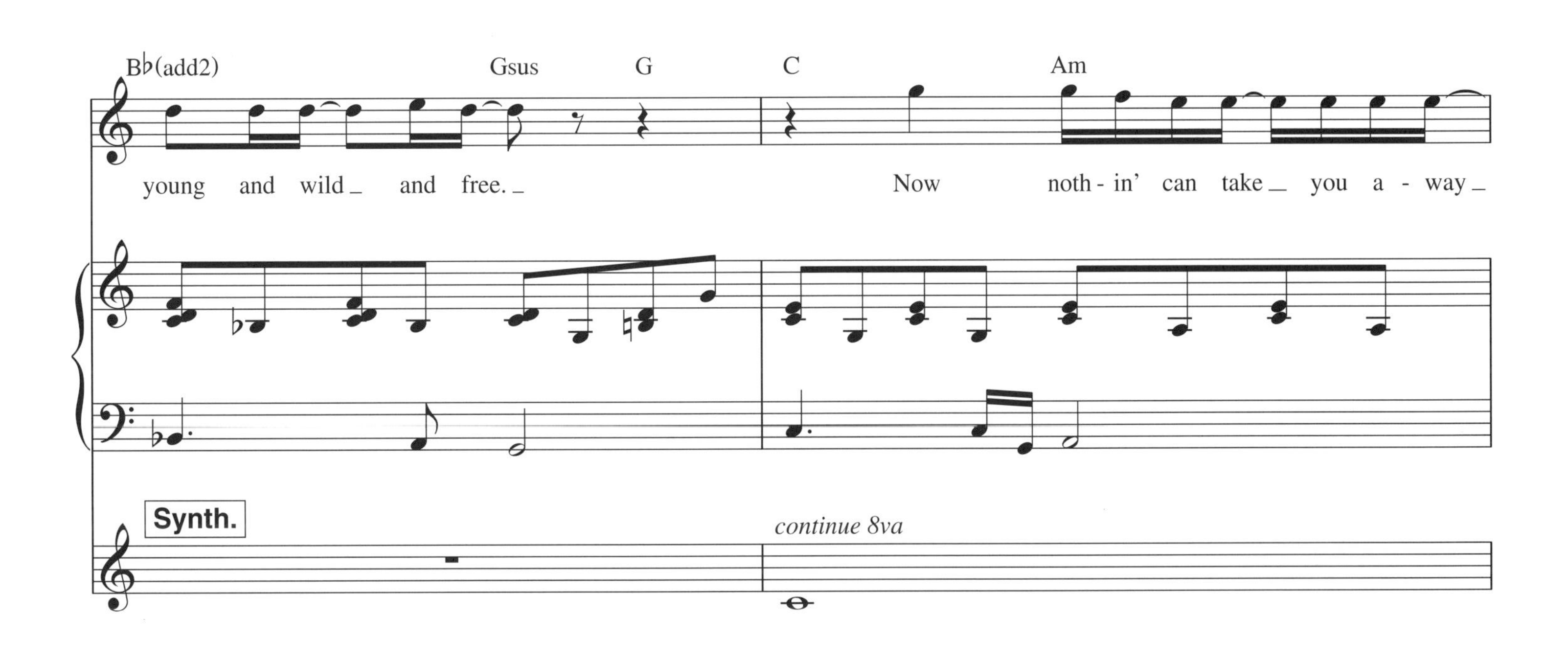
B♭(add2)
Gsus
G
C
Am
young and wild and free. Now noth - in' can take you a - way
Synth.
continue 8va

G
Dm
Am
from me. We've been down that road be - fore, but that's

B♭(add2)
F/A
Gsus
G
o - ver now.
You keep me com - in' back for more.

F
G
Am
C
F
Ba - by, you're all that I want
ba - by, you're all that I want
when you're ly - in' here in my arms. I'm

G
Am
G
find - ing it hard to be - lieve we're in heav - en. And

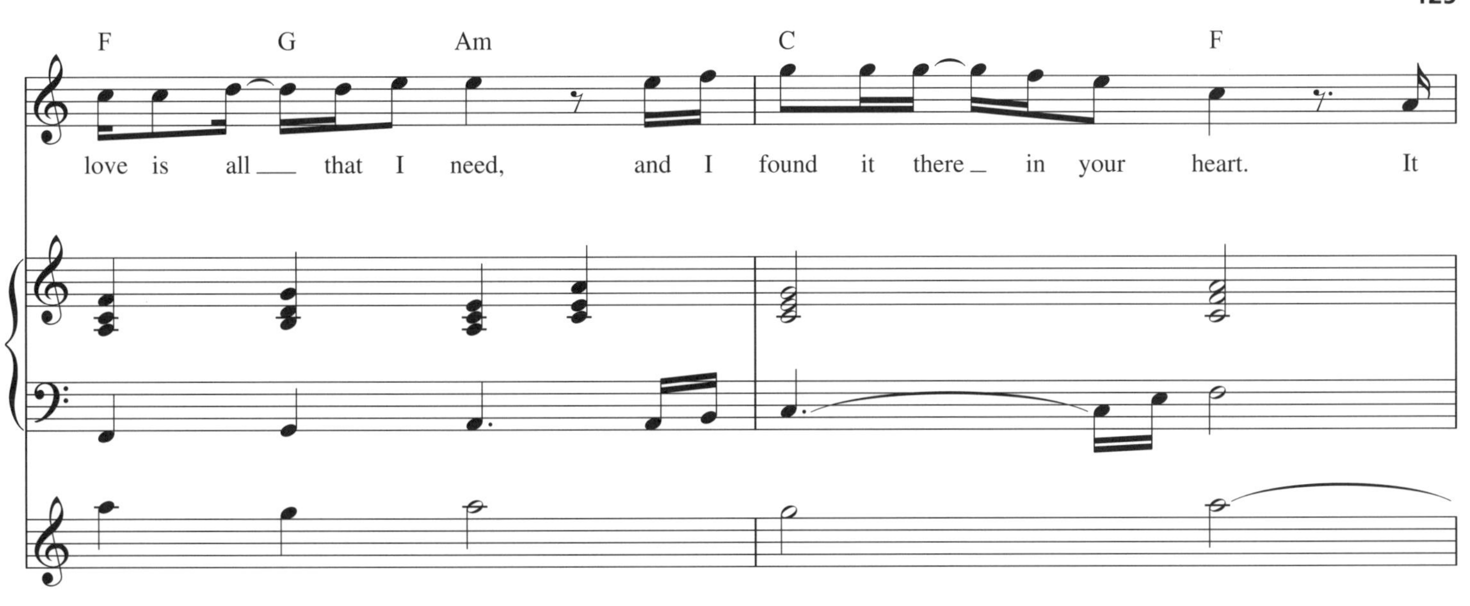
F G Am C F
love is all that I need, and I found it there in your heart. It

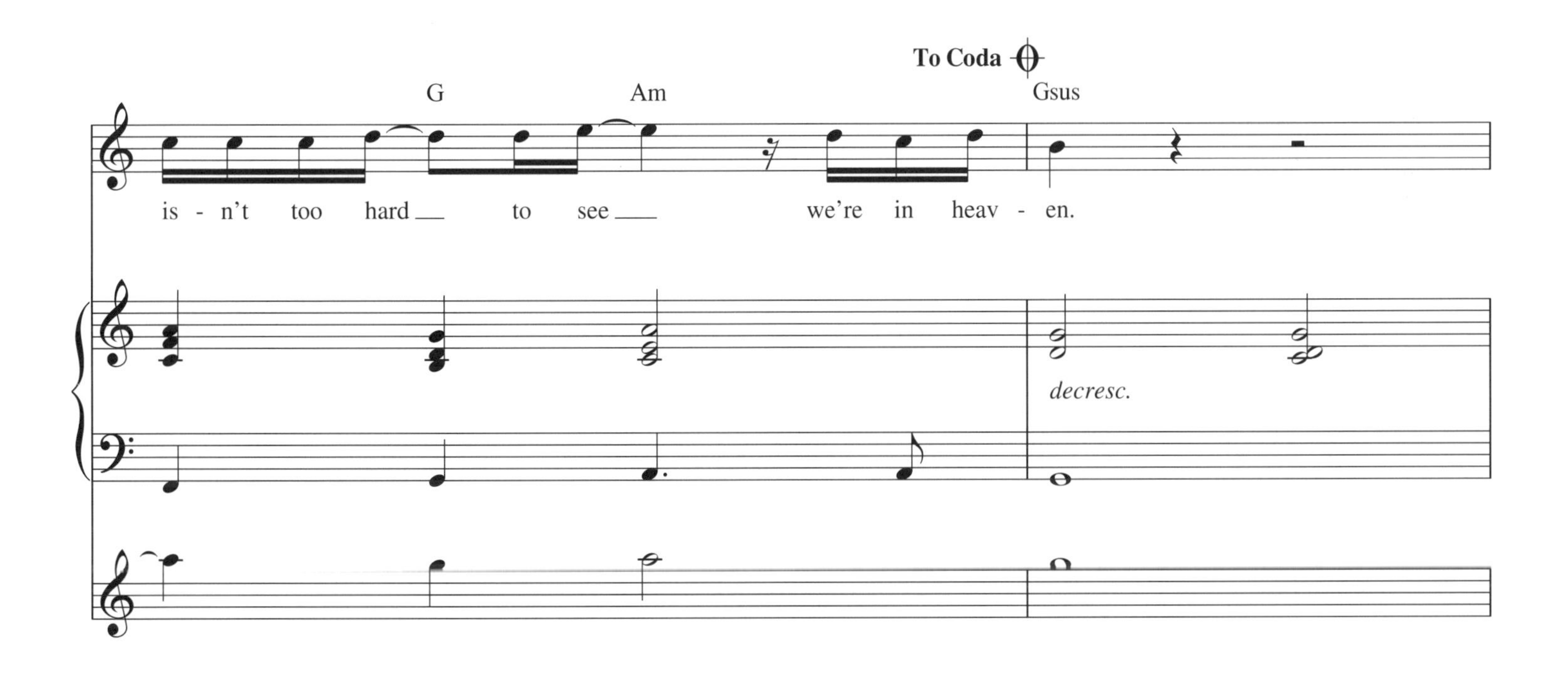
To Coda
G Am Gsus
is - n't too hard to see we're in heav - en.
decresc.

Guitar
C Am7 C/G
mf

Vocal
F(add2)
C
Am
Oh, once in your life you find
loco
G
Dm
Am
some-one who will turn your world a-round, bring you
B♭(add2)
Gsus
C
Am
up when you're feel-in' down.
Yeah, noth-in' can change what you mean

G
Dm
Am
to me. Oh, there's lots that I could say. Just

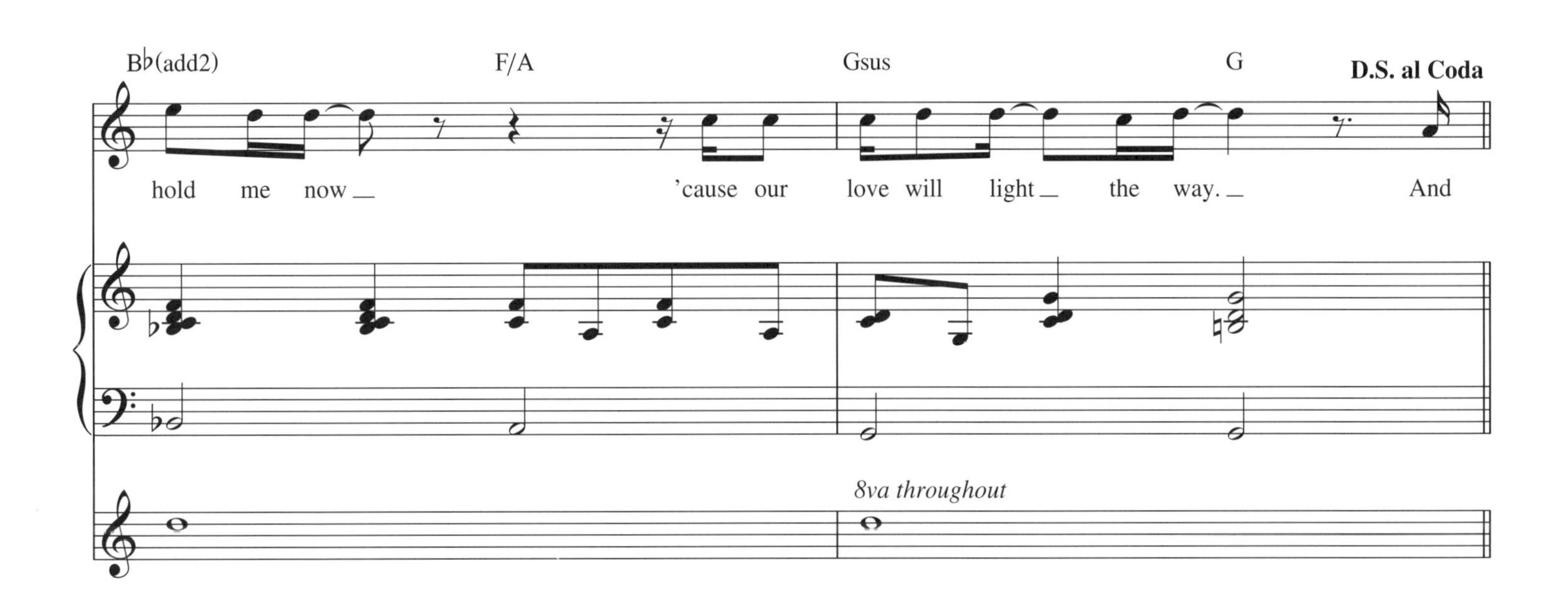
B♭(add2)
F/A
Gsus
G
D.S. al Coda
hold me now 'cause our love will light the way. And
8va throughout

CODA
G
en. Yeah.

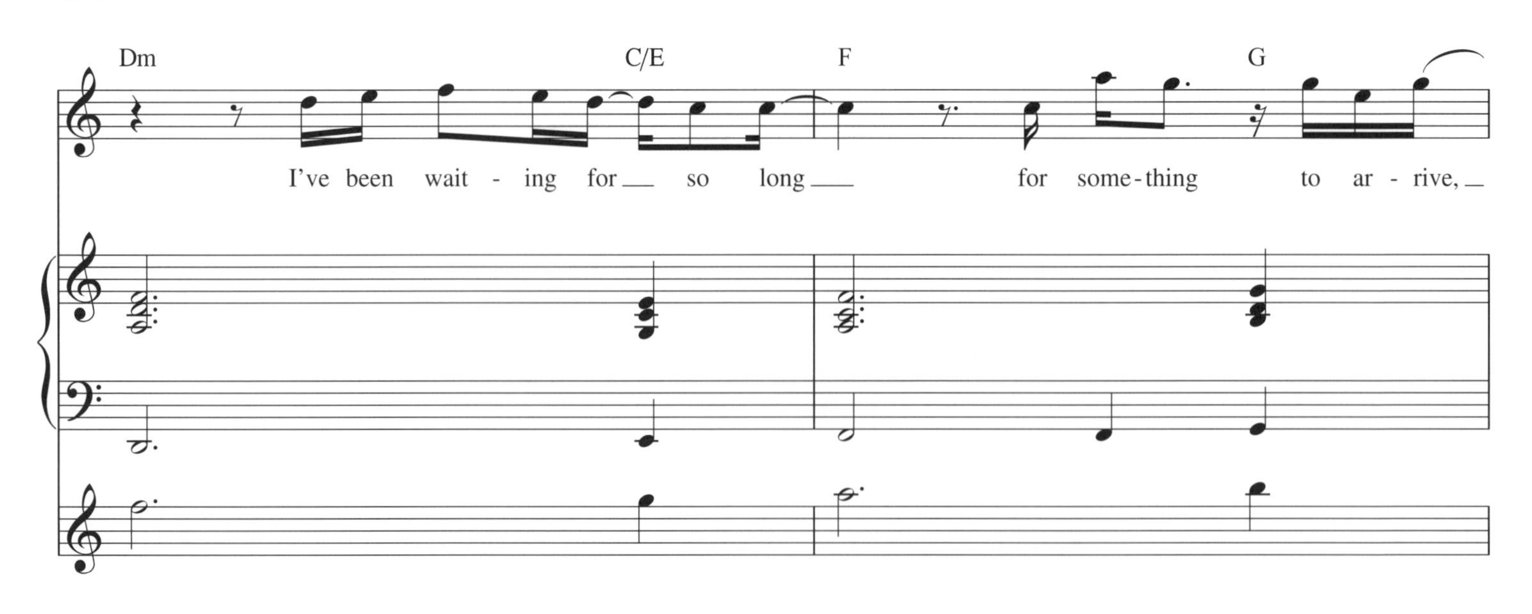
Dm
C/E
F
G
I've been wait - ing for so long for some-thing to ar - rive,

Am
G/B
C
for love to come a - long.

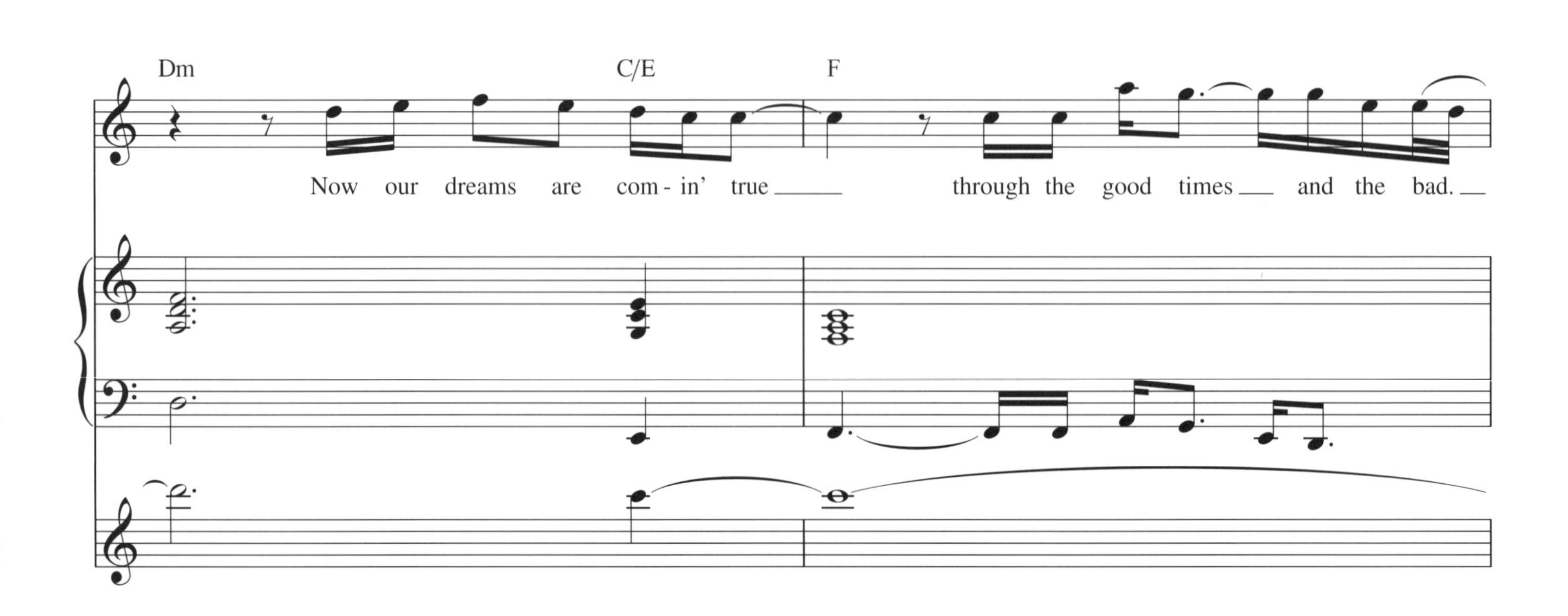
Dm
C/E
F
Now our dreams are com - in' true through the good times and the bad.

C
Gsus
G
Yeah, I'll be stand - in' there by you, oh.
Guitar
F
G
Am
C
F
Vocal
F
G
Am
G
And,

F G Am C F
ba - by, you're all that I want when you're ly - in' here in my arms. I'm

G Am G
find - in' it hard to be - lieve we're in heav - en. And

F G Am C F
love is all that I need, and I found it there in your heart. It

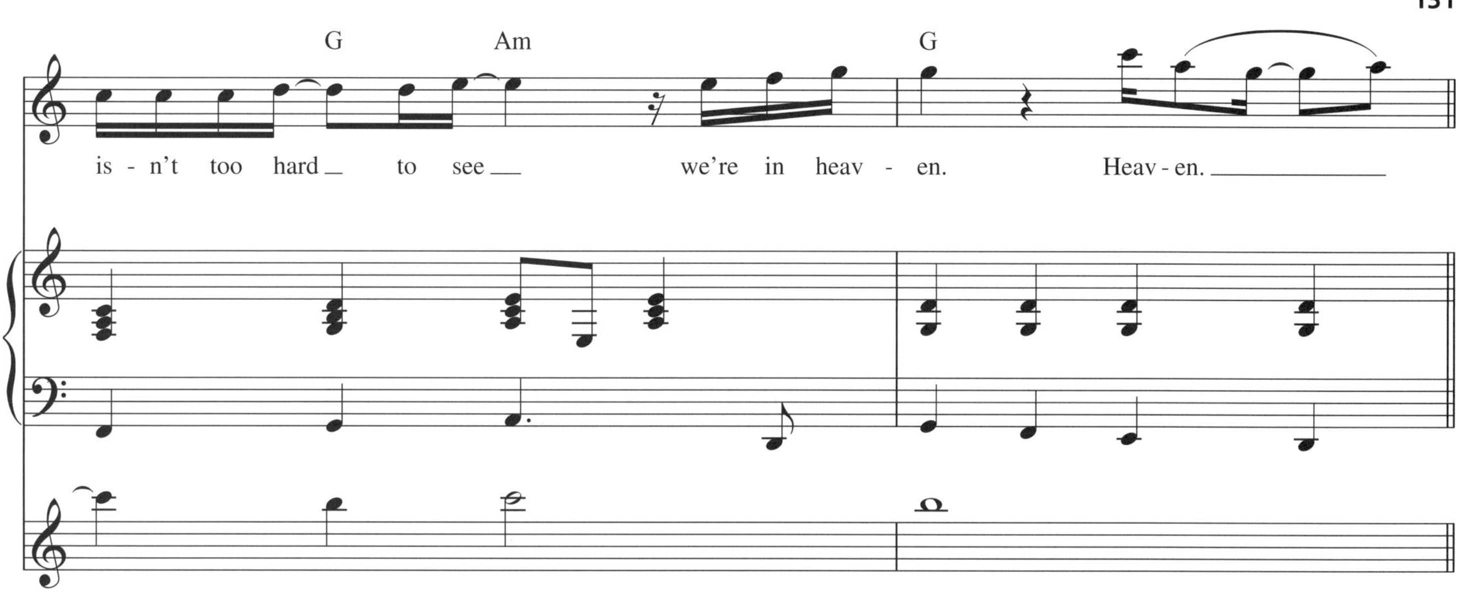
G
Am
G
is - n't too hard to see we're in heav - en. Heav - en.

F
G
Am
C
F
Whoa.
You're

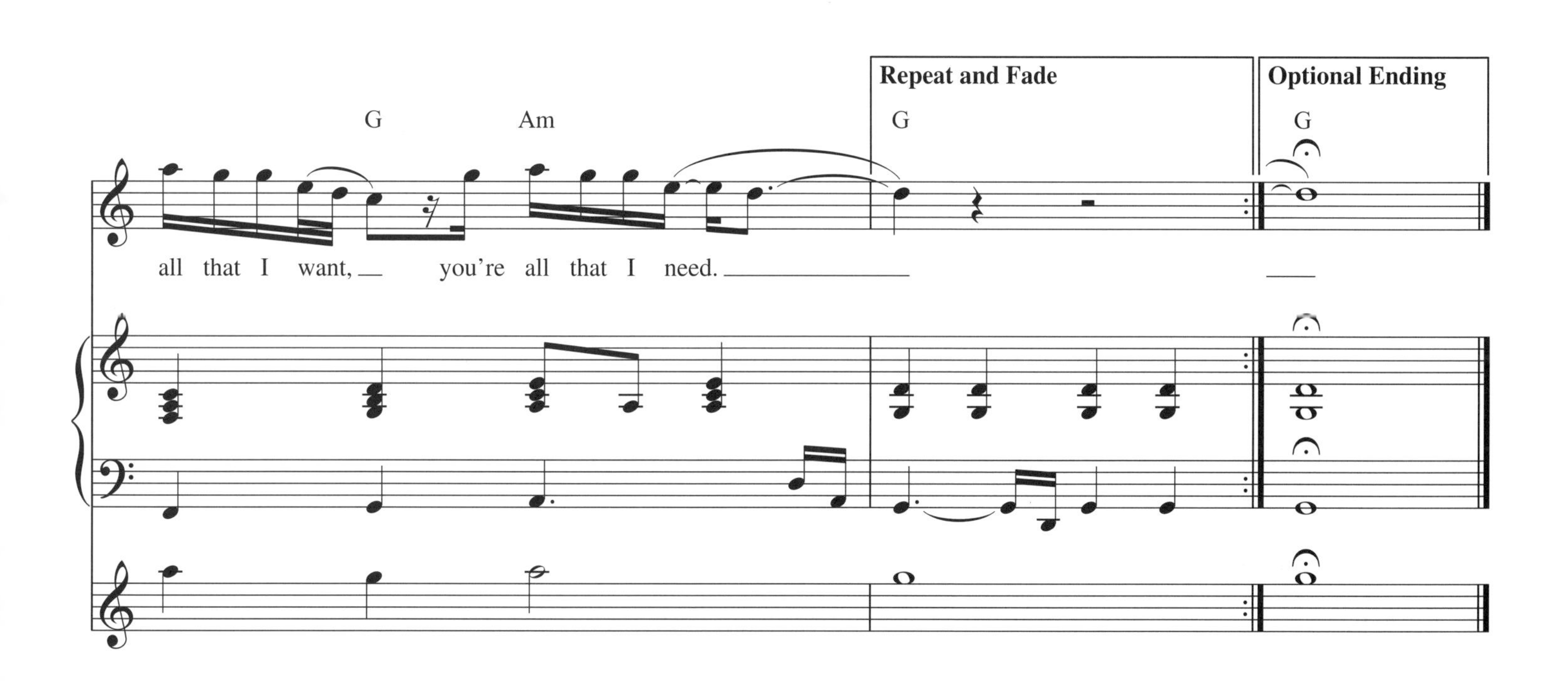
Repeat and Fade
Optional Ending
G
Am
G
G
all that I want, you're all that I need.

Joy to the World

Words and Music by
Hoyt Axton

wine.
Sing - in' joy to the world,
A
D
D7/C
all the boys and girls now.
Joy to the fish - es in the
G/B
B♭
D/A
A/C♯
To Coda
D
C
C♯
D
deep blue sea,
joy to you and me.
N.C.
C
C♯
D
N.C.
If I were the king of the world,
tell you what I'd do.

C C♯ D D7/C G/B B♭
I'd throw a - way the cars and the bars and the wars,
D/A A D
make sweet love to you. Sing it now. Joy to the
A D
world, all the boys and girls.
D7/C G/B B♭ D/A A/C♯ D
Joy to the fish - es in the deep blue sea, joy to you and me.

D
A
D
D7/C
G7/B
B♭
N.C.
D.S. al Coda
C
C♯
D
You

CODA
A7/C♯
D
Joy to the world,

A
D
D7/C
all the boys and girls.
Joy to the fish - es in the
G/B
B♭
D/A
A/C♯
D
deep blue sea,
joy to you and me.
E
A
A/C♯ D D♯
E
Joy to the world,
all the boys
A
E
A
A/C♯
D D♯
and girls.
Joy to the world,

E A G/A D
joy to you and me. Joy to the
A D
world, all the boys and girls now.
D7/C G/B B♭
Joy to the fish - es in the deep blue sea,
Repeat and Fade
D/A A/C♯ D
joy to you and me.
Optional Ending
D/A A D C C♯ D
joy to you and me.

Killer Queen

Words and Music by Freddie Mercury

Ab m
Eb/Bb
Bb11
Bb7
an - y - time _ an in - vi - ta - tion you can't _ de - cline. ___
G7
Cm
Bb
Eb
Ca - vi - ar ___ and ci - ga - rettes, well versed _ in e - ti - quette, ex -
D7
Gm
F
Bb
Dm
Gm
Dm
tr'or - di - na - ri - ly nice. She's a Kil - ler Queen, ___ gun - pow - der, ge - la - tine, _
(Backing vocals)
She's a Kil - ler Queen, ___ gun pow - der, gel - a - tine, _
Gm
A7
Dm
G7
F/A
G7/B
C
dy - na - mite __ with a la - ser beam. _ N' gua - ran - teed __ to blow __ your mind. ______
dy - na - mite __ with a la - ser beam. _ Ba, ba, ba, ba,

B♭
A
Dm
Ooh
re-com-mend-ed at the price,
in-
an-y-time,
G7
C
B♭
F
B♭/F
F11
sa-tia-ble an ap-pe-tite,
wan-na try?
wan-na try?
B♭/F
F11
F
B♭
E♭/G
F11
F
B♭
E♭/G
To a-
Cm
B♭7/D
void com-pli-ca-tions she nev-er kept the same ad-dress,

Cm
Bb7/D
Eb
in con - ver - sa - tion she spoke just like a ba - ron - ess.
Gm/D
Eb7/Db
Ab
Met a man from Chi - na, went down to Gei - sha Mi - nah, but
(Backing Vocals)
Ooh A kil - ler, a
Abm
Eb/Bb
Bb11
Bb7
then a - gain in - ci - dent - 'ly if you're that way in - clined. Per - fume came
kil - ler, she's a Kil - ler Queen.
G7
Cm
Bb
Eb
nat - 'ral - ly from Pa - ris, for cars she could - n't care less, fas -
Nat - 'ral - ly.

D7
Gm
F
B♭
Dm
ti - di - ous and pre - cise. She's a Kil - ler Queen,
She's a Kil - ler Queen,
Gm
Dm
Gm
A7
Dm
gun - pow - der, ge - la - tine, dy - na - mite with a la - ser beam.
gun - pow - der, ge - la - tine, dy - na - mite with a la - ser beam.
G7
F/A
G7/B
C
B♭
Gua - ran - teed to blow your mind.
Ba, ba, ba, ba, an - y - time.
A
Dm
A
Dm
G
Cm
(Guitar solo)

G
Cm
F11
Cm
B♭7/D
Cm
B♭7/D
E♭
Gm/D
E♭7/D♭
A♭
A♭m
E♭/B♭
B♭11
B♭7
E♭/B♭
B♭11
B♭7
Drop _ of a

G7
Cm
G7
Cm
hat she's as will-ing as,
play-ful as a pus-sy cat, then
(Backing Vocals)
Ooh,
B♭
E♭
B♭
E♭
mo-men-ta-ri-ly out of ac-tion,
tem-po-ra-ri-ly out of gas, to
ooh,
da,
da,
D7
Gm
F
B♭
F
ab-so-lute-ly drive...
drive you wild,

B♭m F B♭ Dm
She's all out to get you. She's a Kil-ler Queen,
wild. She's a Kil-ler Queen,
Gm Dm Gm A7 Dm
gun - pow - der, ge-la-tine, dy-na-mite with a la-ser beam.
gun - pow - der, ge-la-tine, dy-na-mite with a la-ser beam.
G7 F/A G7/B C B♭
Gua-ran-teed to blow your mind. Ooh
Ba, ba, ba, ba, a-ny-time,
A Dm G7 C
re-com-mend - ed at the price, in - sa - tia - ble an ap-pe-tite,

Bb
F
Bb/F
F11
F
Bb
Eb/G
wan-na try?
You wan-na try...
(Backing Vocals)
wan-na try?
F11
F
Bb
Eb/G
F
Bb
Eb7
Repeat and Fade
Optional Ending

Lady Madonna

Words and Music by John Lennon
and Paul McCartney

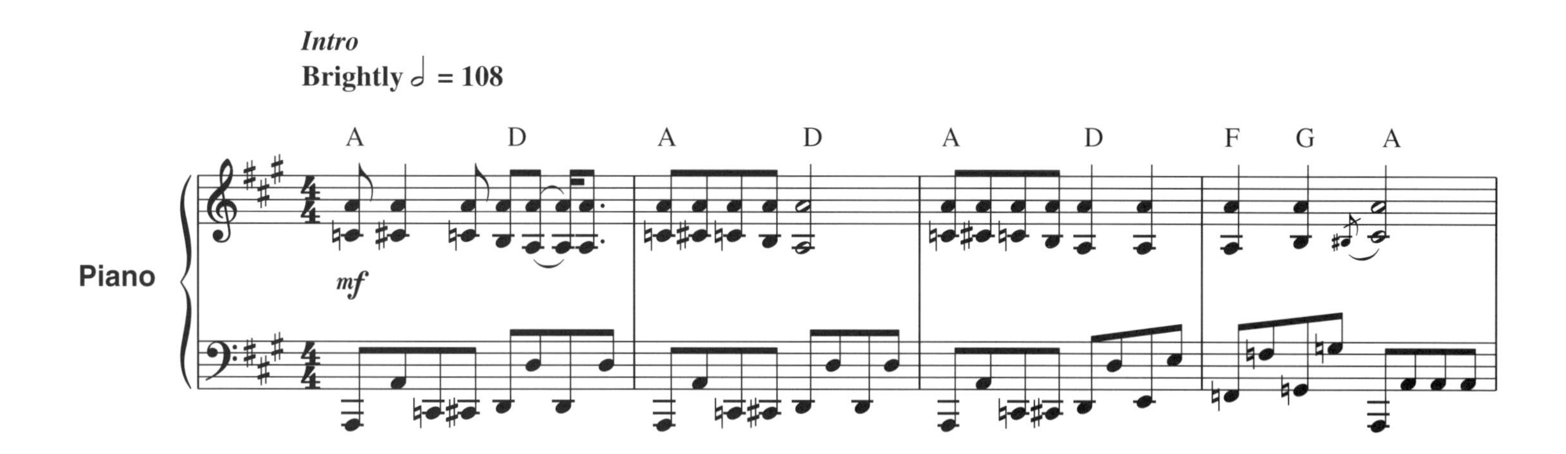

Chorus
A D F G A Dm7
Did you think that mon-ey was heav - en sent? Fri-day night ar-rives with-out a
G7 C Am
suit - case. Sun-day morn - ing creep-ing like a nun.
Dm7 G7 C Bm7 E7sus E7
Mon-day's child has learned to tie his boot lace. See how they run.
Verse
A D A D A D
La - dy Ma-don - na, ba - by at your breast, won-ders how you man-age to feed
La - dy Ma-don - na, ly - ing on the bed, lis - ten to the mu - sic play-ing

To Coda
F G A
D
A D
A D
the rest.
in your head.
Chorus
F G A
Dm7
G7
C
Pa pa pa pa pa pa pa pa pa.
Pa pa pa pa pa pa
D.S. al Coda
Am7
Dm7
G7
C Bm7 E7sus E7
pa pa pa pa pa.
Pa pa pa pa pa pa
pa pa pa.
See how they run.

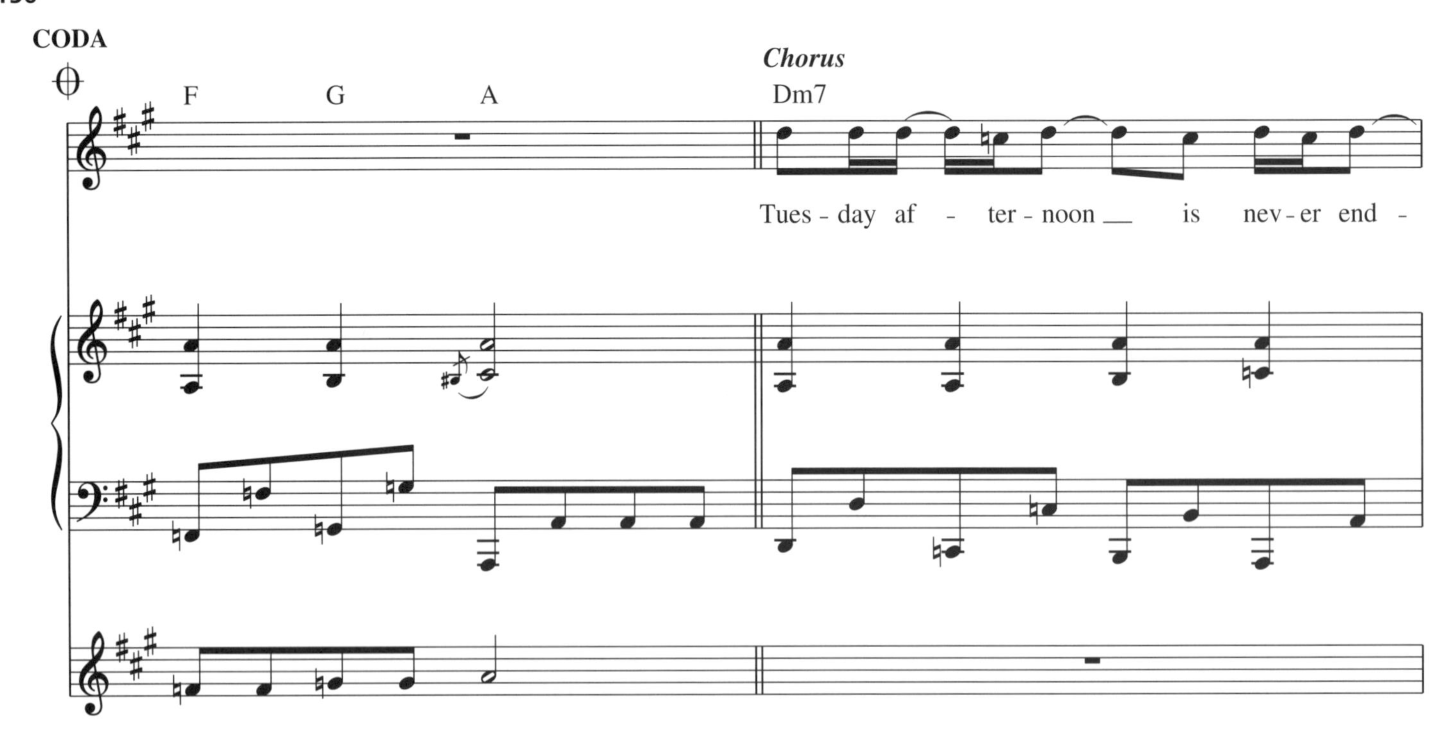
CODA
Chorus
F G A Dm7
Tues - day af - ter - noon is nev - er end -

G7 C Am7
- ing. Wednes - day morn - ing pa - pers did - n't come.

Dm7 G7 C Bm7
Thurs - day night your stock - ings need - ed mend - ing. See how they

E7sus
E7
A
D
A
D
run.
La - dy ___ Ma - don - na,
chil - dren at ___ your feet.
A
D
F
G
A
Bm7
Won - der how you man - age to make ___ ends meet. ___
Cm6
Bm7
A
Bm7
Cm6
Bm7
A

King of Pain

Written and Composed by G.M. Sumner

Gmaj7 A5 Gmaj7 A5 F#sus F#7sus Gmaj7 G6
same old thing as yes - ter - day. There's a
B5 Asus2 B5 Asus2 B5 Asus2 B5 Asus2
black hat caught in a high tree top. There's a
Gmaj7 Asus2 Gmaj7 Asus2 F#sus F#7sus Gmaj7 G6
flag - pole rag and the wind won't stop. I have

D5
A/E
D/F♯
G(add2)
stood here be - fore in - side the pour - ing rain with the world turn - ing cir - cles run - ning
'round my brain. I guess I'm al - ways hop - ing that you'll end this reign. But it's
my des - ti - ny to be the king of pain. There's a
Synth
dry plucked sound
mf

Bm
lit - tle black spot on the sun to - day. (That's my soul up there.)
fos - sil that's trapped in a high cliff wall. (That's my soul up there.)
(Synth)
A/G
It's the same old thing as yes - ter - day.
There's a dead sal - mon fro - zen in a wat - er - fall.
F♯m
G
Bm
(That's my soul up there.) There's a black hat caught in a high
(That's my soul up there.) There's a blue whale beached by a spring -
tree top. (That's my soul up there.) There's a
- tide's ebb. (That's my soul up there.) There's a
A/G
F♯m
flag - pole rag and the wind won't stop. (That's my soul up there.)
but - ter - fly trapped in a spi - der's web. (That's my soul up there.)

G
D
G
I have stood here be - fore in - side the pour - ing rain with the
(Piano)
sustained sound
D
G
D
world turn - ing cir - cles run - ning 'round my brain. I guess I'm al - ways hop - ing that you'll
G
D
1
G
end this reign. But it's my des - ti - ny to be the king of pain.

2
G
A
Gmaj7
A
There's a king of pain. There's a king on a throne
plucked sound:
Gmaj7
A
Gmaj7
A
Gmaj7
with his eyes torn out. There's a blind man look ing for a sha-dow of doubt.
A
Gmaj7
A
Gmaj7
A
Gmaj7
A
There's a rich man sleep - ing on a gold - en bed. There's a skel-e-ton chok -

A Gmaj7
Bm
- ing on a crust of bread.
Synth
sustained sound
A
King of pain.
F♯m
G
Csus
Piano/Synth Bells
sustained sound

Bsus
There's a red fox torn by a hunts - man's pack. (That's my soul up there.)
A
There's a black-winged gull with a bro - ken back. (That's my soul up there.)
F♯m
G
N.C.
There's a lit - tle black spot on the sun today.
(slow fall off)
It's the same old thing as yes - ter - day.
(slow fall off)

D/F#
Gsus2
D
I have stood here be - fore in - side the
cresc.
f
Synth - plucked sound
Synth - sustained sound
G
D
G
pour - ing rain with the world turn - ing cir - cles run - ning 'round my brain. I guess
D
G
D
I'm al - ways hop - ing that you'll end this reign. But it's my des - ti - ny to be the

G
D
G
king of pain.
King of pain.
D
G
D
King of pain.
Repeat and Fade
Optional Ending
G
D
G
D
King of pain.
I'll al - ways be king of pain.

Light My Fire

Words and Music by The Doors

Fm
A♭m7
Fm
"Girl, we could-n't get much high - er."
and our love be-come a fun-'ral pyre.

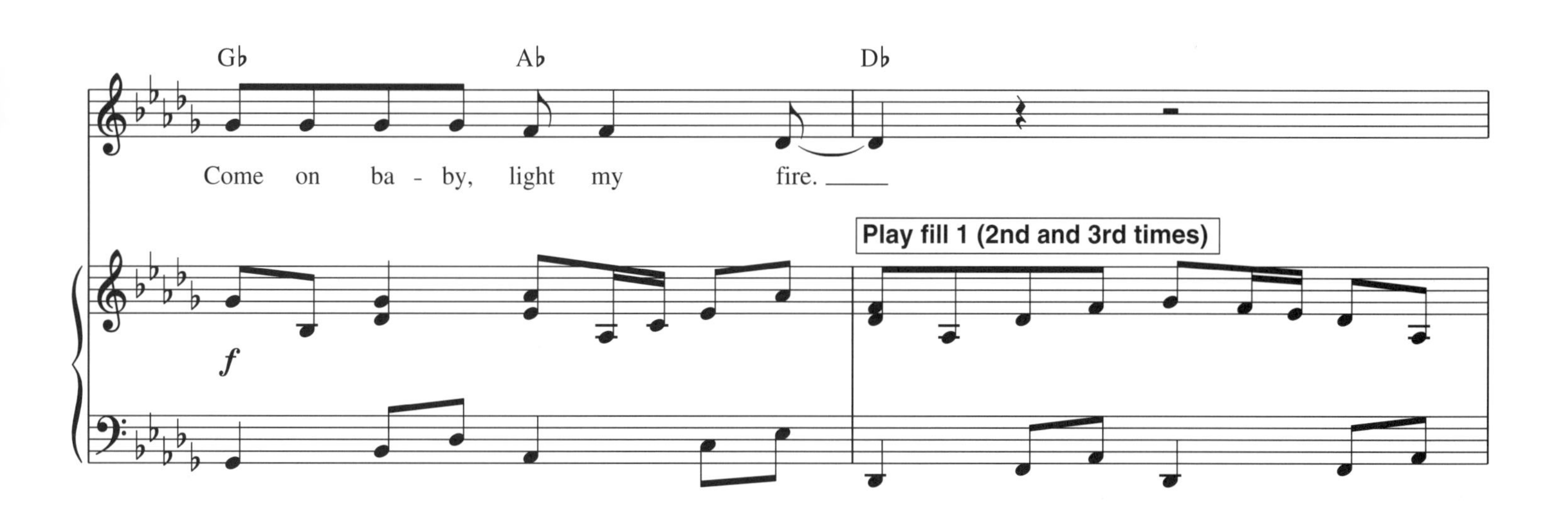
G♭
A♭
D♭
Come on ba - by, light my fire.
Play fill 1 (2nd and 3rd times)
f

To Coda
G♭
A♭
D♭
B♭
G♭
D♭
Come on ba - by, light my fire.
Try to set the night on

Fill 1

1
Eb
fi - re.
2. The
2
Eb
fi - re,
yeah.
Abm7
Bbm7
Organ solo (R.H.) + Bass (L.H.)
3

Abm7
Bbm7
Abm7
Bbm7
Abm7
Bbm7
Abm7
Bbm7
Abm7
Bbm7
Abm7
Bbm7
Abm7
Bbm7
Abm7
Bbm7
Abm7
Bbm7
Abm7
Bbm7
Abm7
Bbm7
Abm7
Bbm7
Abm7
Bbm7
Abm7
Bbm7

Abm7
Bbm7
Abm7
Bbm7
Abm7
Bbm7
Abm7
Bbm7
Abm7
Bbm7
Abm7
Bbm7
Abm7
Bbm7
Abm7
Bbm7
Abm7
Bbm7
Abm7
Bbm7
Abm7
Bbm7
Abm7
Bbm7
Abm7
Bbm7
Abm7
Bbm7
Abm7
Bbm7

A♭m7 B♭m7 A♭m7 B♭m7 A♭m7 B♭m7
A♭m7 B♭m7 A♭m7 B♭m7 A♭m7 B♭m7
A♭m7 B♭m7 A♭m7 B♭m7 A♭m7 B♭m7
A♭m7 B♭m7 A♭m7 B♭m7 A♭m7 B♭m7
A♭m7 B♭m7 A♭m7 B♭m7 A♭m7 B♭m7

Abm7
Bbm7
decrescendo
Repeat ad lib.
F#
C#
Guitar solo
Organ comps freely
mf – f

E
A
D
G

D.S. al Coda
A♭
The

CODA
E♭
A♭m7
fi - re,
yeah.
You know that it would be un - true;

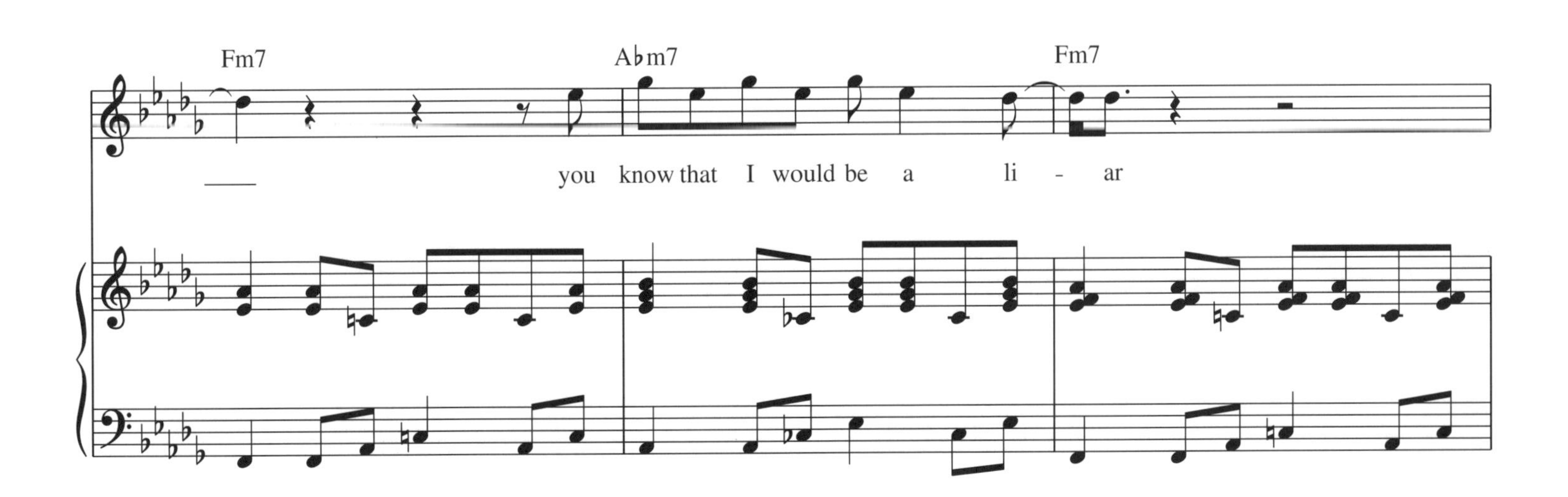
Fm7
A♭m7
Fm7
you know that I would be a li - ar

A♭m7
Fm7
A♭m7
if I was to say to you,
"Girl, we could-n't get much high -
Fm7
G♭
A♭
D♭
- er."
Come on, ba - by, light my fi - re.
G♭
A♭
D♭
Come on, ba - by, light my fi - re.
E
B
D♭
Try to set the night on fi - re.

E
B
D♭
Try to set the night on fi - re.
E
B
D♭
E
B
Try to set the night on fi - re.
Try to set the night on
D♭
F♯
C♯
fi - re.
E
A
D
G
A♭

Mandolin Rain

Words and Music by B.R. Hornsby
and John Hornsby

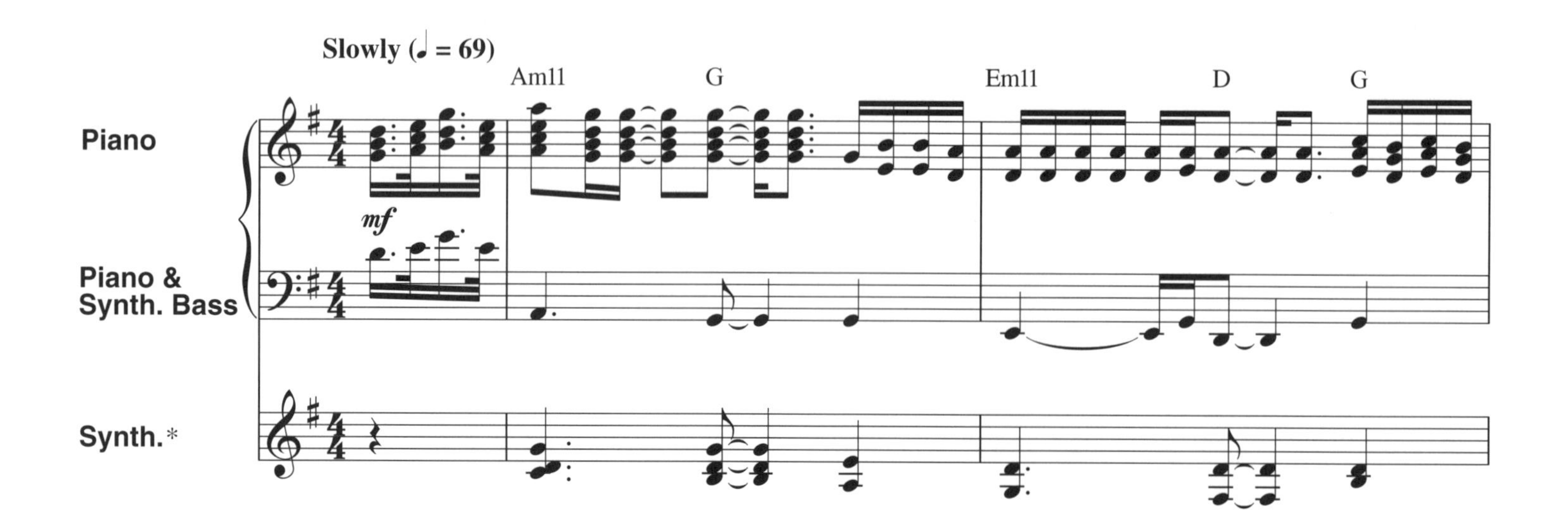

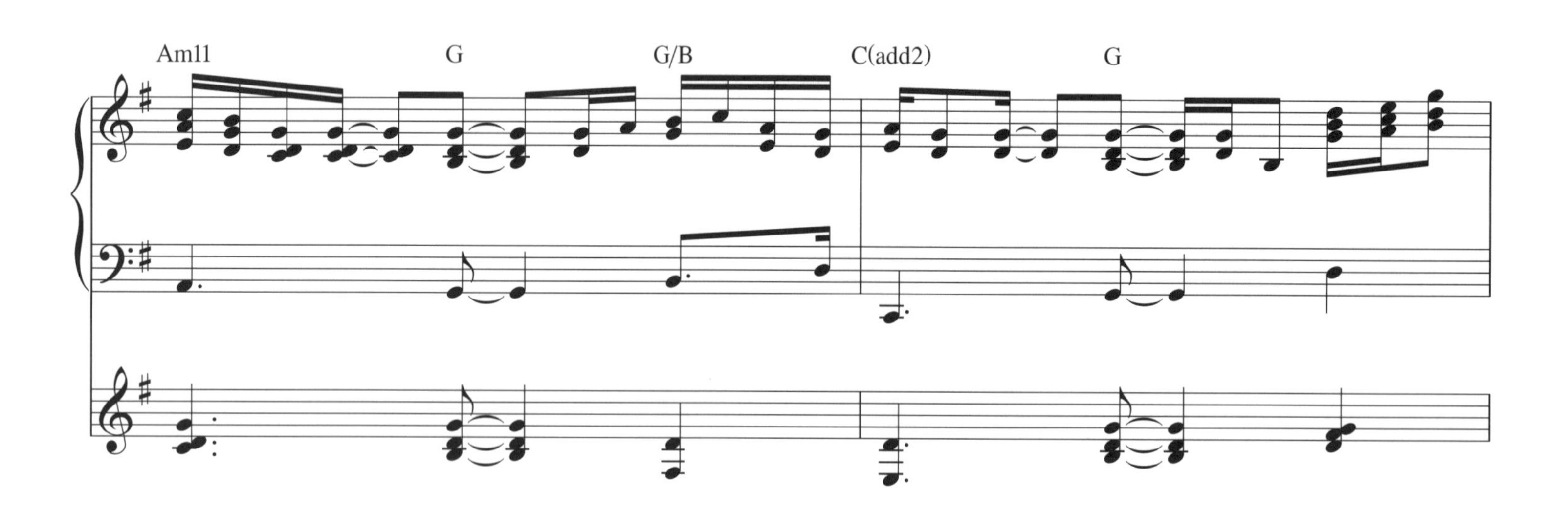

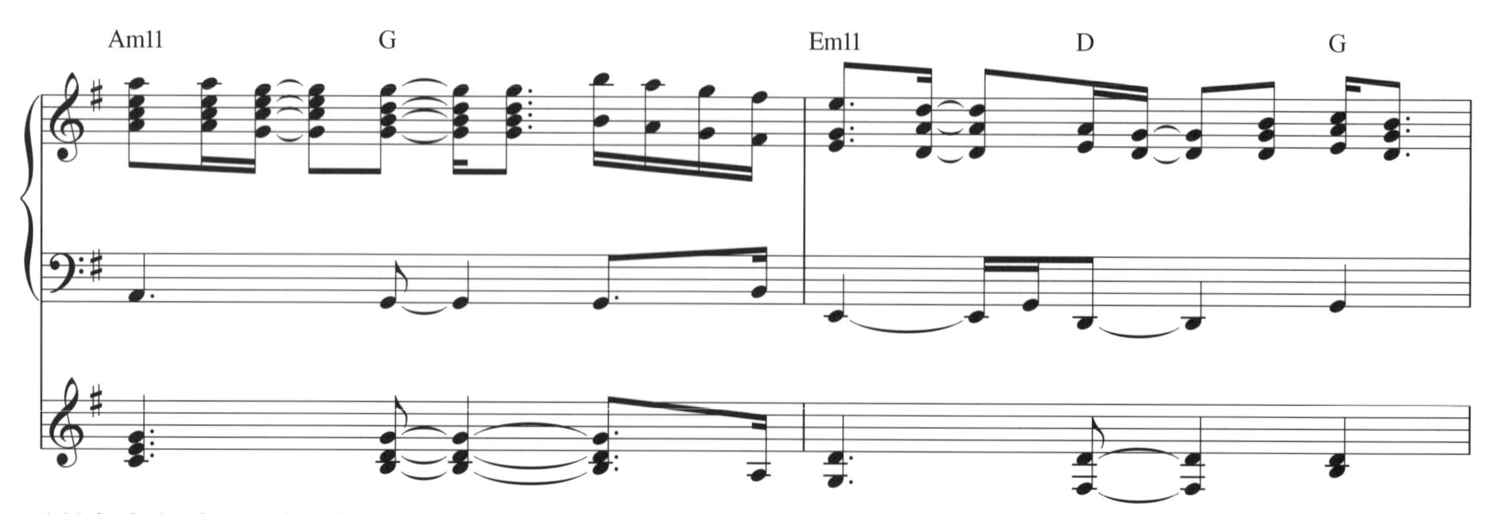

* *Multiple Synth. parts have been combined to be playable by one keyboard.*

Vocal
Am11
G
C(add2)
G
D
The
G
Am
G/B
D
Am
G/B
song came and went like the times that we spent hid - ing out
cool eve - ning dance, lis - tening to the blue - grass band takes the chill
boat's steam - ing in, oh, watch the side - wheel spin, and I
C(add2)
D
Cmaj9/E
G
D
from the rain un - der the car - ni - val tent. I
from the air un - til they play the last song.
think a - bout her when I hear that whis - tle blow. But

G
Am
G/B
D
Am
G/B
laughed and she'd smile; it would last for a - while. You don't
I'll do my time for keep - ing you off my mind, but there's
I can't change my mind, oh, I knew all the time that she'd
Analog Synth.
(Play 3rd time)
C(add2)
D
Cmaj9/E
G
D
To Coda
know what you got till you lose it all a - gain.
mo - ments that I find I'm not feel-ing so strong.
go, but that's a choice I made long a - go.
Lis-ten to the
Play Fill 1 (3rd time)

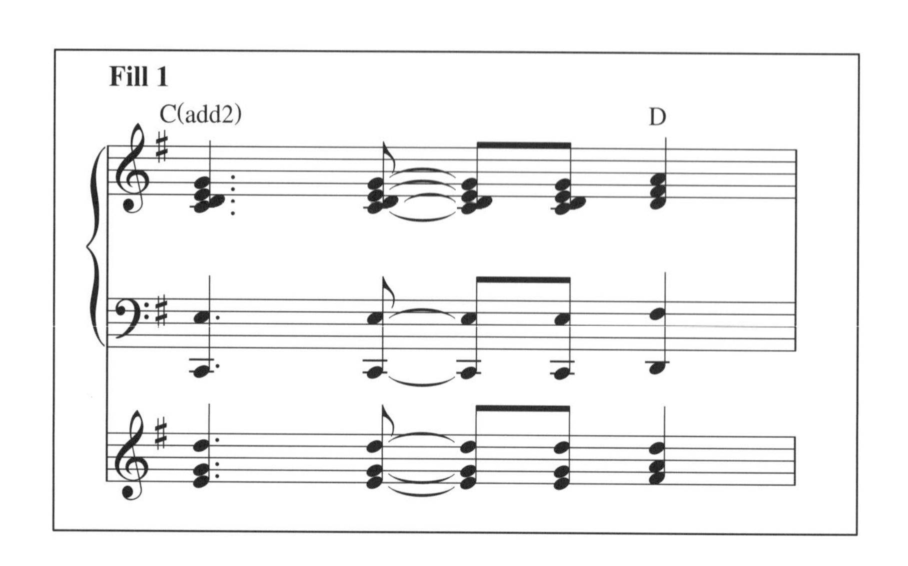
Fill 1
C(add2)
D

Am11
G
Em11
D
G
man-do-lin rain, lis-ten to the mu-sic on the lake. Ah, lis-ten to my

Am11
G
C(add2)
G
D
3
3
heart break ev-'ry time she runs a-way. Oh, lis-ten to the

Am11
G
Em11
D
G
ban-jo wind, a sad song drift-in' low. Lis-ten to the

Am11
G
C(add2)
G
D
tears roll down my face as she turns to go.
(1st time) A

F
C(add2)/E
Bm7(add4)
Cmaj9/E
C
D
Run-ning down by the lake - shore, she did love the sound of a sum-mer storm. It

F
C(add2)/E
Bm7(add4)
Cmaj9/E
C
D
played on the lake like a man - do - lin, now it's wash - ing her a - way once a -

C/E
D/F♯
G
Am7(add4)
G
Piano Solo
gain,
whoa,
a - gain.
Em11
D
G
Am11
G
C(add2)
G
Am11
G
Em11
D
G
Am11
G

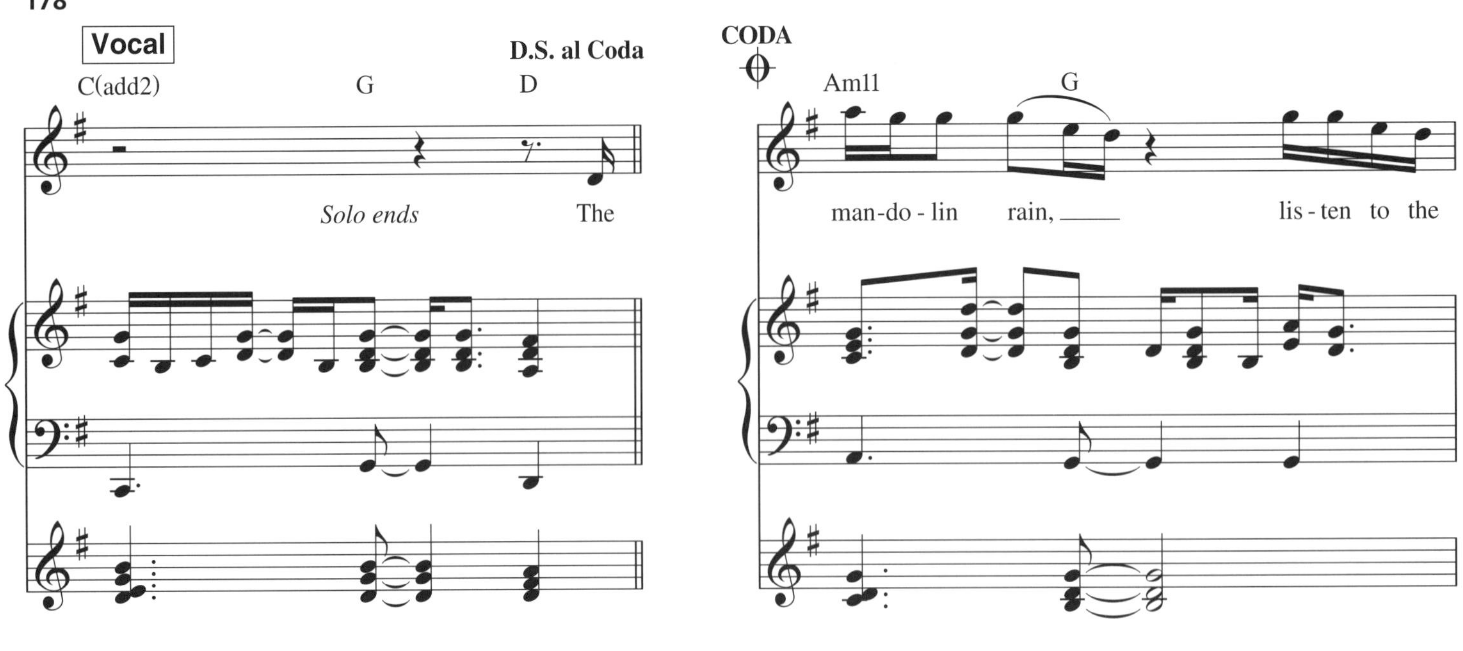
Vocal
D.S. al Coda
CODA
C(add2)
G
D
Am11
G
Solo ends
The
man-do-lin rain,
lis-ten to the

Em11
D
G
Am11
G
mu-sic on the lake.
Ah,
lis-ten to my
heart
break
ev-'ry
time
she

C(add2)
G
D
Am11
G
runs
a - way.
Whoa,
lis-ten to the
ban - jo
wind,
a sad song

Em11 D G Am11 G
drift - ing low. Lis - ten to the tears roll down my face as she
Cmaj9 G D Am11 G G/B
turns to go, as she turns to go.
3
Em11 D G Am11 G
Lis - ten to the, lis - ten to the man - do - lin rain,
3

C(add2)
G
D
Am11
G
to the wom - an, oh.

Em11
D
G
Am11
G

C(add2)
G
D
Am7
G
D(add4)
Lis - ten to the tears roll down my face as she

C(add2)
G
D(add4)
Am7
G
D(add4)
turns to go. Lis - ten to the tears roll down my face as she
3

C(add2)
G
D(add4)
C(add2)
turns to go.
3

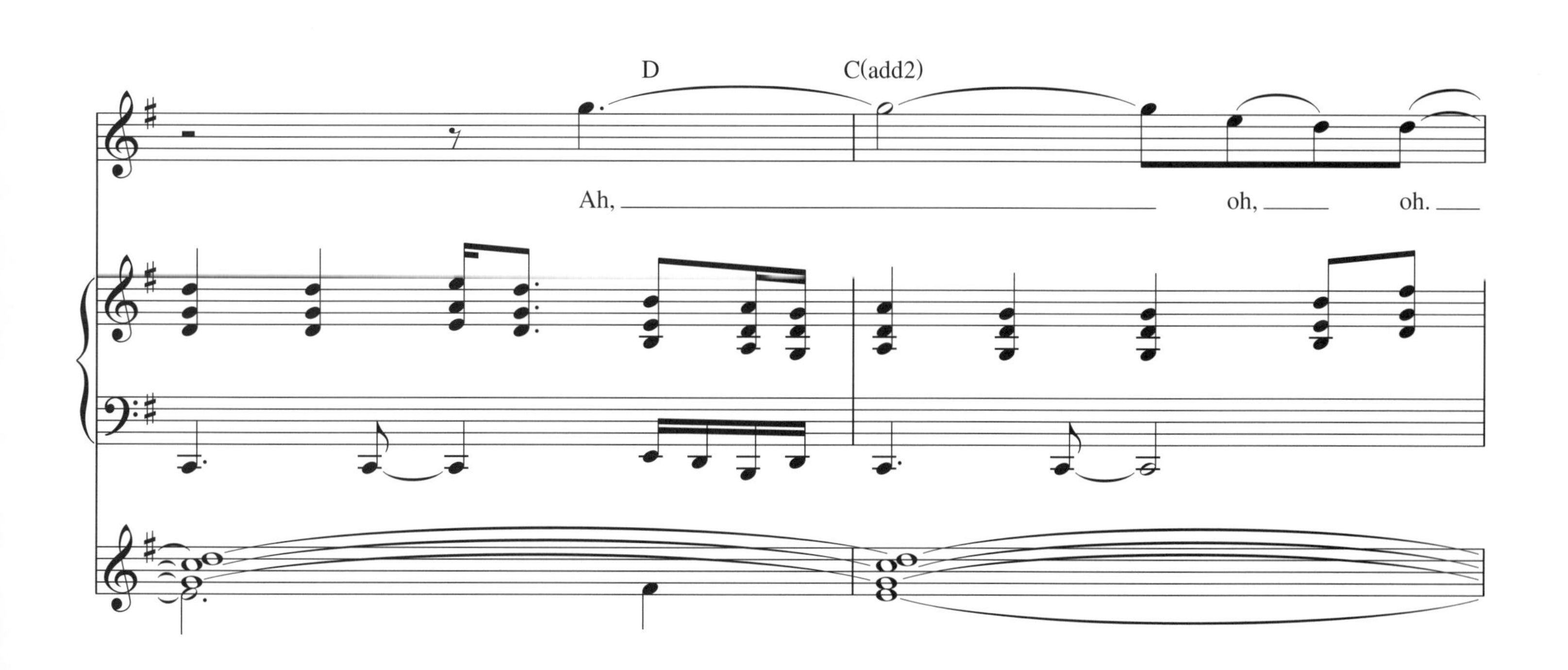
D
C(add2)
Ah, oh, oh.

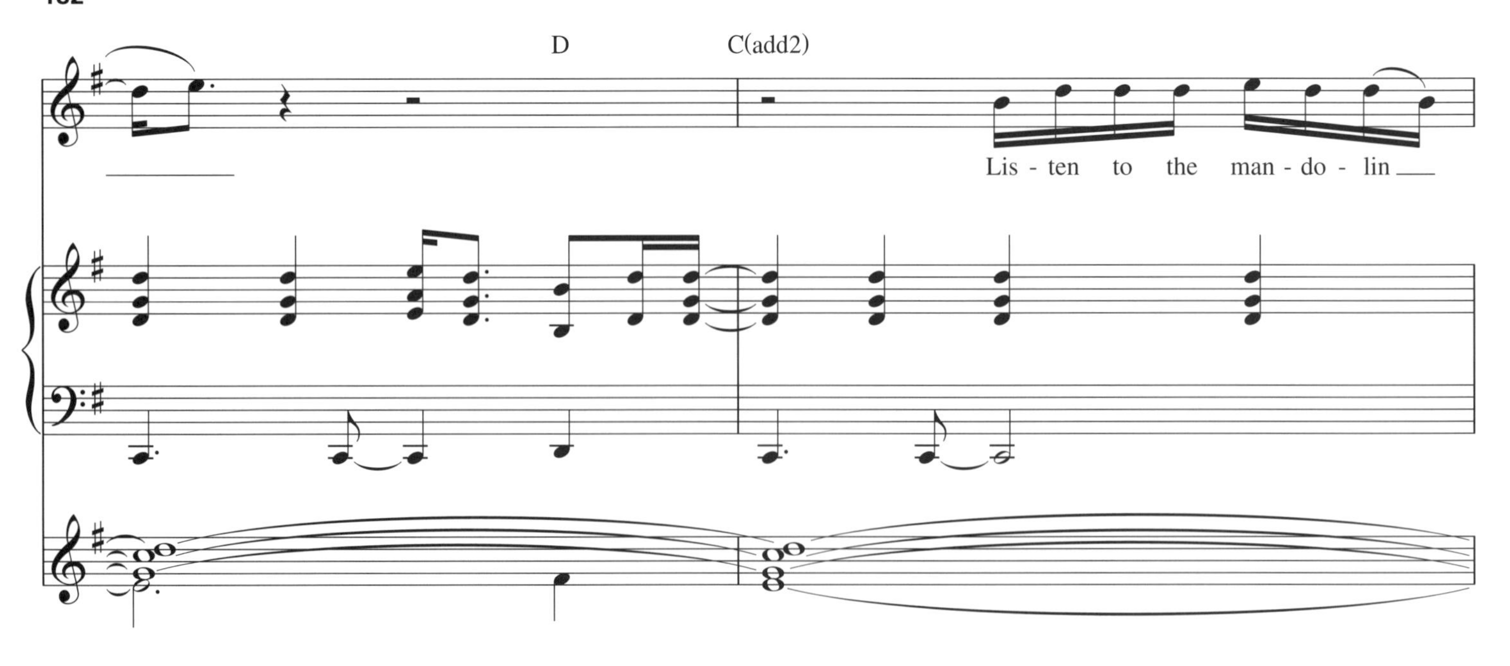
D
C(add2)
Lis - ten to the man - do - lin

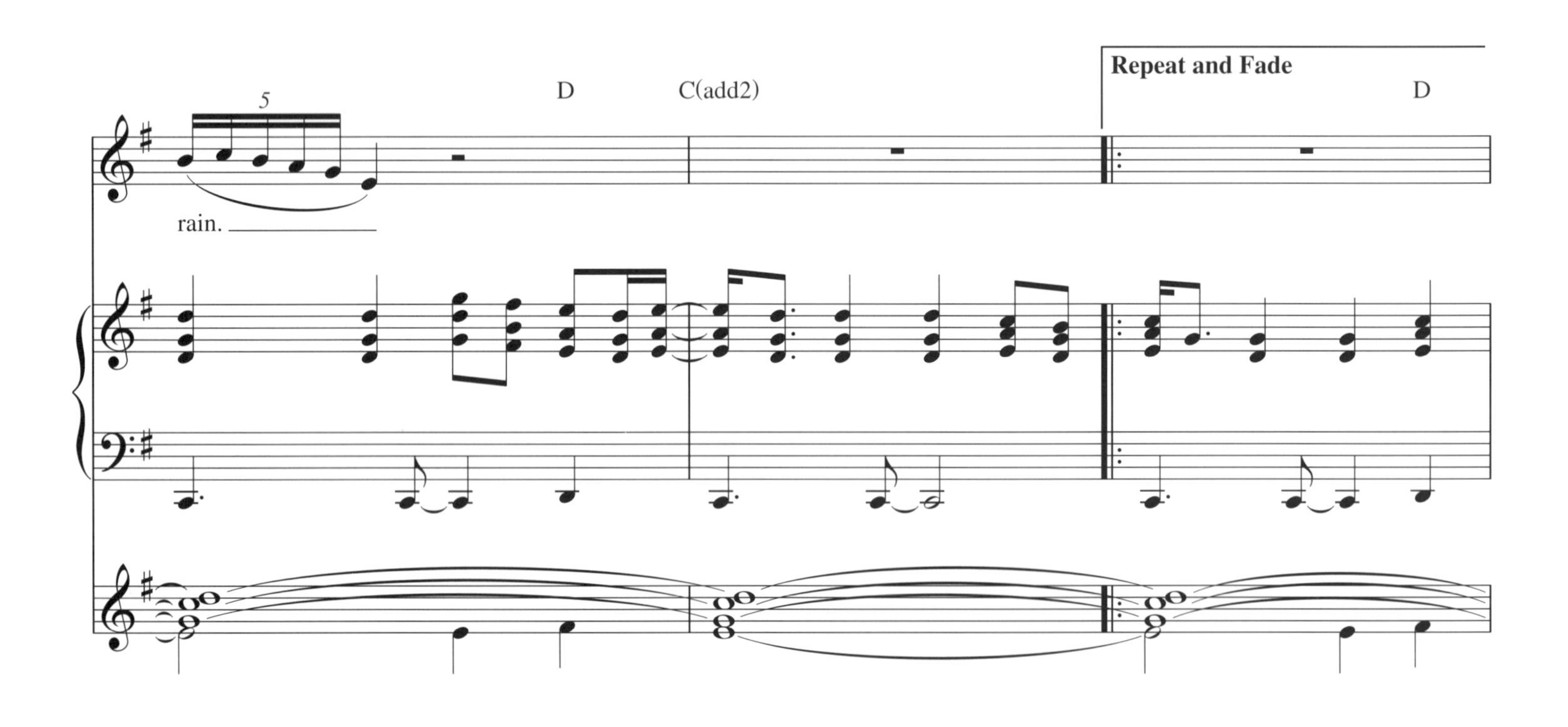
5
D
C(add2)
Repeat and Fade
D
rain.

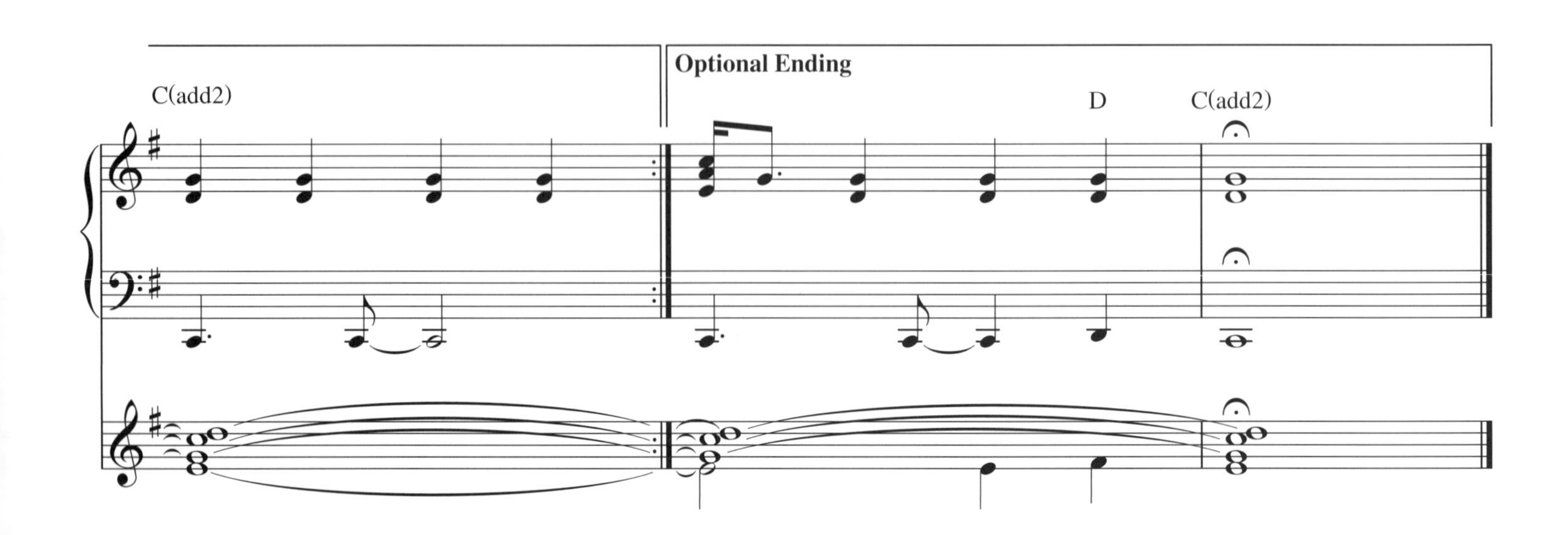
C(add2)
Optional Ending
D
C(add2)

My Life

Words and Music by Billy Joel

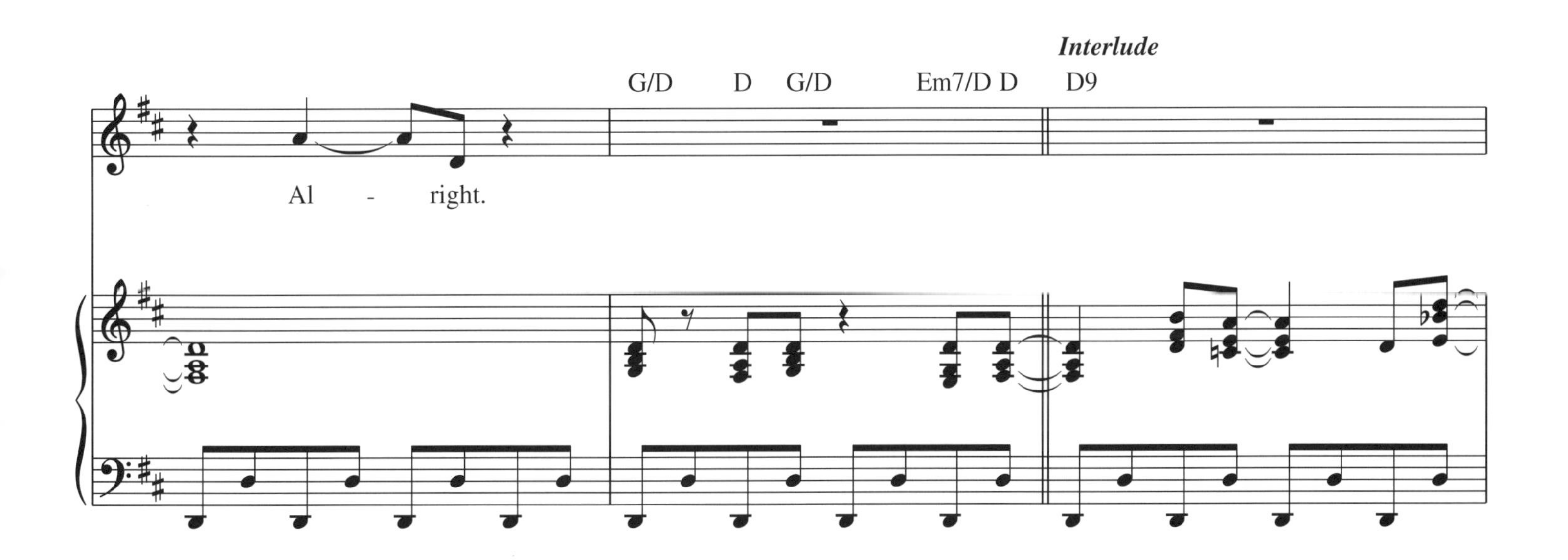

C9
E♭maj7/F
F7
B♭
Woo.
8vb
D9
C9
E♭maj7/F
F7
8vb
B♭
Verse
D
D(add9)/F♯
Got a call from an old friend, we used to be real
They will tell you you can't sleep a - lone in a strange
2nd time - sim.
mf
8vb
G
A
close.
place,
Said he could - n't go on
then they'll tell you you can't
Play Fill 1 (2nd time)

D
G/D
D
the A - mer - i - can way.
sleep with some - bod - y else.
Play Fill 2 (2nd time)

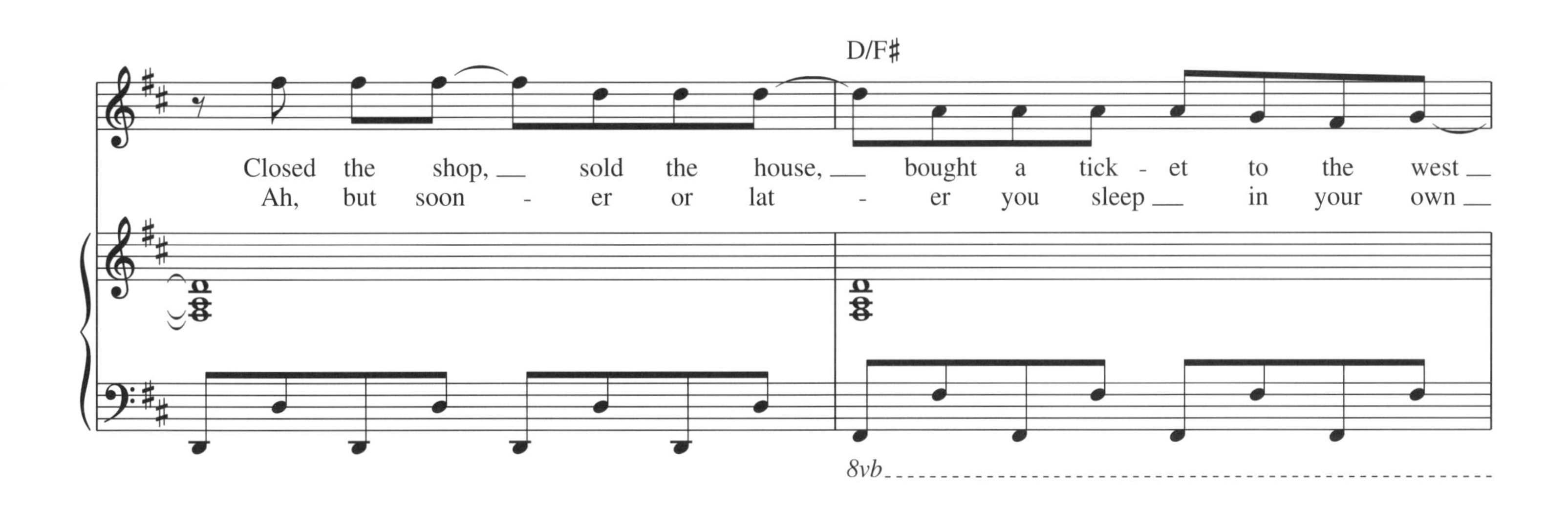
D/F♯
Closed the shop, sold the house, bought a tick - et to the west
Ah, but soon - er or lat - er you sleep in your own
8vb

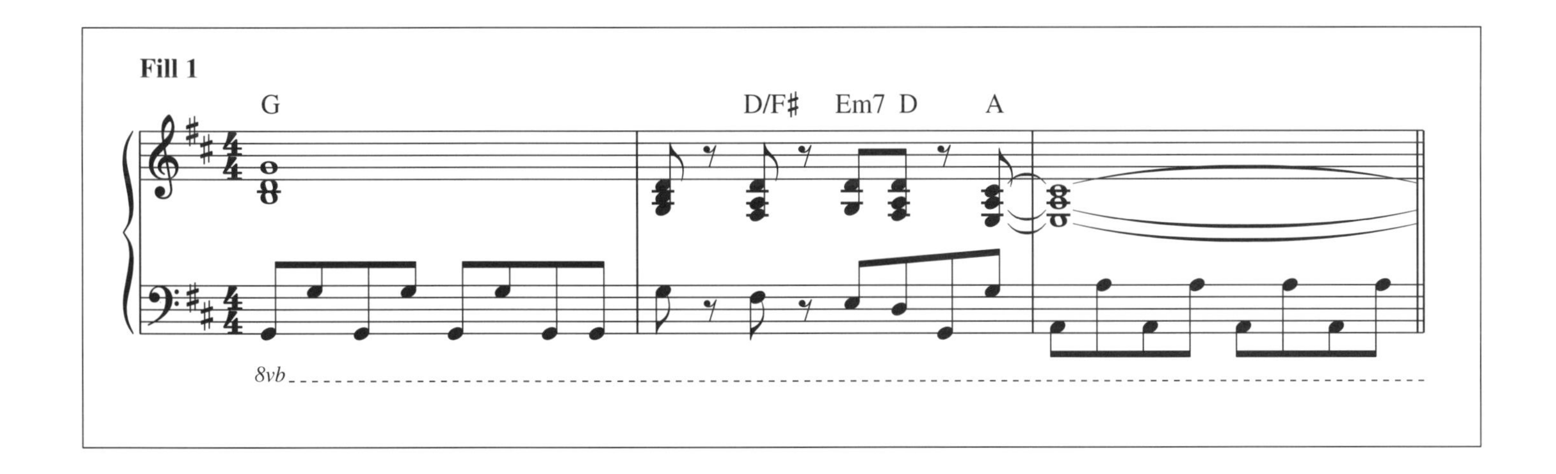
Fill 1
G
D/F♯
Em7
D
A
8vb

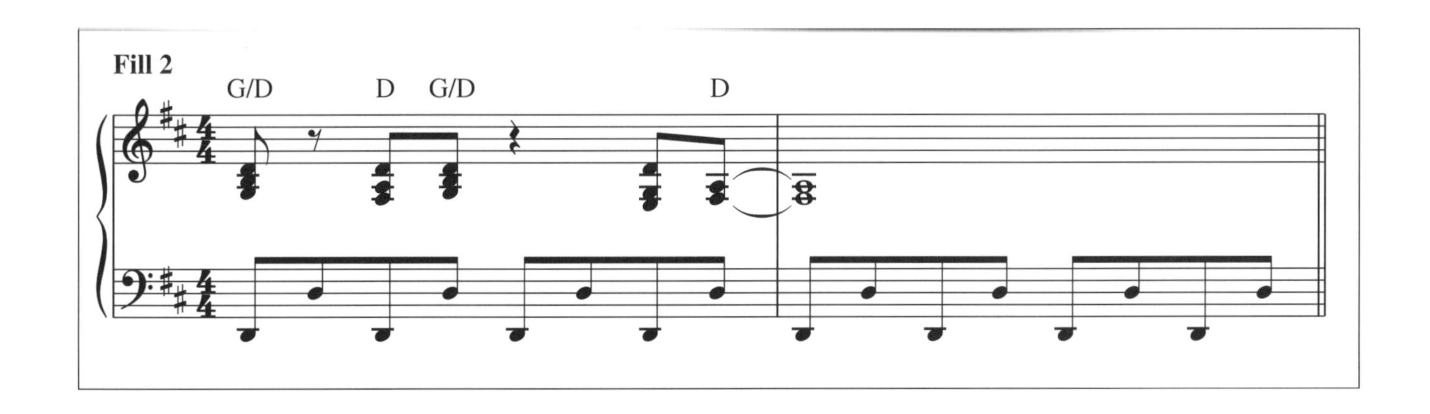
Fill 2
G/D
D
G/D
D

G
A
coast.
space.
Now, he gives _ them a stand -
Eith - er way, _ it's o - kay, _
Play Fill 1 (2nd time)

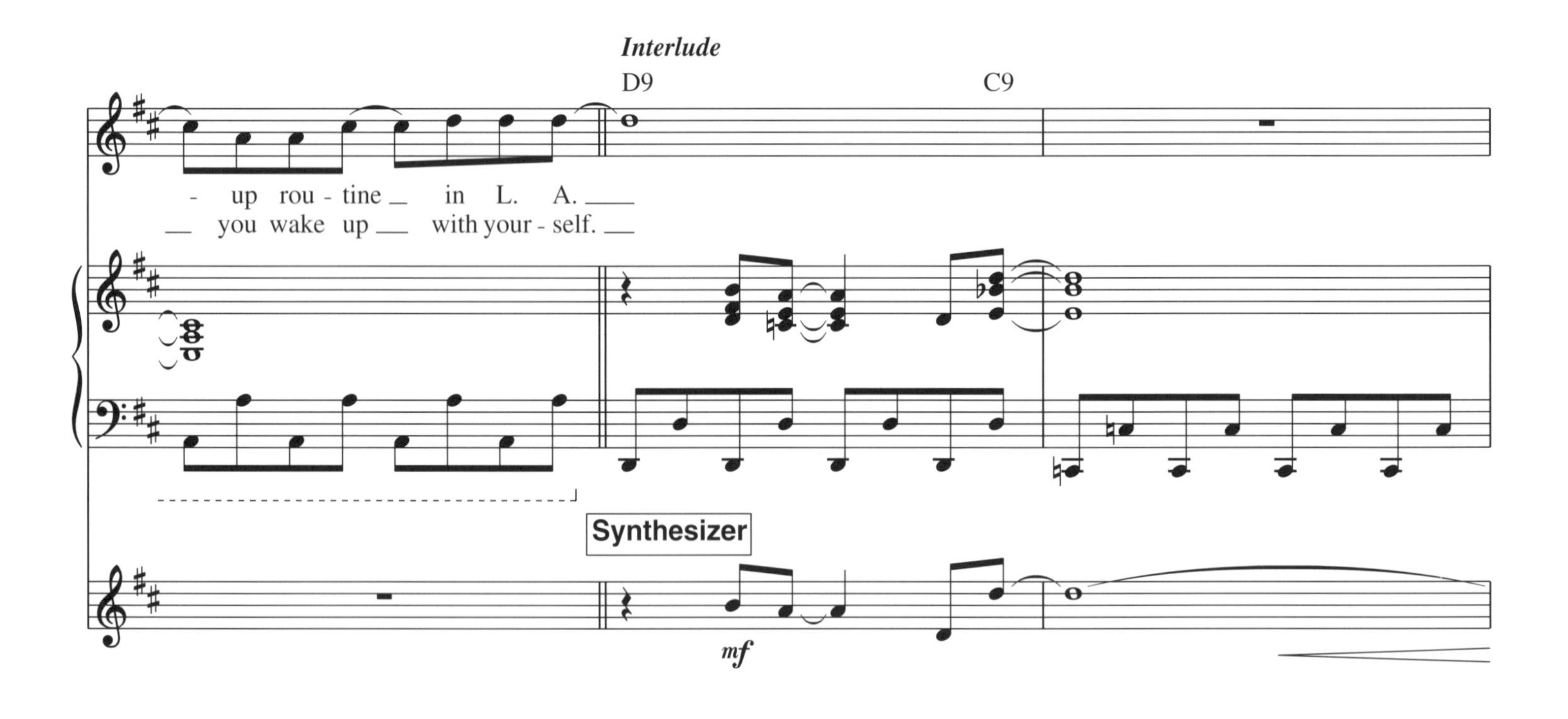
Interlude
D9
C9
- up rou - tine _ in L. A. _
_ you wake up _ with your - self. _
Synthesizer
mf

E♭maj7/F
F7
B♭
D7
C9
8vb

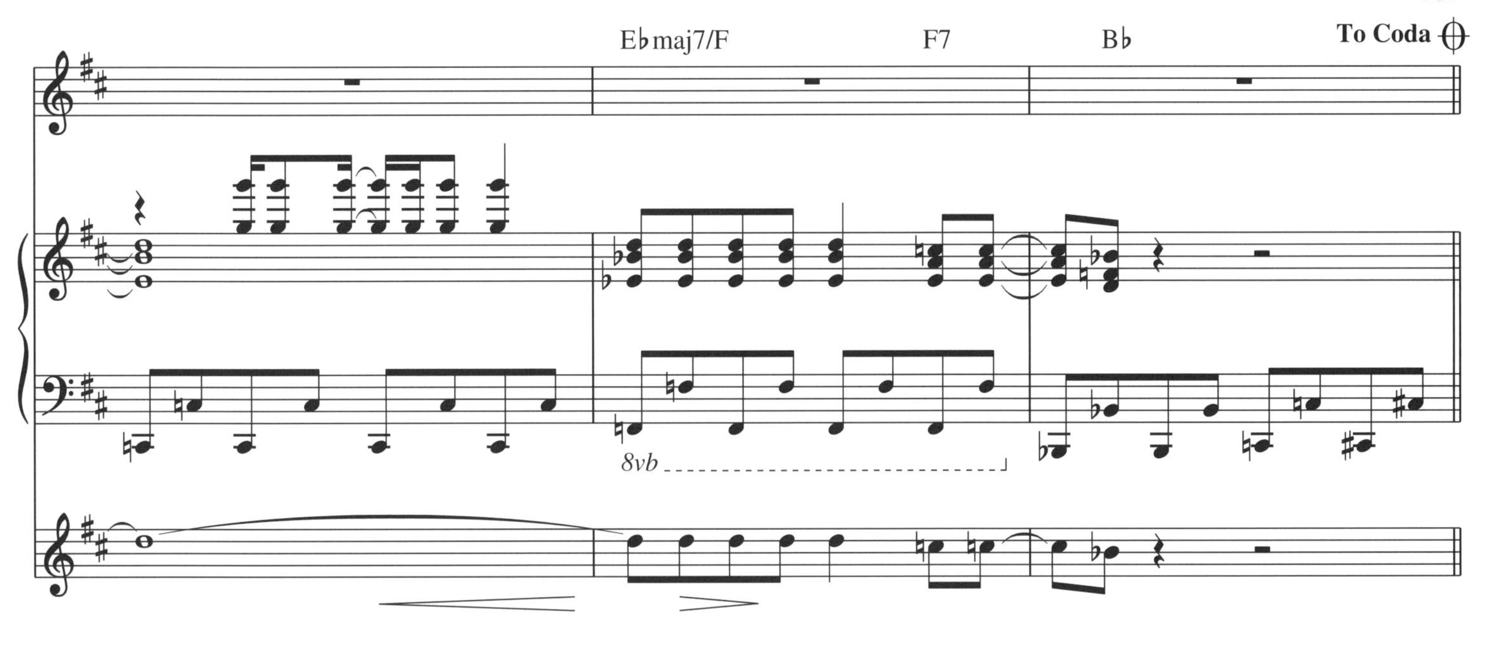
E♭maj7/F
F7
B♭
To Coda
8vb

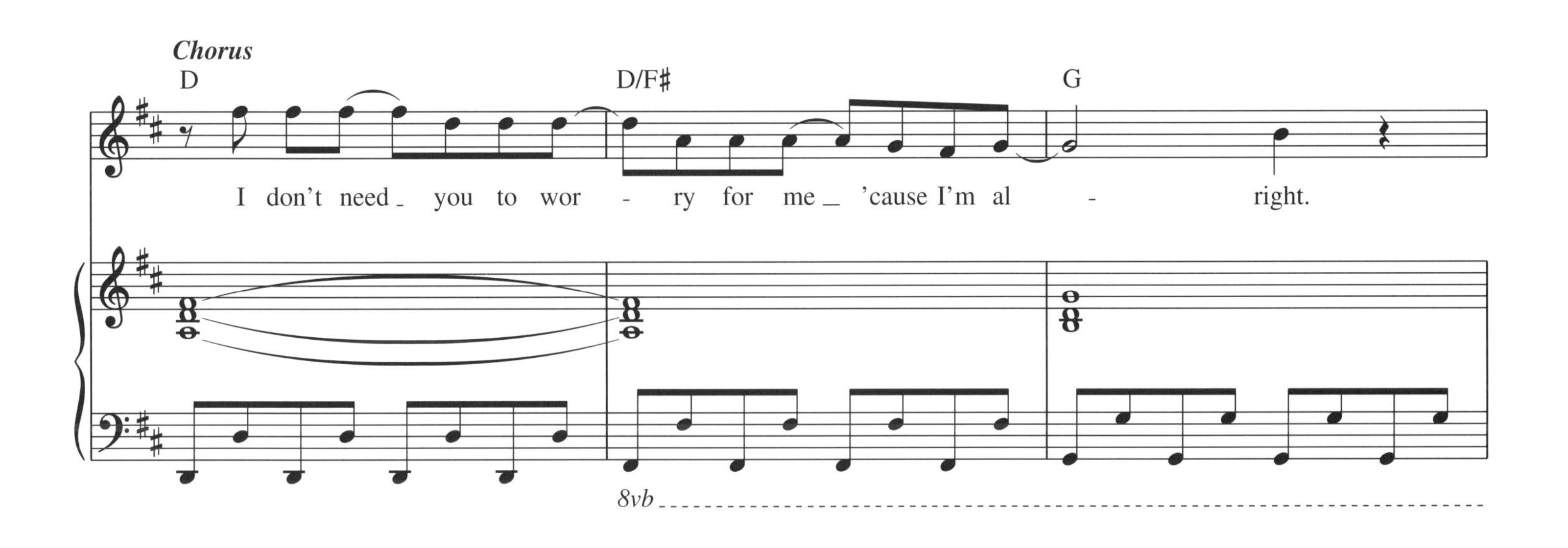
Chorus
D
D/F♯
G
I don't need you to wor - ry for me 'cause I'm al - right.
8vb

A
I don't want you to tell me it's time to come home.

D
G/D D G/D D
I don't care what you say
D/F#
G
D/F# Em7 D A
anymore, this is my life.
8vb
Go ahead with your own life. Leave me alone.
Bridge
Bm
I never
2nd time - sim.
F#7/C#
said you had to offer me a second chance.
mp
mf
mp

D7
E9
I never said I was a victim of circumstance.
N.C.
G
D/F♯
I still belong.
8vb
F♯7
Bm
E7sus
Don't get me wrong.
And you can speak
E7
G/A
A
G/A
A
To Coda
D.S. al Coda
your mind, but not on my time.

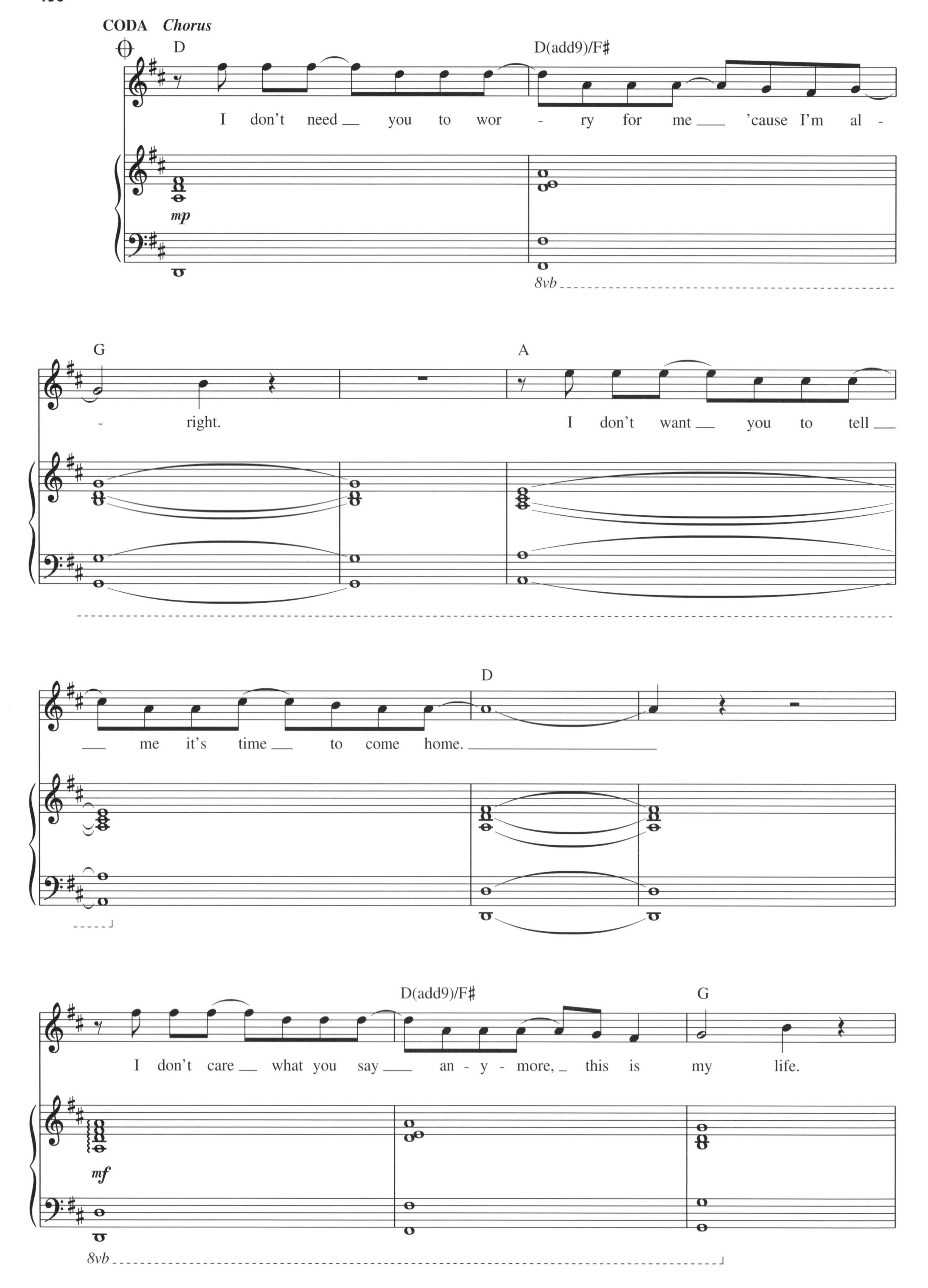
CODA Chorus
D
D(add9)/F♯
I don't need you to wor - ry for me 'cause I'm al -
mp
8vb
G
A
- right.
I don't want you to tell
me it's time to come home.
D
D(add9)/F♯
G
I don't care what you say an - y - more, this is my life.
mf
8vb

D/F♯
Em7 D
A
D.S.S. al Coda
Go a - head with your own life. Leave me a - lone.
8vb
CODA
Chorus
D
D/F♯
mf
8vb
G
A
D
G/D
D G/D
Em7/D D

D/F♯
I don't care what you say any-more, this is
8vb

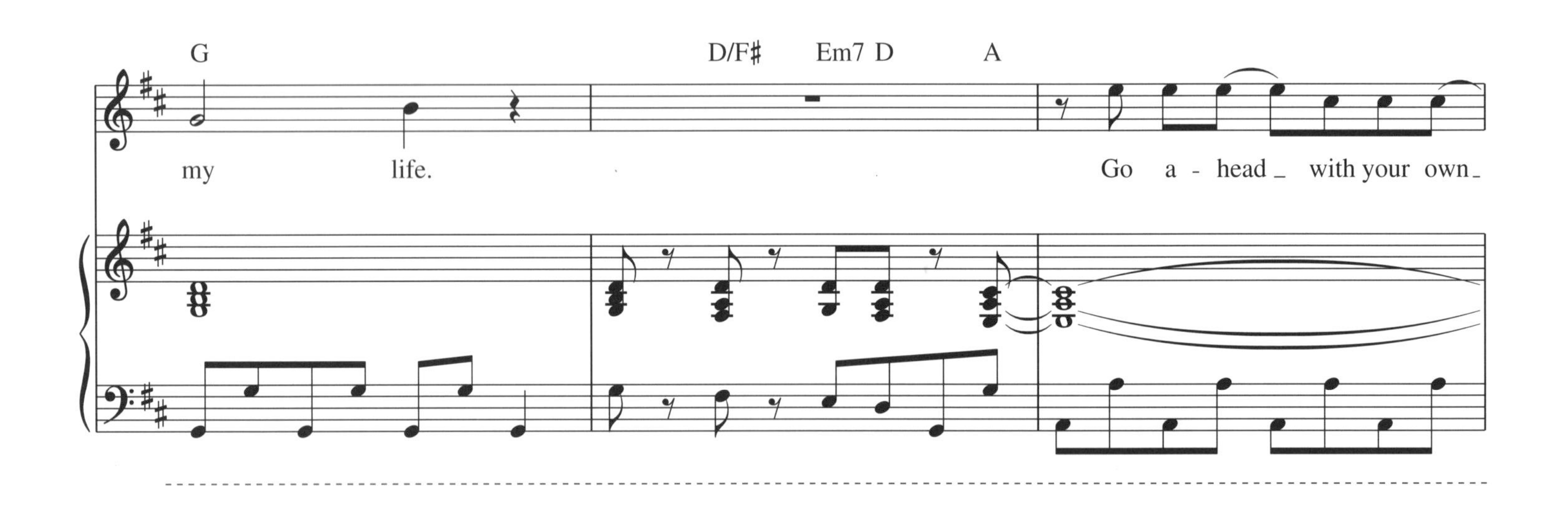
G
D/F♯
Em7 D
A
my life.
Go a-head with your own

Ending (Begin Fade 2nd time)
D9
C9
life. Leave me a-lone.
Lead vocal 1st time only
Synthesizer
mf

E♭maj7/F
F7
B♭
D9
C9
(Keep it to your - self, it's my ___ life.)
8vb

E♭maj7/F
F7
B♭
Repeat and Fade
Play Fill 3 (2nd time)
(Keep it to your - self, it's my ___ life.)
8vb

Fill 3

Oye Como Va

Words and Music by
Tito Puente

Am7
D7
Am
Bue - no pa go - zar,
mu - la - ta.
D Am
Am7
D7
Guitar
Am7
D7
1
2
Am7
D7
1
Am7
D7

2
Am7
D7
Am7
D7
Am7
D7
3
Am7
D7
Play 3 times
Am7
D7

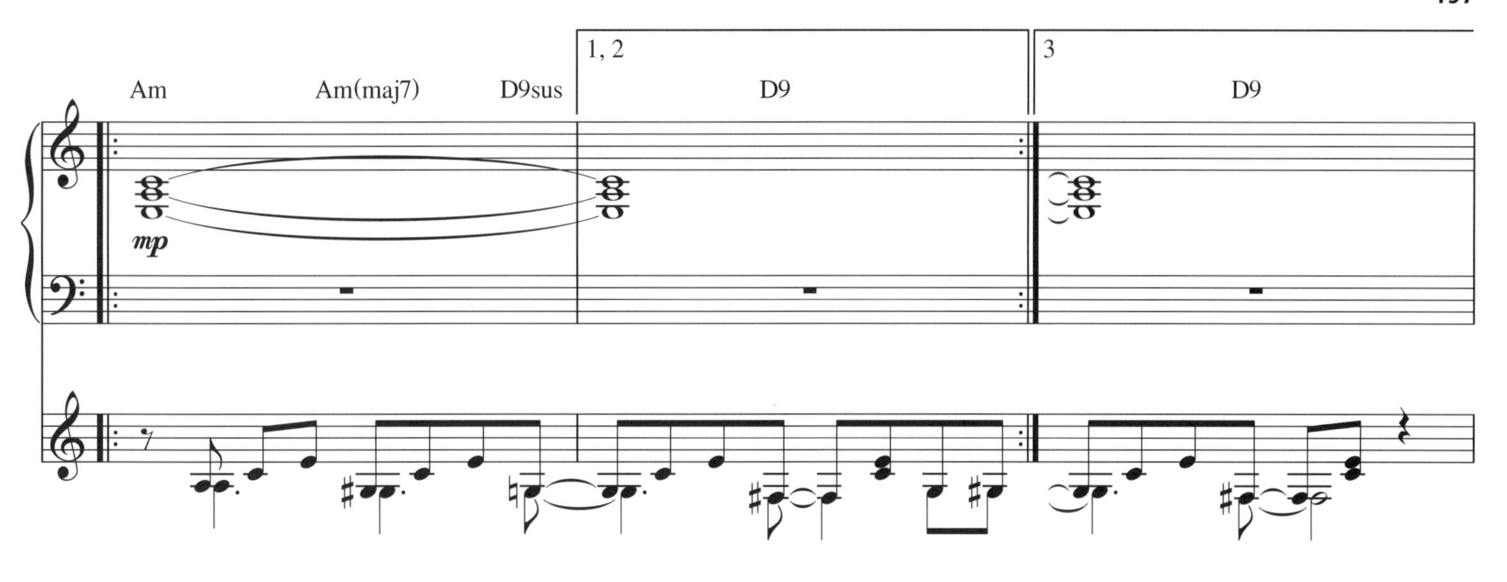
1, 2
3
Am
Am(maj7)
D9sus
D9
D9
mp

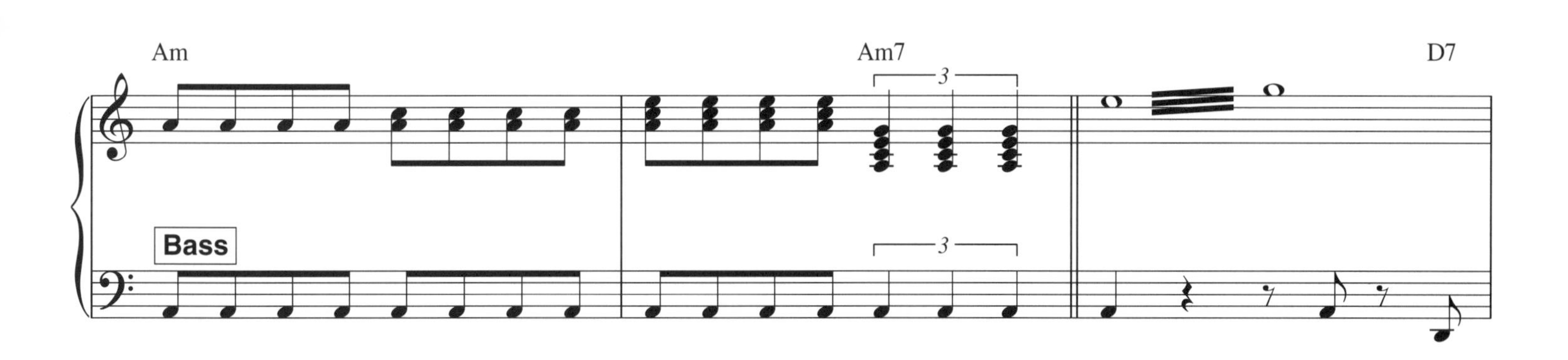
Am
Am7
D7
Bass
3
3

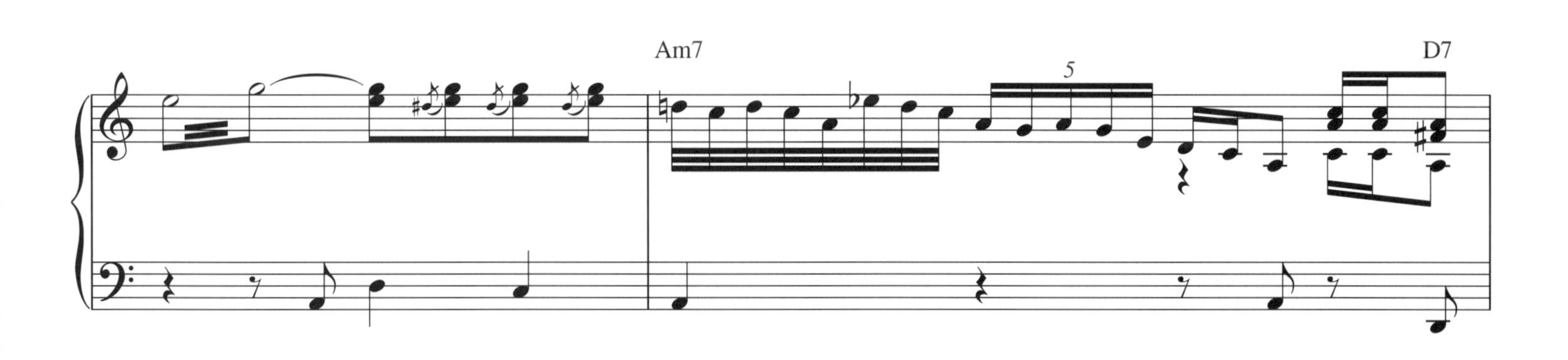
Am7
D7
5

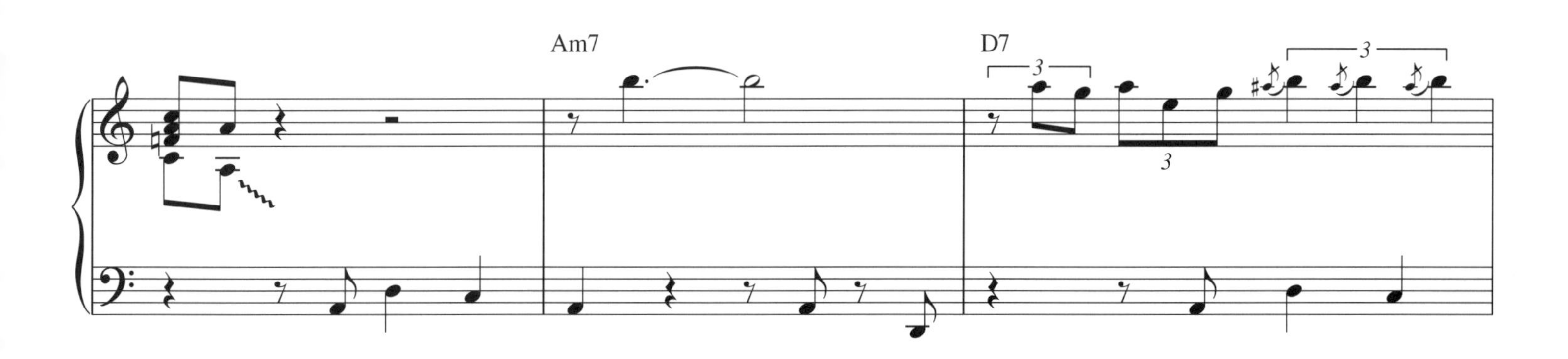
Am7
D7
3
3
3

Am7
D7
6
Am7
D7
Am7
D7
Am7
3
D7
5
5
7
Am7
D7

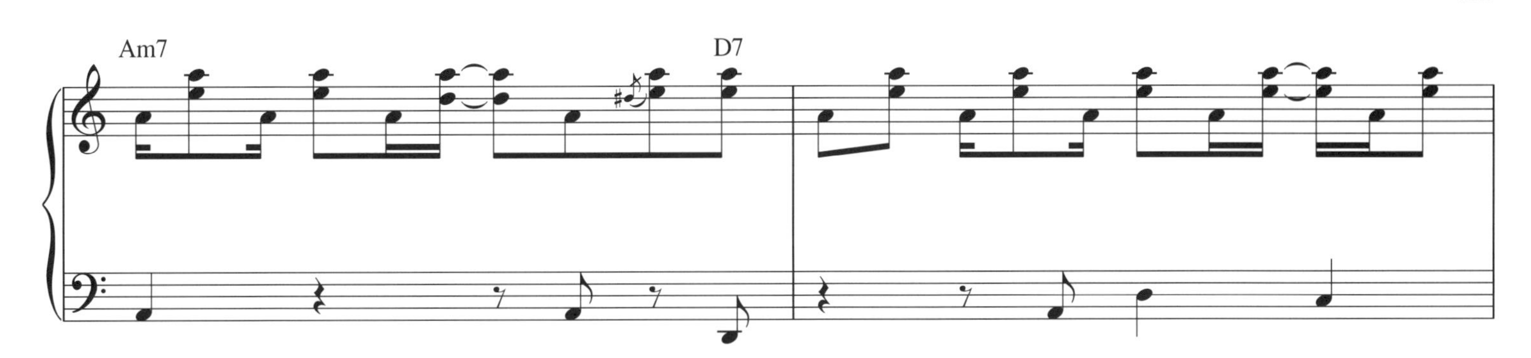
Am7
D7

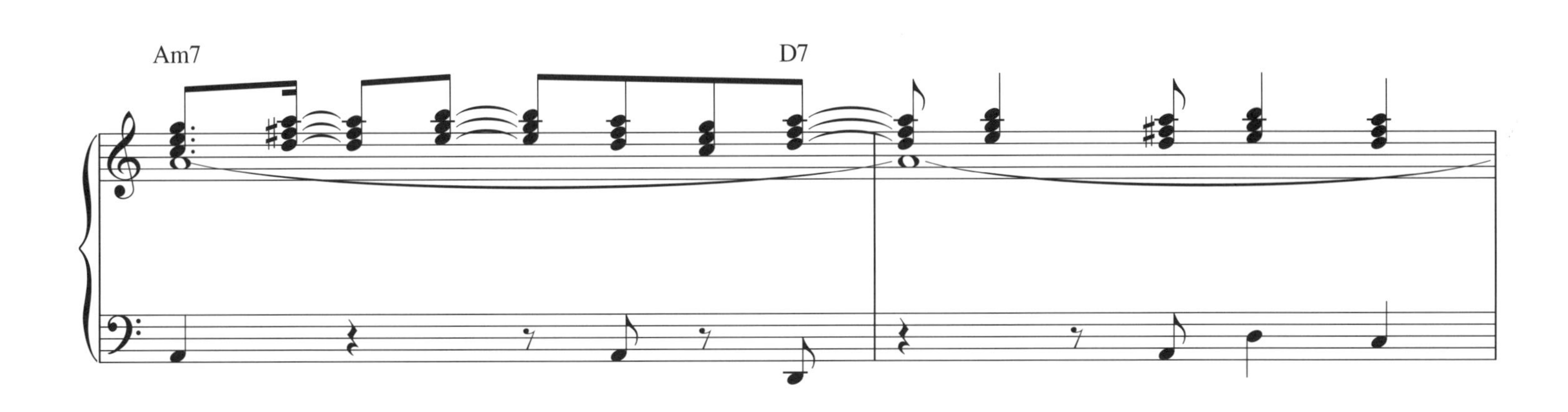
Am7
D7

Am7
D7
Am7
D7
Organ

Am
D
Am

Vocal
Am7
D7
Am7
D7
O - ye co - mo va,
mi rit - mo.
Bue - no pa go - zar,
mu - la - ta.
D
D7
D9
3
Am7
D7
Guitar
Am7
D7

Am7
D7
Am7
D7
Am7
D7
Am7
D7
Am7
D7
Am7
D7

Am7
D7
Am7
D7
Am7
D7
Am7
D7
Am
D
Am
D
Am

Piano Man

Words and Music by Billy Joel

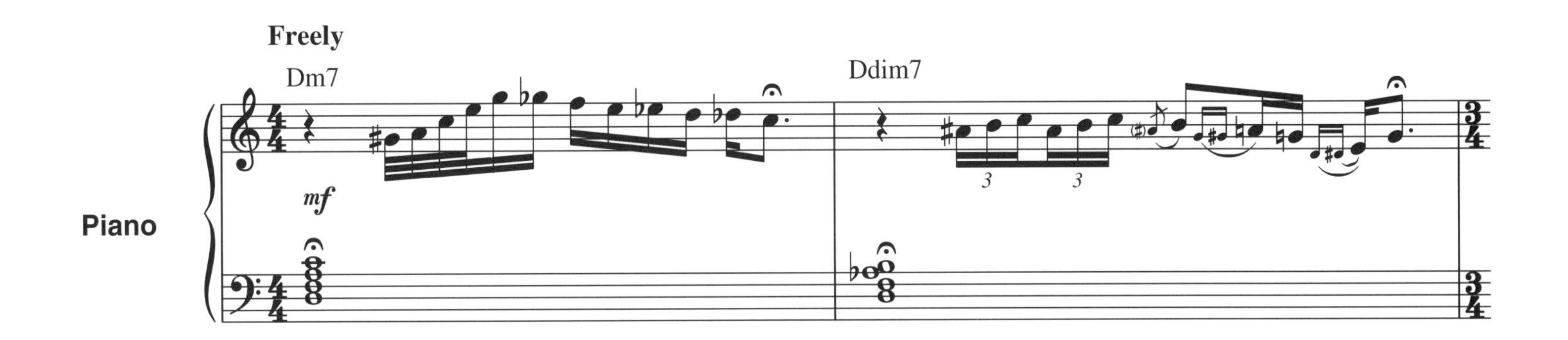

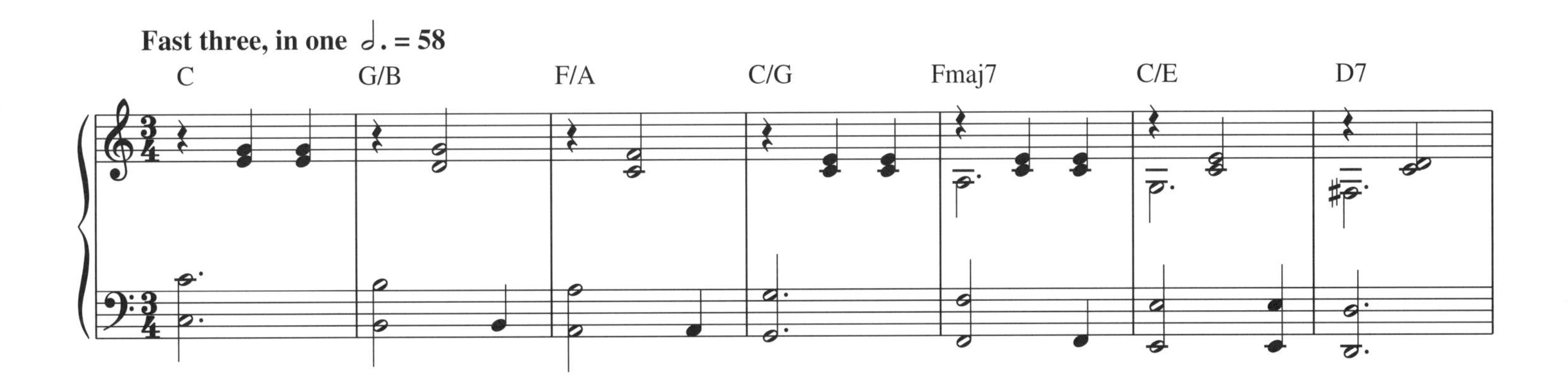

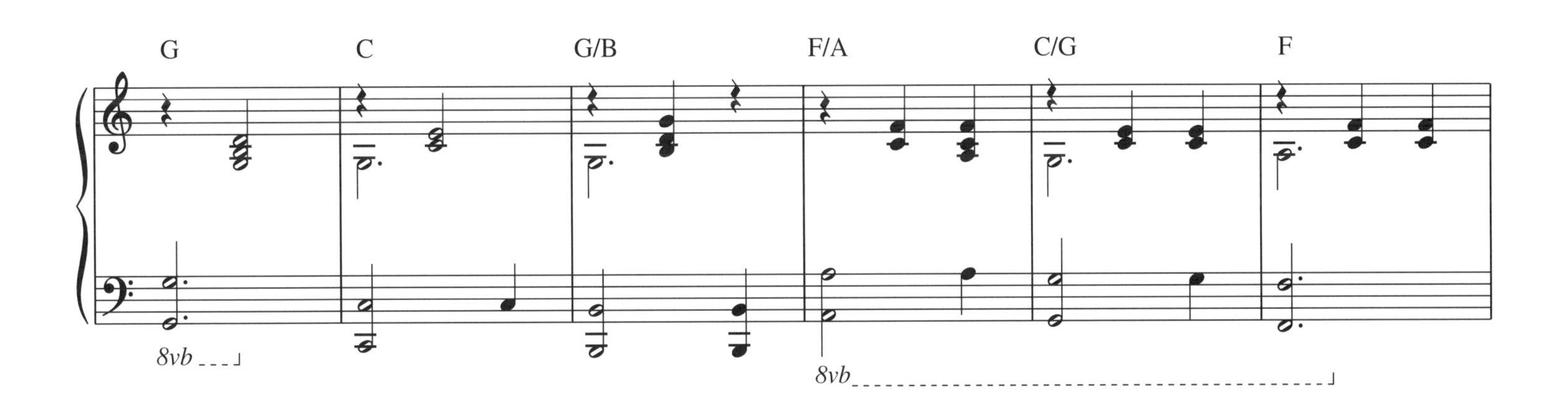

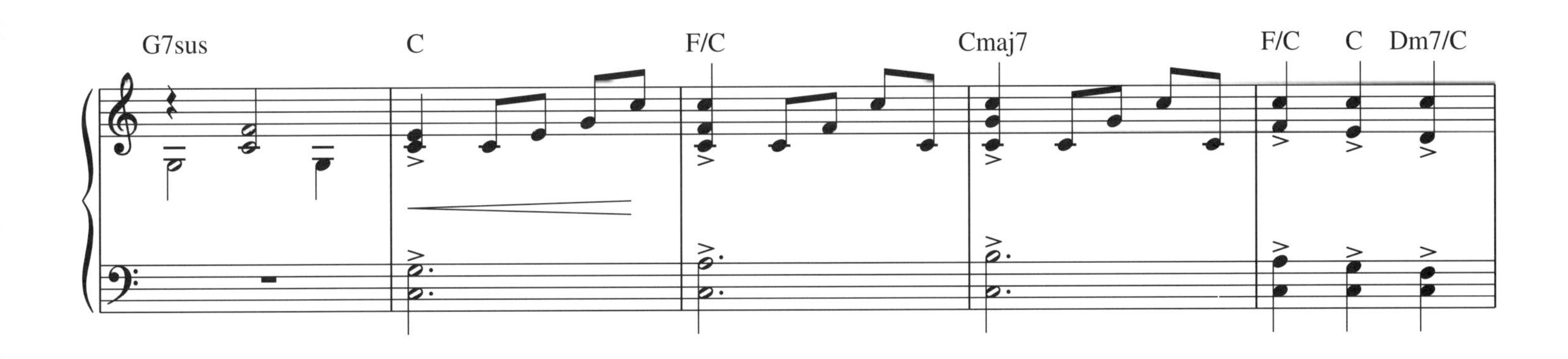

Vocal
C F/C Cmaj7 F/C C Dm/C C G/B
It's nine o' - clock on a
Paul is a real es - tate
2nd time - sim.
F/A C/G F C/E D
Sat - ur - day, the reg - u - lar crowd shuf - fles in.
nov - el - ist who nev - er had time for a wife
Play Fill 1 (2nd time)
G C G/B F(add9)/A C/G
There's an old man sit - ting next to me mak - in'
and he's talk - in' with Dav - y who's still in the Nav - y and
Fill 1
D
3
4

*Octaves are played in L.H. 2nd time.

F
C/E
D
G
C
G/B
not real-ly sure how it goes,
but it's sad and it's sweet and I
- 'ness-men slow - ly get stoned._
Yes, they're shar - ing a drink they call
Play Fill 3 (2nd time)

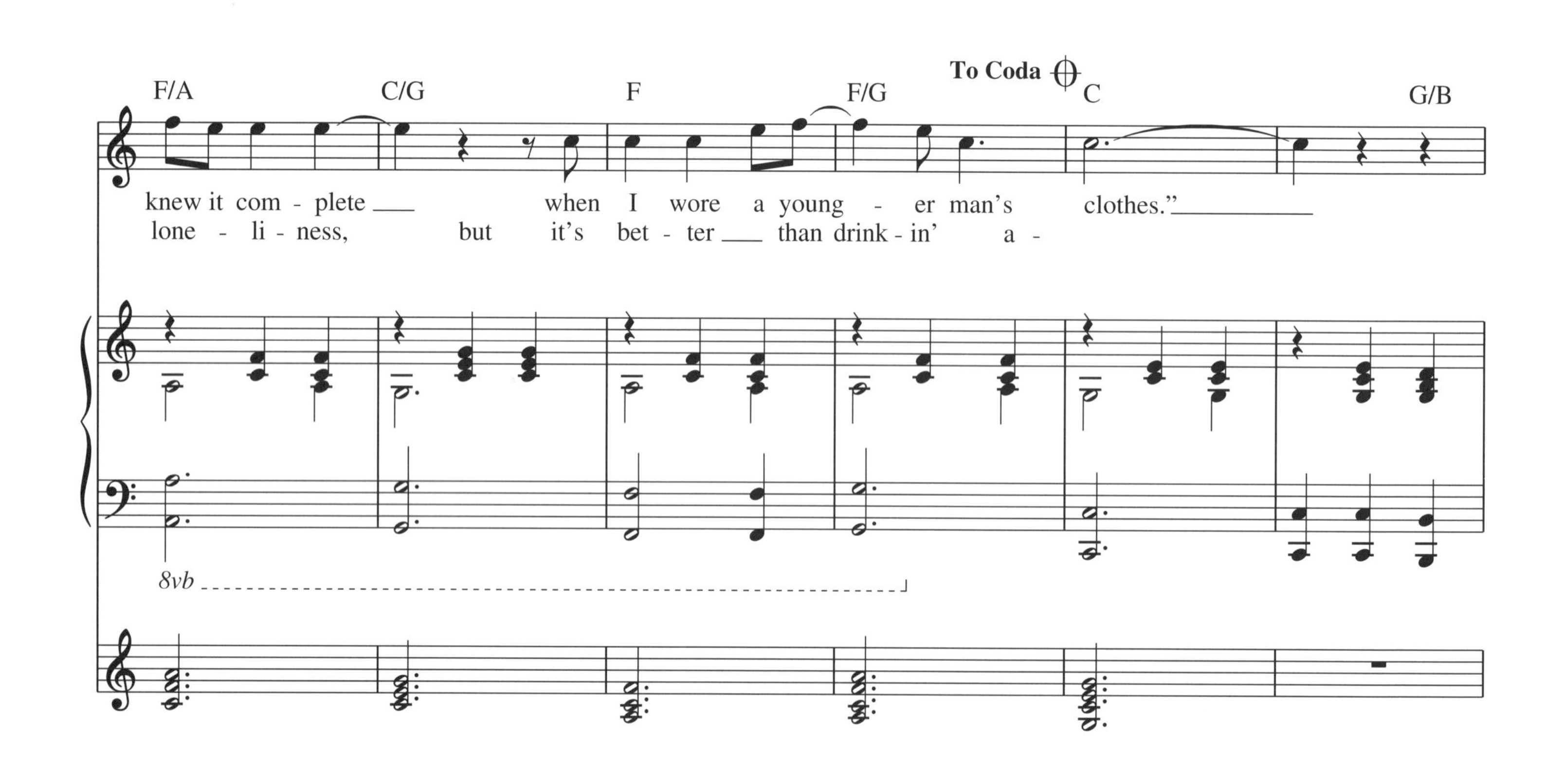
F/A
C/G
F
F/G
To Coda
C
G/B
knew it com - plete when I wore a young - er man's clothes."
lone - li - ness, but it's bet - ter than drink - in' a -
8vb

Fill 3
D
G

Am
Am/G
D/F♯
F
Am
Am/G
La, la, la, li, di, da.
La, la, li, di,
mf
8vb
D/F♯
D
G
G/F
C/E
G7/D
da, da, dum.
cresc.
𝄋𝄋
C
G/B
F/A
C/G
F
C/E
Sing us a song, you're the pia-no man.
Sing us a song to-night.
2nd time - sim.
f
Play 2nd time only
8vb

D
G
C
G/B
F(add9)/A
C/G
Well, we're all in the mood for a mel-o-dy and
Play Fill 4 (2nd time)
8vb
F(add9)
F/G
C
G/B
you've got us feel-in' al - right.
mf
F(add9)/A
C/G
F
F/G
C
F/C
8vb

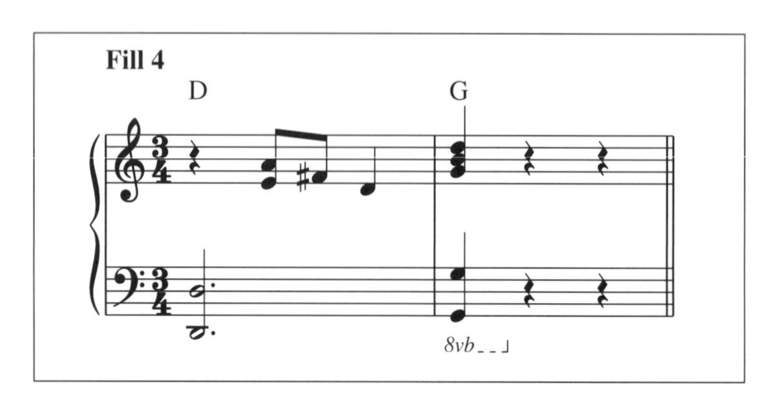
Fill 4
D
G
8vb

Cmaj7
F/C C Dm7/C C
F/C
Cmaj7
Play Fill 5 (2nd time)
F/C C Dm/C C G/B F/A C/G
Now, John at the bar is a friend of mine. He
It's a pret-ty good crowd for a Sat - ur - day and the
mf
F C/E D G C
gets me my drinks for free. And he's quick with a joke
man - a - ger gives me a smile 'cause he knows that it's
To Coda
G/B F/A C/G F(add9) G9sus
3
or to light up your smoke, but there's some - place that he'd rath - er be.
me they've been com - ing to see to for - get a - bout life for a - while.
Fill 5
Cmaj7 F/C C Dm/C

C
F/C
C
G/B
He says, "Bill, I be - lieve this is
cresc.
Accordion
Play 1st time
F/A
C/G
F
C/E
D
kill - ing me," as a smile ran a - way from his face.
8vb
G
C
G/B
F(add9)/A
C/G
"Well, I'm sure that I could be a mov - ie star if
8vb

F
F/G
C
Am
I could get out of this place.
Oh, la, la, la,
mf
8vb
Am/G
D/F#
F
Am
Am/G
di, di, da.
La, la di, di,

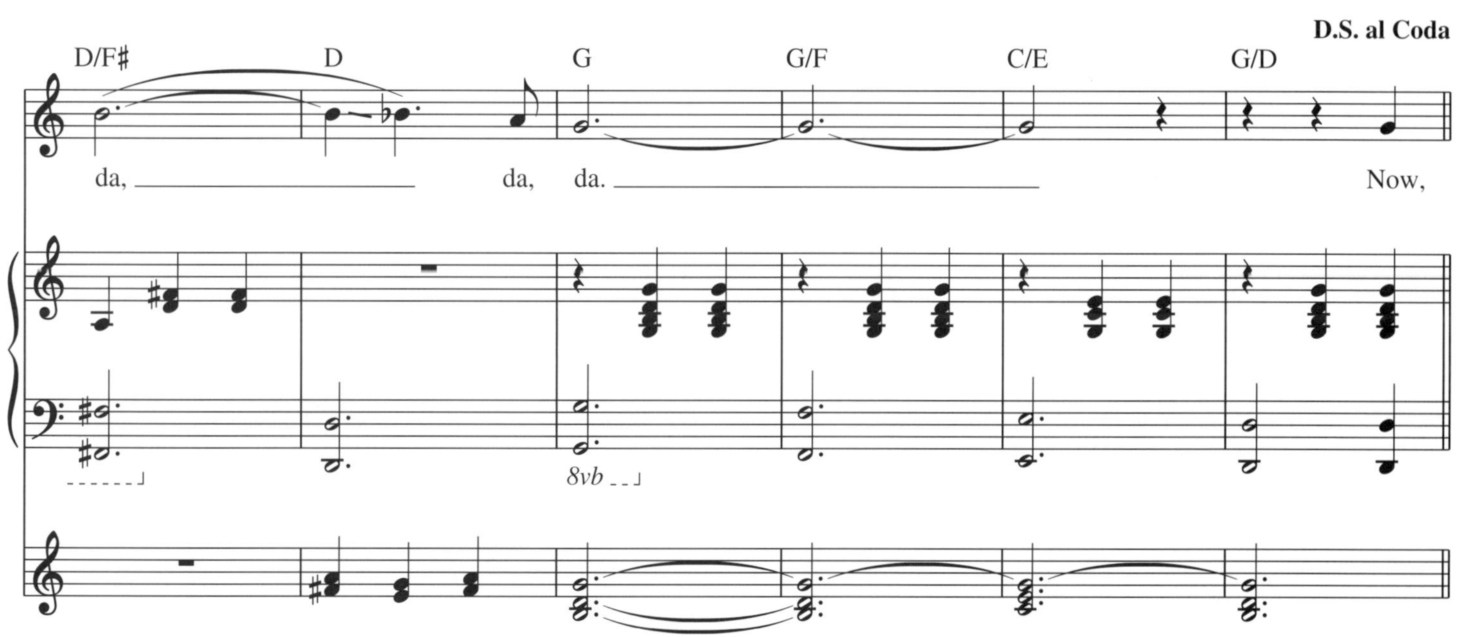
D.S. al Coda
D/F#
D
G
G/F
C/E
G/D
da, da, da.
Now,
8vb

CODA
C
Am
Am/G
D
F
lone.
8vb
Am
Am/G
D
F
Am
Am/G
D.S.S. al Coda
D
G
G/F
C/E
G7/D
CODA
C
F/C
C
G/B
And the pia - no, it sounds like a
cresc.
ff
p
mf

F/A
C/G
F
C/E
D
G
car - ni - val
and the mi - cro-phone
smells like a beer
and they
8vb
C
G/B
F/A
C/G
F
F/G
sit at the bar
and put
bread in my jar
and say, "Man,
what are you
do - in' here?"
8vb
C
Am
Am/G
D/F♯
F
Oh,
la,
la, la,
di, di,
da.
mf
8vb

Am Am/G D/F# D G G/F
La, la, di, di, da, da, dum.
C/E G7/D C G/B F/A C/G
Sing us a song, you're the pia - no man.
8vb
F C/E D G C G/B
Sing us a song to - night.
Well, we're all in the mood for a

F/A C/G F(add9)/A G9sus C
mel - o - dy
and you've got us feel - in' al - right.
8vb

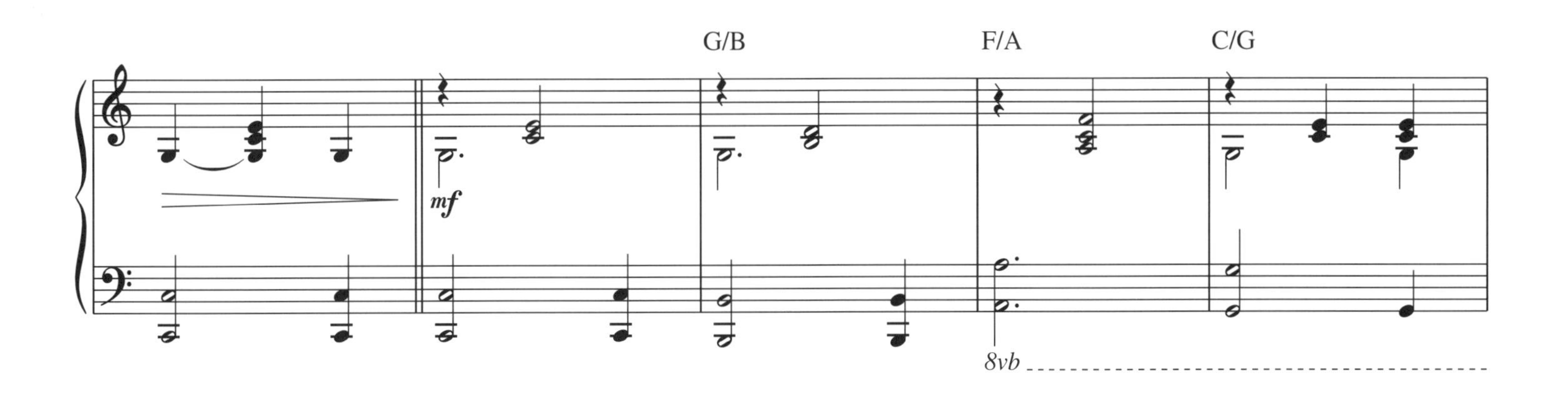
G/B F/A C/G
mf
8vb

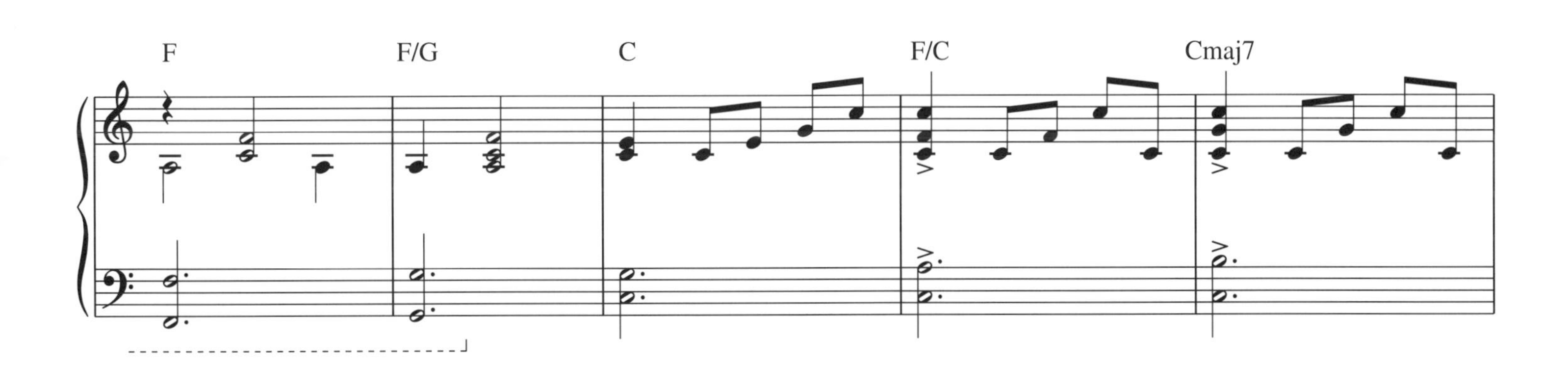
F F/G C F/C Cmaj7

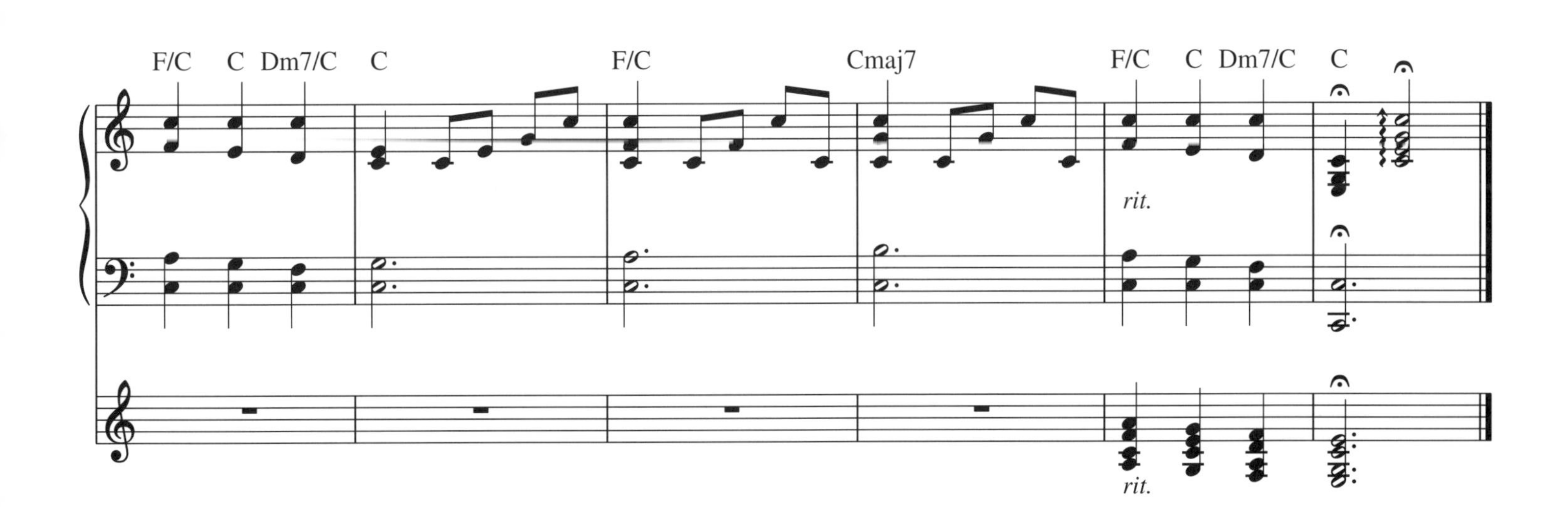
F/C C Dm7/C C F/C Cmaj7 F/C C Dm7/C C
rit.
rit.

Point of Know Return

Words and Music by Steve Walsh,
Phil Ehart and Robert Steinhardt

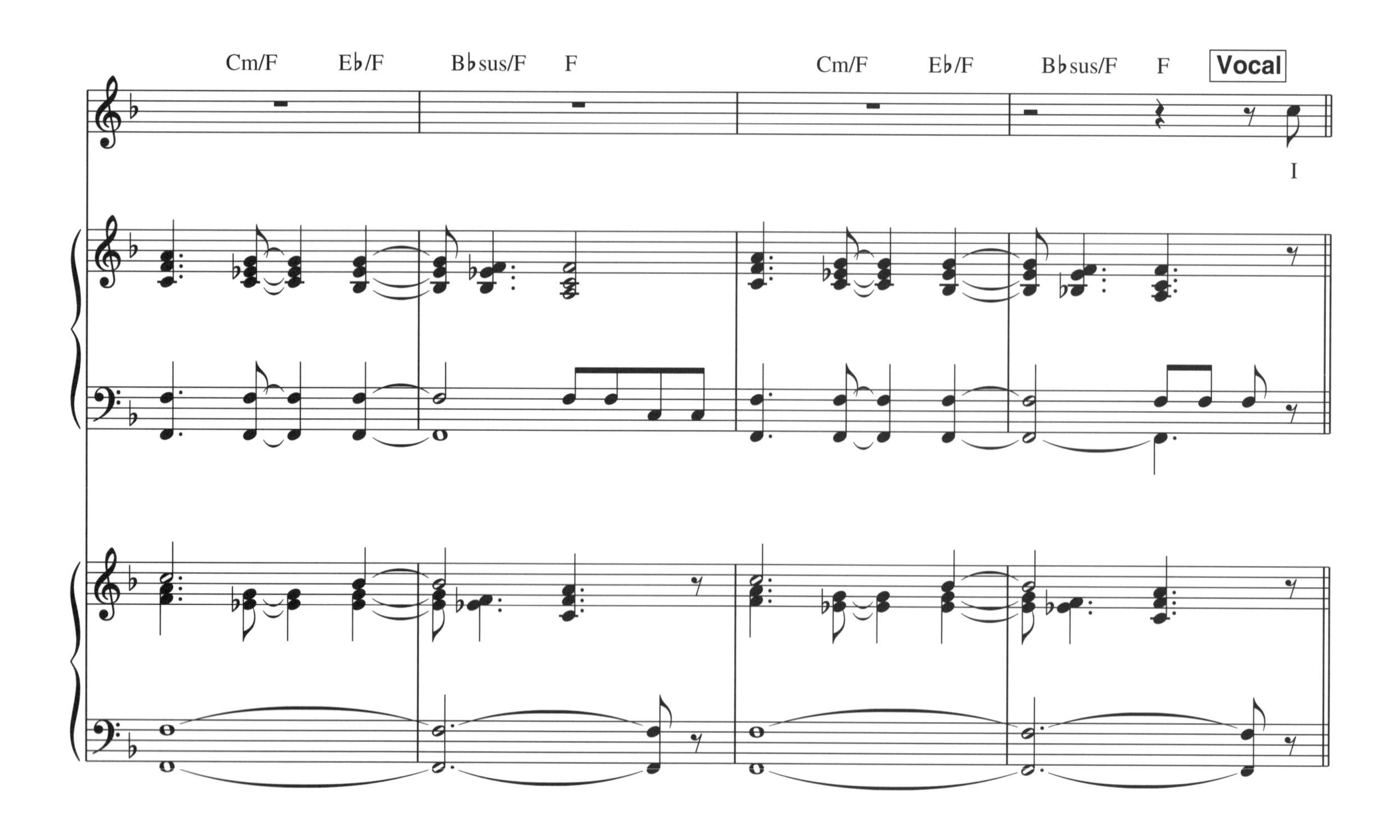

C F/C C7(no3rd) F/C C Bb F/A Gm7
heard the men say - ing some - thing. The cap - tains tell they pay
F C F/C C7(no3rd) F/C C
you well. And they say they need sail - ing men to
Bb F/A Gm7 F A/C# Dm C
show the way and leave to - day. Was it you that said
Bb/F F Bb/F C/F F
how long?
(Organ)

B♭/F F B♭/F C/F F
How long? They
C F C7(no3rd) F/C C
say the sea turns so dark that you
Synth
B♭ F/A Gm7 F C F/C C7(no3rd)
know it's time you see the sign. They say the point de -

F/C C Bb F/A Gm7 F
-mons guard_ is an o - cean grave for all ___ the brave. Was it
A/C# Dm C Bb/F F Bb/F C/F F
you that __ said how long?
Organ
Bb/F F Bb/F C/F F
How long?

Dm C B♭ F Cm/F E♭/F B♭sus/F F
How long to the point of know - re - turn?
B/C♯ C♯ F♯/C♯ B/C♯ C♯ B/C♯ C♯ B/C♯ C♯ F♯/C♯ B/C♯ C♯ F♯/C♯ B/C♯ C♯ F♯/C♯
3
B E E/F♯ F♯ B/F♯ E/F♯ F♯ E/F♯ F♯
E/F♯ F♯ B/F♯ E/F♯ F♯ B/F♯ E/F♯ F♯ B/F♯ E A
3
3

G
F
Your fath - er,
he said he
needs
you.
(Piano)
(Organ)
C/E
F
Your moth - er,
she said she
loves
you.
G
F
Your broth - ers,
they
ech - o
your
words.
How

C/E
C
E♭sus2
far
to the point of know – re – turn,
to the
(Point of know – re – turn.)
B♭
C
B♭/F
F
B♭/F
point of no re – turn?
Well, how long?
C/F
F
B♭/F
F
B♭/F
How long?

F
C F/C C7 F/C C
To - day I found a mes - sage float - ing
Synth
B♭ F/A Gm7 F C F/C C7 F/C C
in the sea from you to me. You wrote that when you could see it you
B♭ F/A Gm7 F A/C♯ Dm C
cried with fear, the point was near. Was it you that said
Piano

Bb/F F Bb/F C/F F
how long?
Bb/F F Bb/F C/F F
How long?
Dm C Bb Bb/F F Bb/F
How long to the point of know re - turn?

C
F
B♭/F
F
B♭/F
How
long?
C
F
Dm
C
B♭
How long to the point of know re - turn?
B♭/F
F
B♭/F
C
F
Know re -

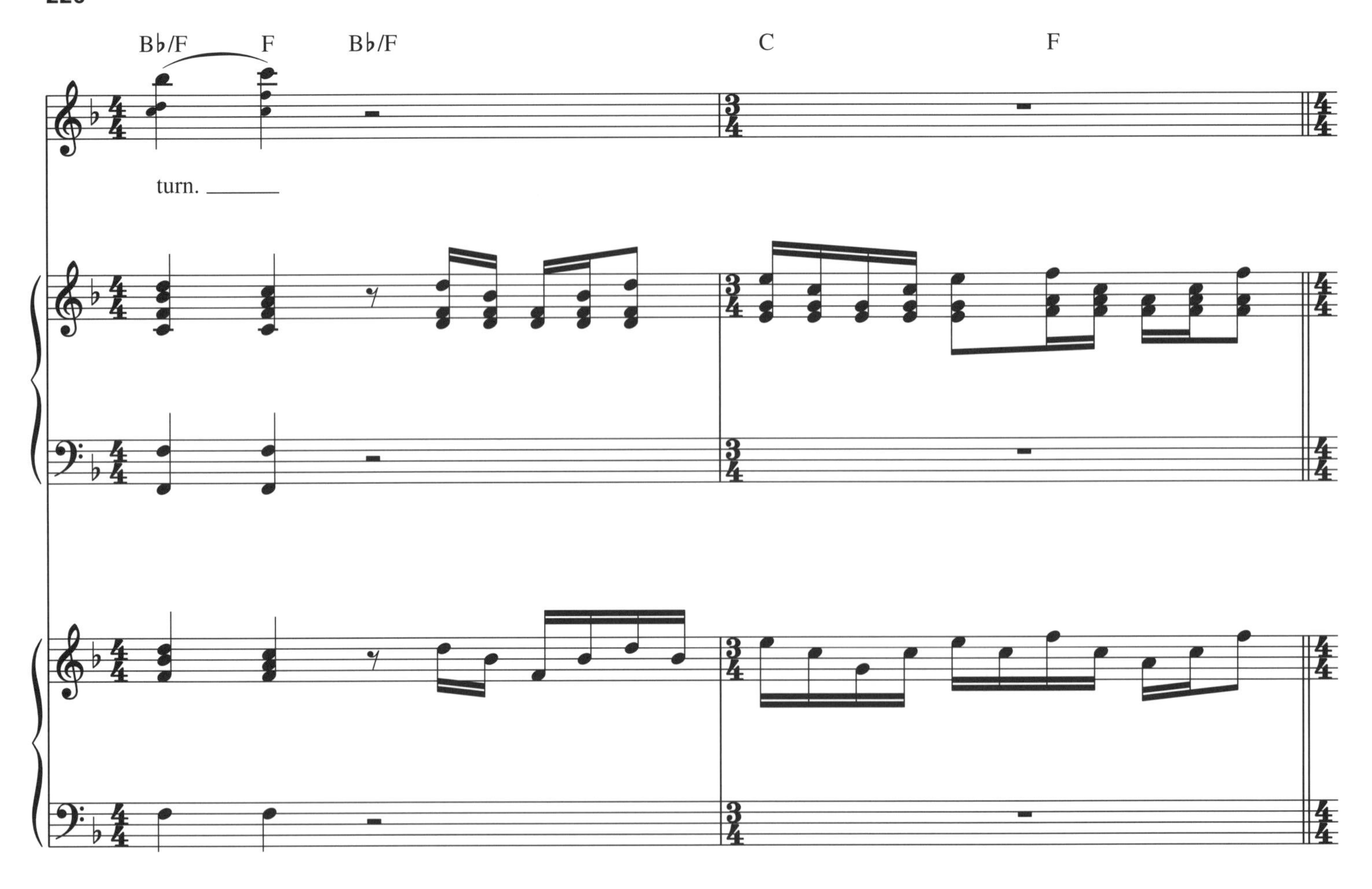
B♭/F
F
B♭/F
C
F
turn.

Repeat and Fade
Optional Ending
B♭/F
F
B♭/F
C
F
B♭/F
F
How long?
How long?

Runaway

Words and Music by Jon Bon Jovi
and George Karakoglou

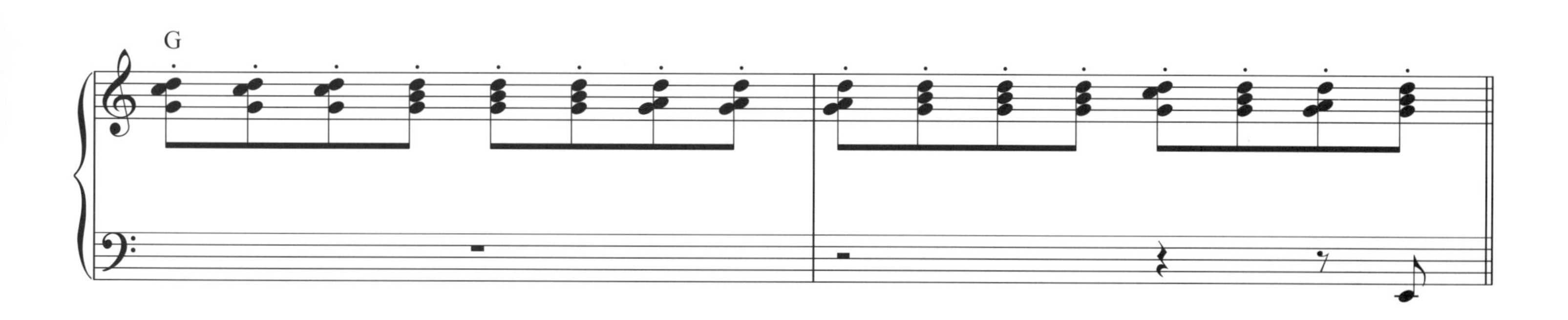

G
live girls talk a - bout their so - cial lives. They're made of
night, guar - an - teed to blow your mind.
Em F G Am
lip - stick, plas - tic and paint, a touch of sa - ble in their eyes.
I see you out on the streets, call me for a wild time.
Play Fill 1 (2nd time)
(All your life.) All your life all you've asked when's your dad - dy gon - na
So you sit home a - lone 'cause there's noth - in' left that
f
Guitar
Fill 1
Am

G
Em
talk to you. But you were liv - in' in an - oth - er world,
you can do. There's on - ly pic - tures hung in the
G
Am
try - in' to get a mes - sage through.
shad - ows left there to look at you.
Bass
Em
G
Am
No one heard a sin - gle word you said.
You know she likes the lights at night on the ne - on Broad - way signs.
Guitar
Dm
They should have seen it in your eyes, what was
She don't real - ly mind. It's on - ly

C
G
Am
go - in' 'round your head.
love she hoped to find.
Ooh,
Synth.
G
she's a lit - tle run - a - way.
simile
C
Em
G
Am
Dad - dy's girl learned fast all those things he could - n't say.
To Coda
G
Em
N.C.
Ooh,
she's a lit - tle

Am
D.S. al Coda
run - a - way.
mf
CODA
Em
N.C.
she's a lit - tle run - a - way.
Am
mf
Guitar Solo
f

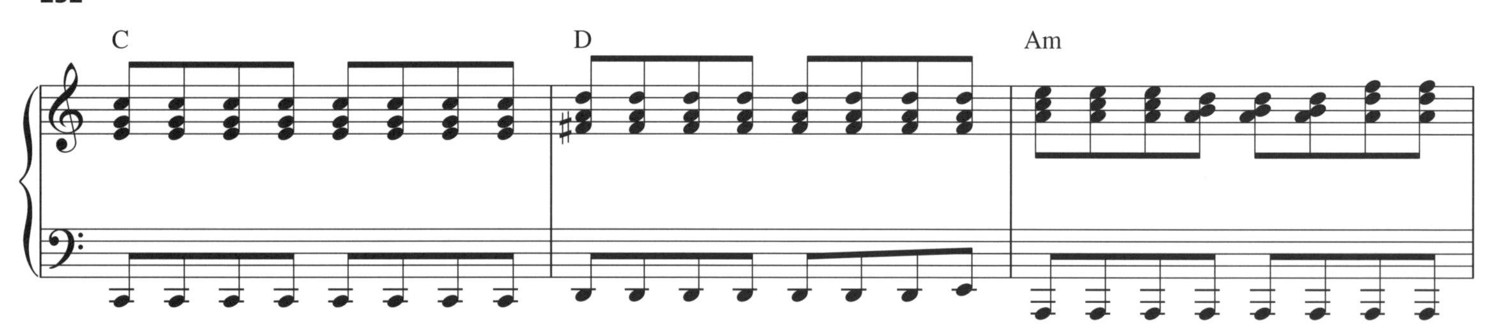
C
D
Am

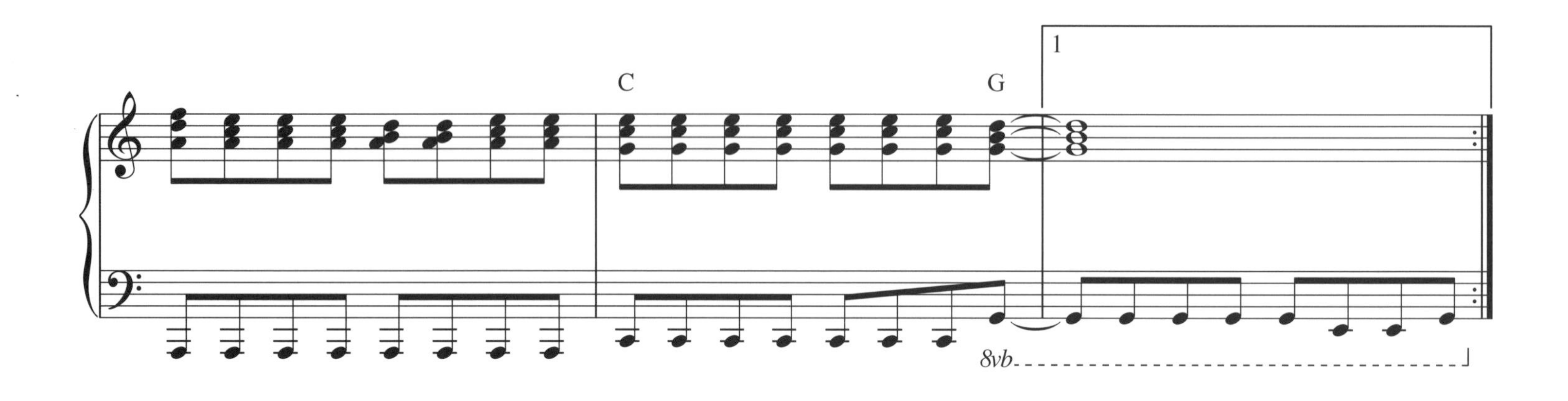
C
G
1
8vb

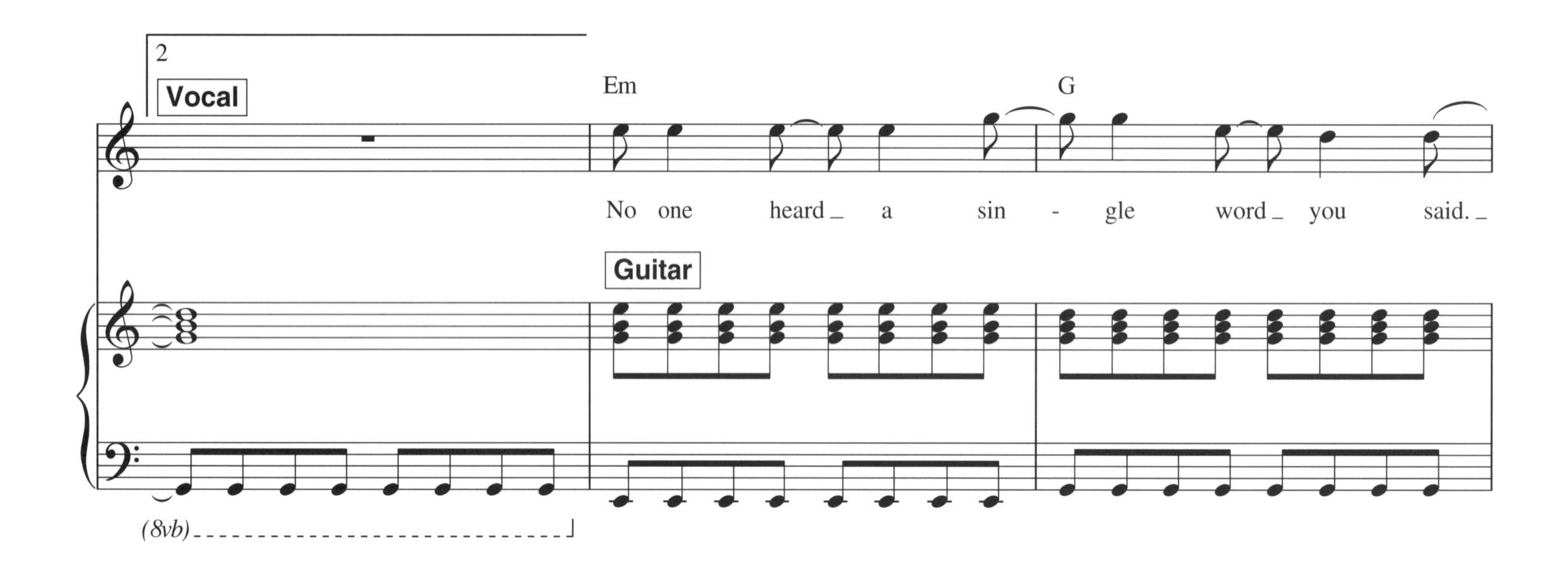
2
Vocal
Em
G
No one heard a sin - gle word you said.
Guitar
(8vb)

Am
Dm
They should have seen it in your eyes,

C
G
what was go - in' 'round your head.
Am
G
Ooh, she's a lit - tle run - a - way.
Synth.
simile
C
Em
G
Dad - dy's girl learned fast all those things he
Dad - dy's girl learned fast, now she works the
Am
could - n't say.
night a - way.
Repeat and Fade
Optional Ending

Roll with the Changes

Words and Music by
Kevin Cronin

C
F/C
- ble, woman, I am will - ing to make
- pen, felt the ta - bles turn - ing.
B♭/C
F/C
C
the break that we are on the brink of. My cup is on the ta -
Got me through my dark - est hour. I heard the thun - der clap -
F/C
- ble, my love is spill - ing, wait -
- ping, felt the des - ert burn - ing, un -

B♭/C
F/C
C
- ing here for you to take and drink of.
til you poured on me like a sweet sun show - er.
B♭
Dm
C
C/E
G7/D
C
So if you're tired of the same old sto - ry,
B♭
Dm
C
oh, turn some pag - es.
B♭
Dm
C
C/E
G7/D
C
I'll be here when you are read - y to roll with the chang -

1
G7
- es,
yeah.

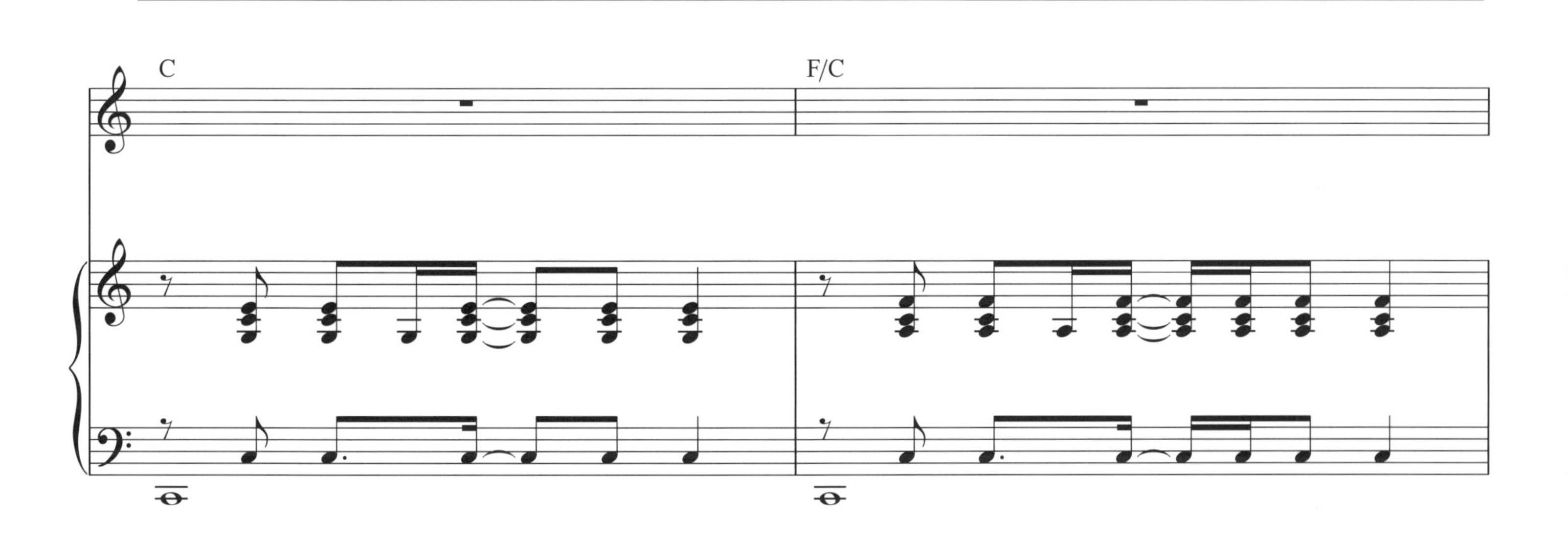
C
F/C

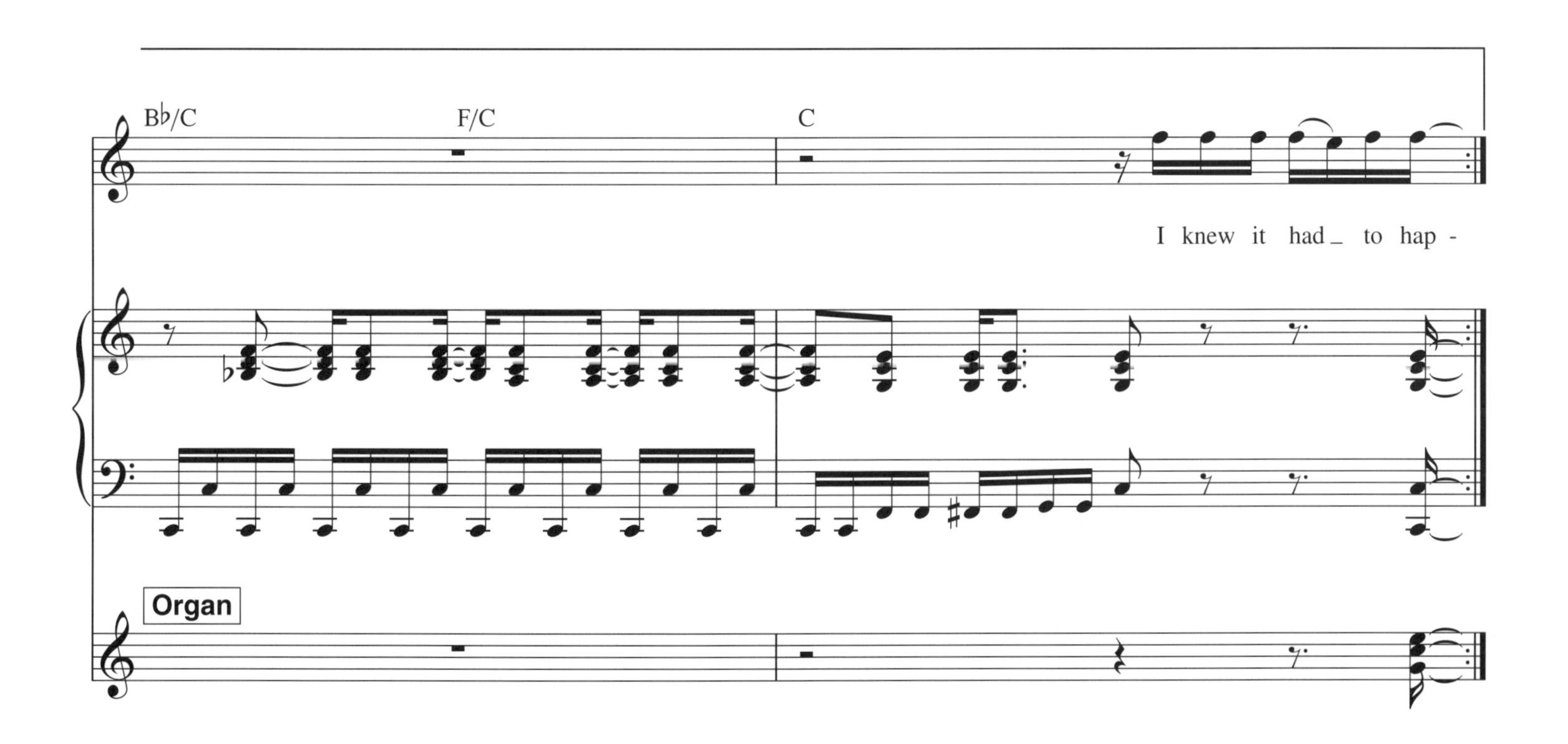
B♭/C
F/C
C
I knew it had to hap -
Organ

2
G7
- es, oh,
C
F/C
yeah.
(Vocal 1st time only)
B♭/C
F/C
1
C
2
C
B♭
Dm
So, if you're tired of the same

C C/E G7/D C B♭ Dm
old sto - ry, oh, ba - by, turn some pag -
C B♭ Dm
- es. I'll be here when you are read -
C C/E G7/D C G7
- y to roll with the chang - es, ba -
- by, roll with the chang - es. Oh, you know,

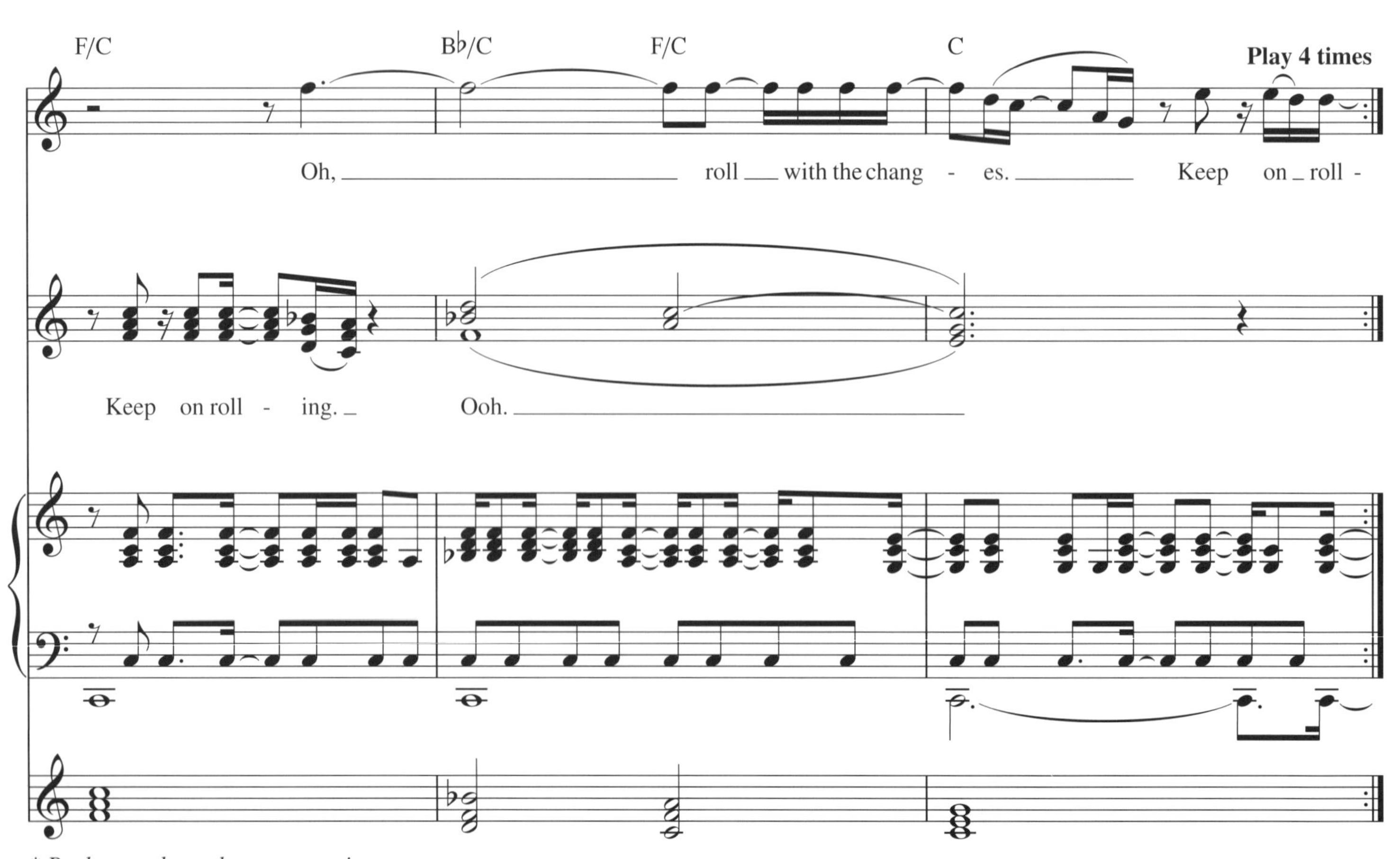

* Background vocals sung as written.

Guitar Solo
(2nd time)
C
F/C
Organ
(Play 1st time only)
B♭/C
F/C
C
F/C
B♭/C
F/C
C

F/C
B♭/C
F/C
C
F/C
B♭/C
F/C
1
C

2
Vocal
C
F/C
Keep on roll - ing.
Keep on roll - ing.
1-3
B♭/C
F/C
C
Ooh.
4
B♭
F
C
Ooh,
ah!
8vb

Say You Love Me

Words and Music by
Christine McVie

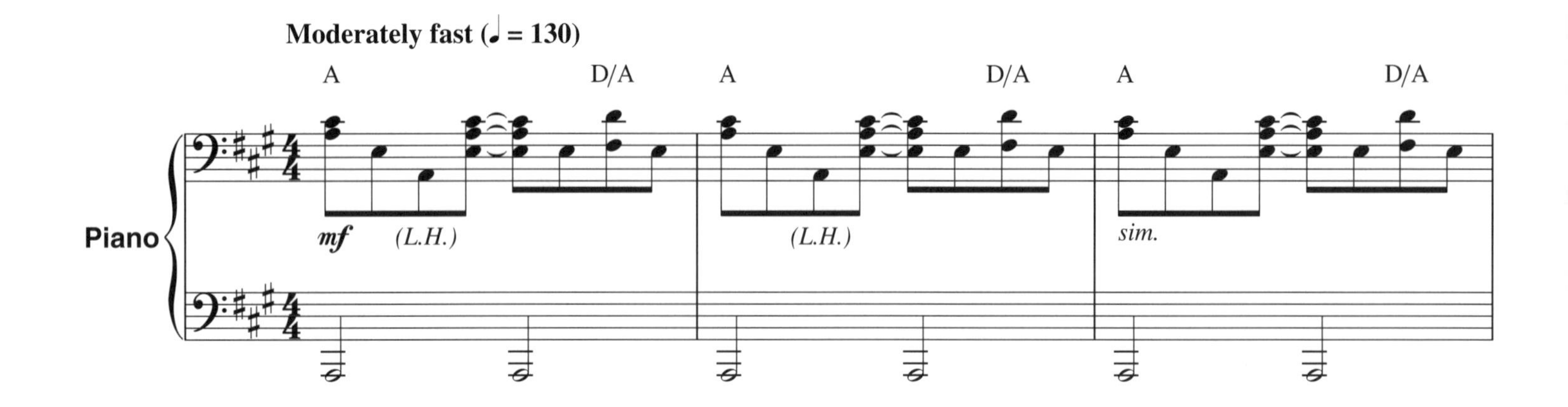

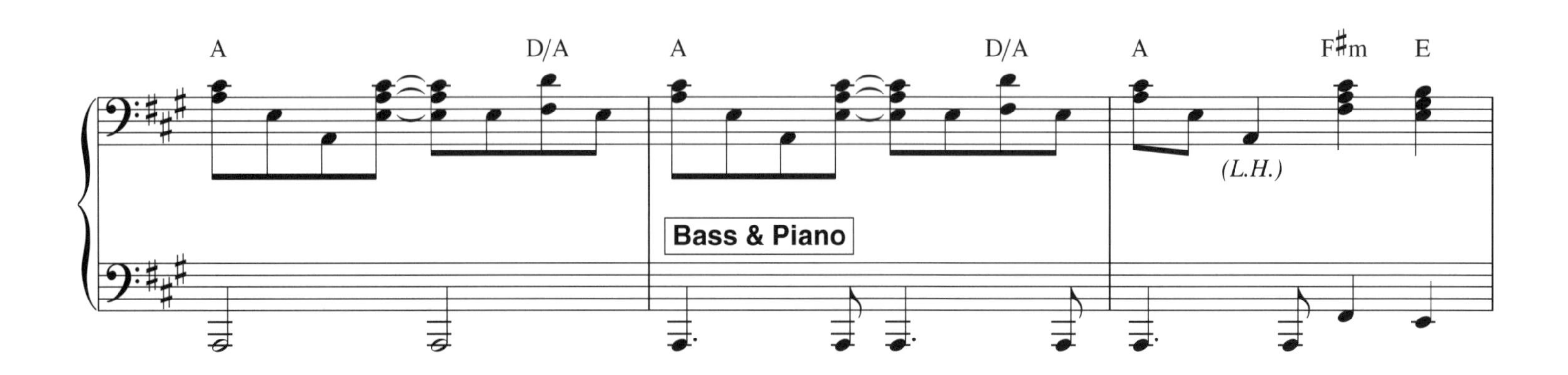

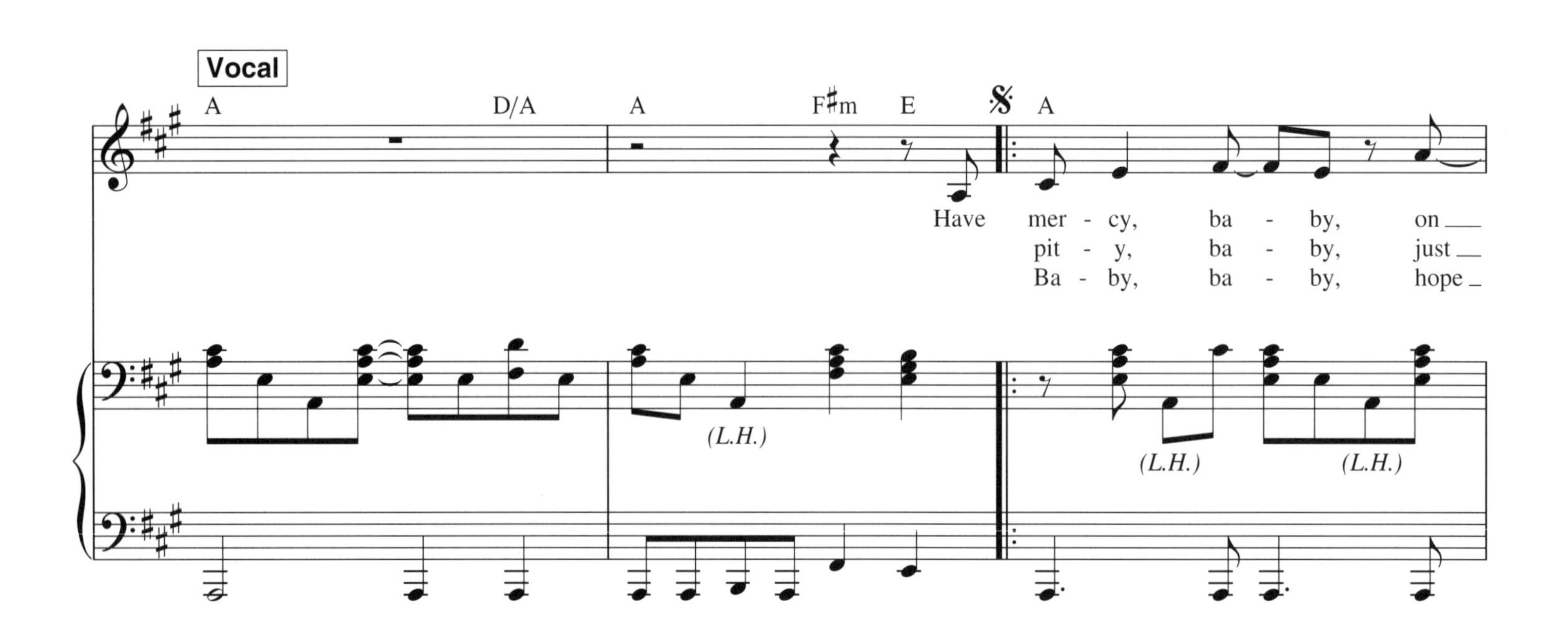

D/A
A
D/A
A
a poor girl like me.
when I thought it was o - ver,
you're gon - na stay a - way
You know I'm
and now you
'cause I'm
Play Fill 1 (2nd time)
(L.H.)
sim.

E
A/E
E
A
D/A
fall - ing, fall - ing, fall - ing at your feet.
got me run - ning, run - ning, run - ning for cov - er.
get - ting weak - er, weak - er ev - er - y day.

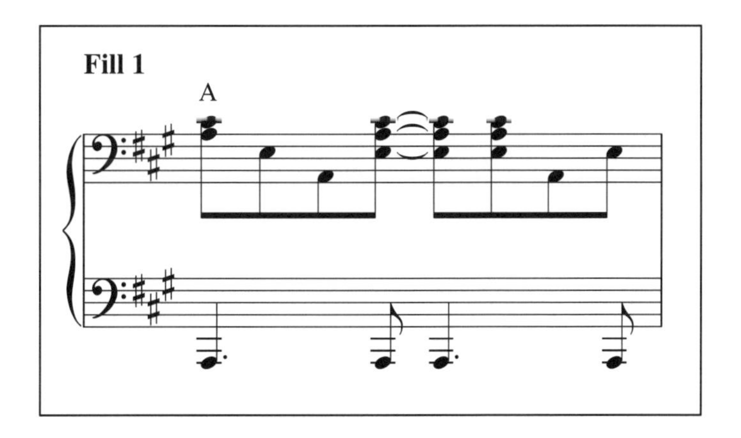
Fill 1
A

A
Play Fill 2 (2nd & 3rd time)
I'm tin-gling right from my head to my toes,
I'm beg-ging you for a lit-tle sym-pa-thy,
I guess I'm not as strong as I used to be,

D/A A
A/C♯ D
E A/E
so help me, help me, help
and if you use me a-gain, it-'ll be
and if you use me a-gain, it-'ll be

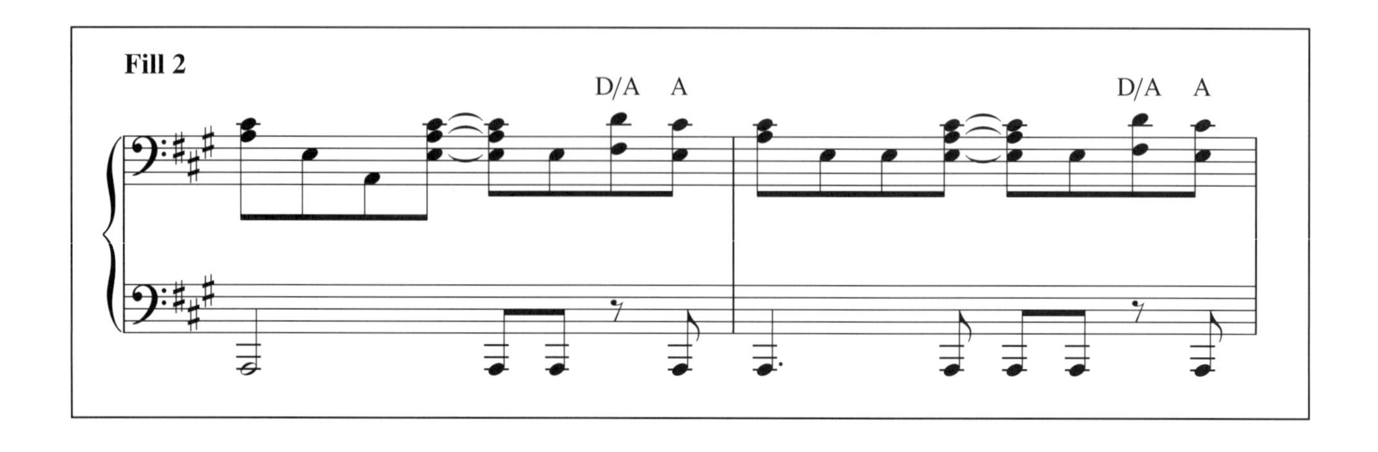
Fill 2
D/A A
D/A A

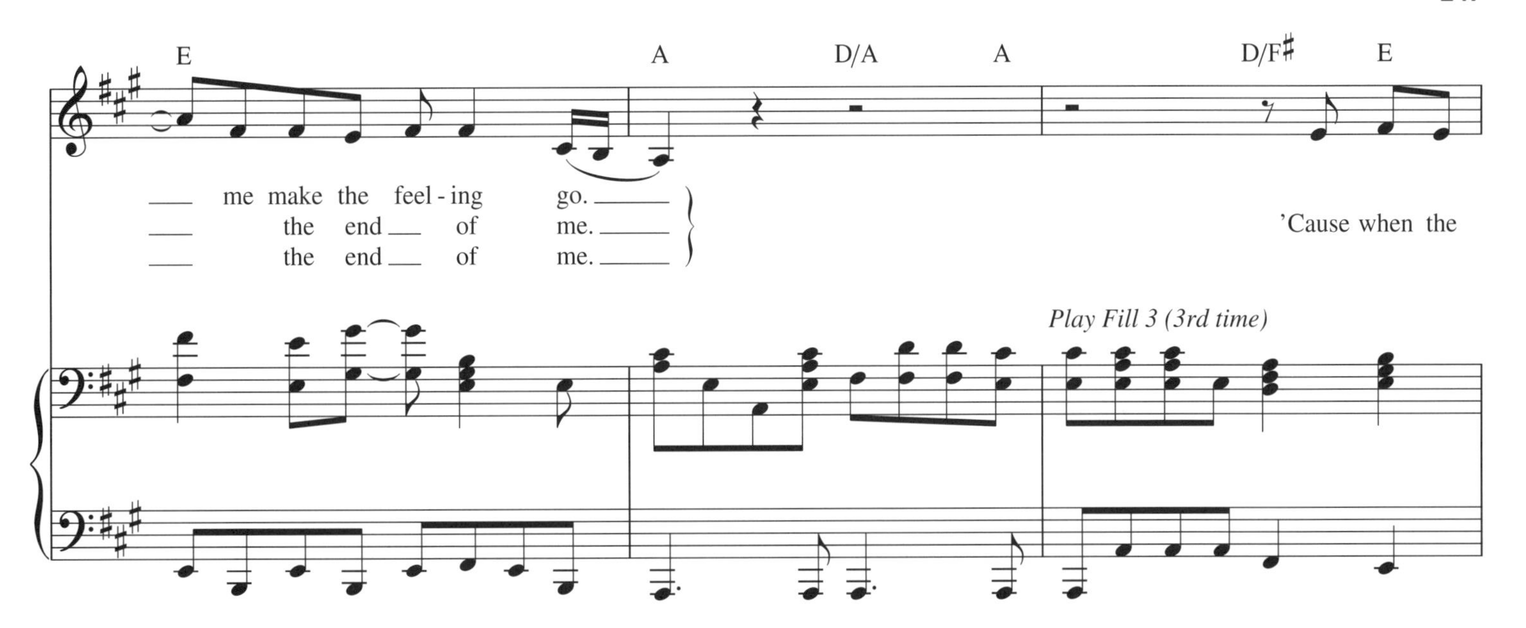
E
A
D/A
A
D/F♯
E
me make the feel - ing go.
the end of me.
the end of me.
'Cause when the
Play Fill 3 (3rd time)

F♯m
E
D
A
F♯m
E
lov - ing starts and the lights go down and there's not an - oth - er liv - ing

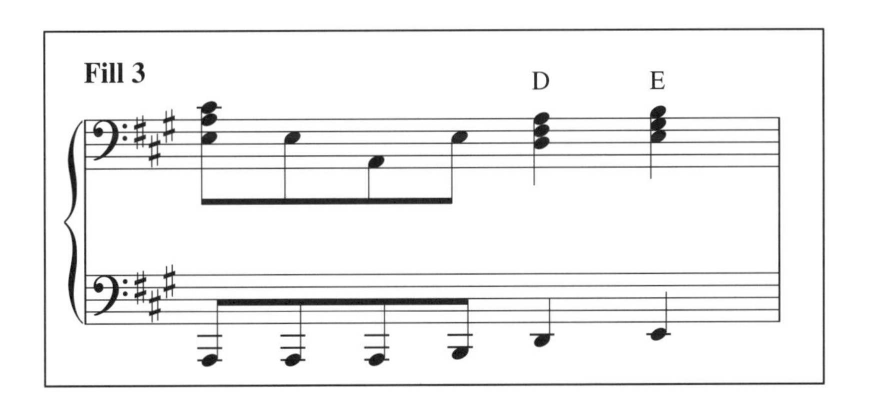
Fill 3
D
E

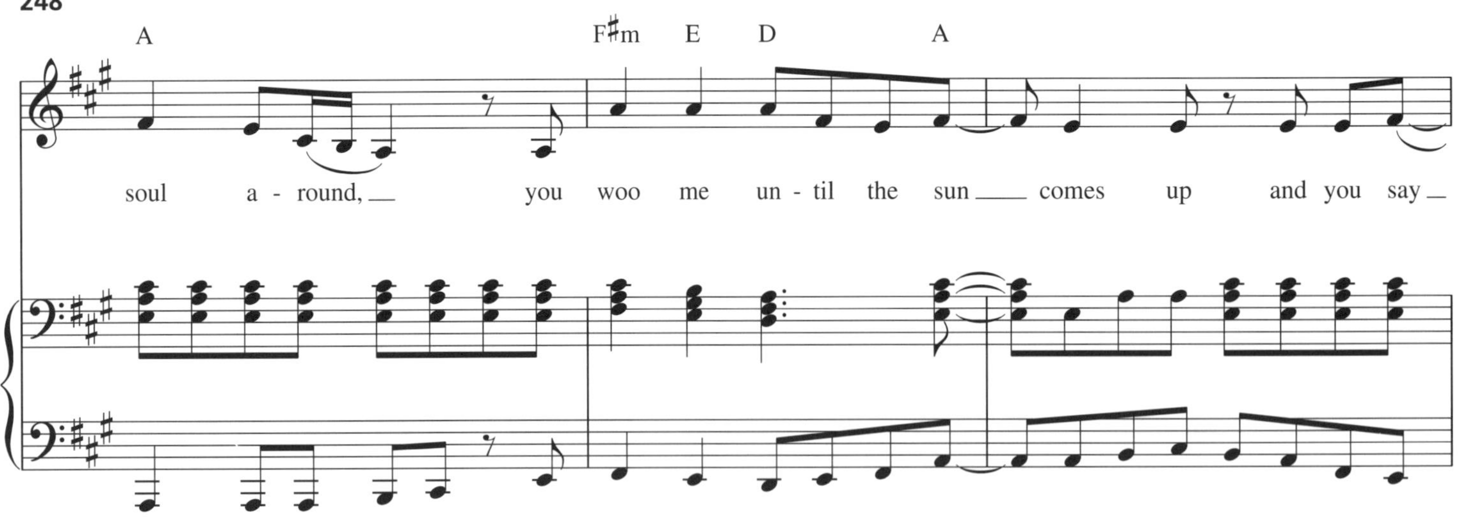
A
F♯m
E
D
A
soul a - round, you woo me un - til the sun comes up and you say

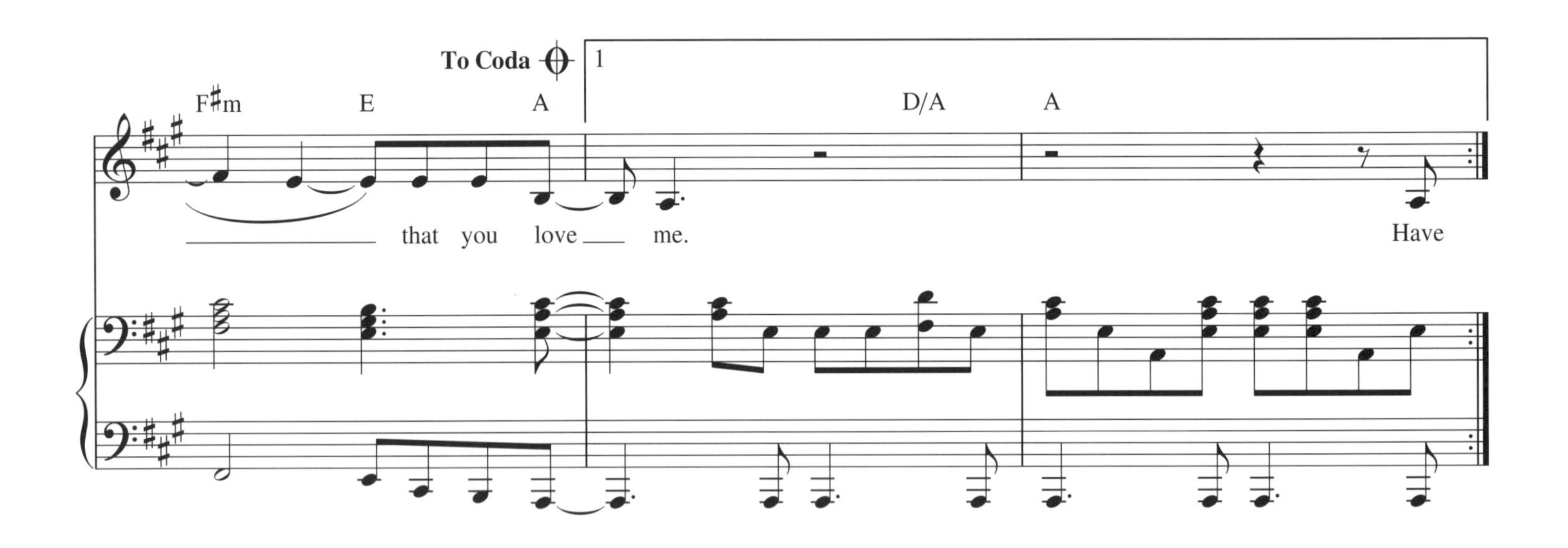
To Coda
1
F♯m
E
A
D/A
A
that you love me.
Have

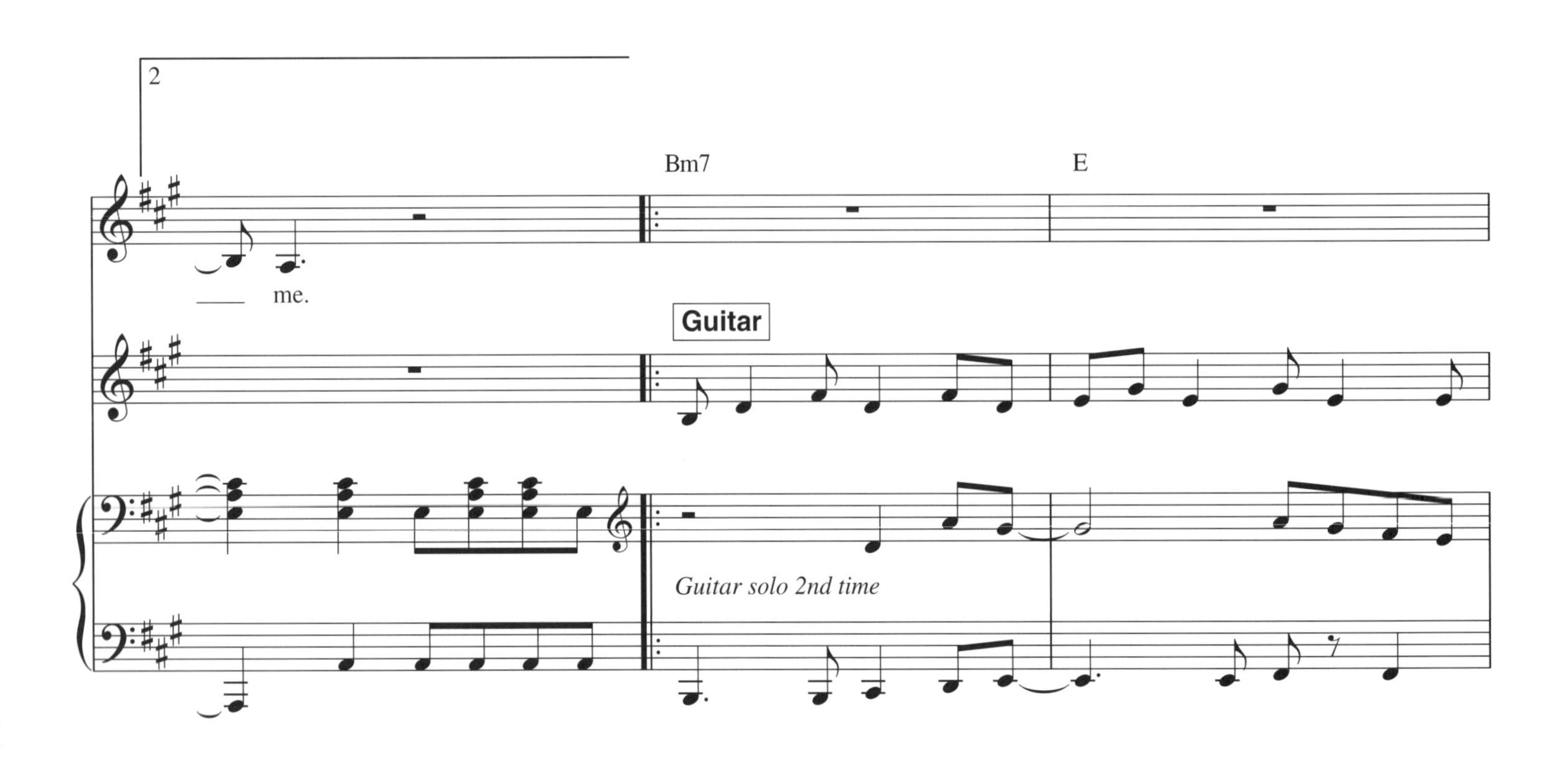
2
Bm7
E
me.
Guitar
Guitar solo 2nd time

Bm7
E
Bm7
Play Fill 4 (2nd time)

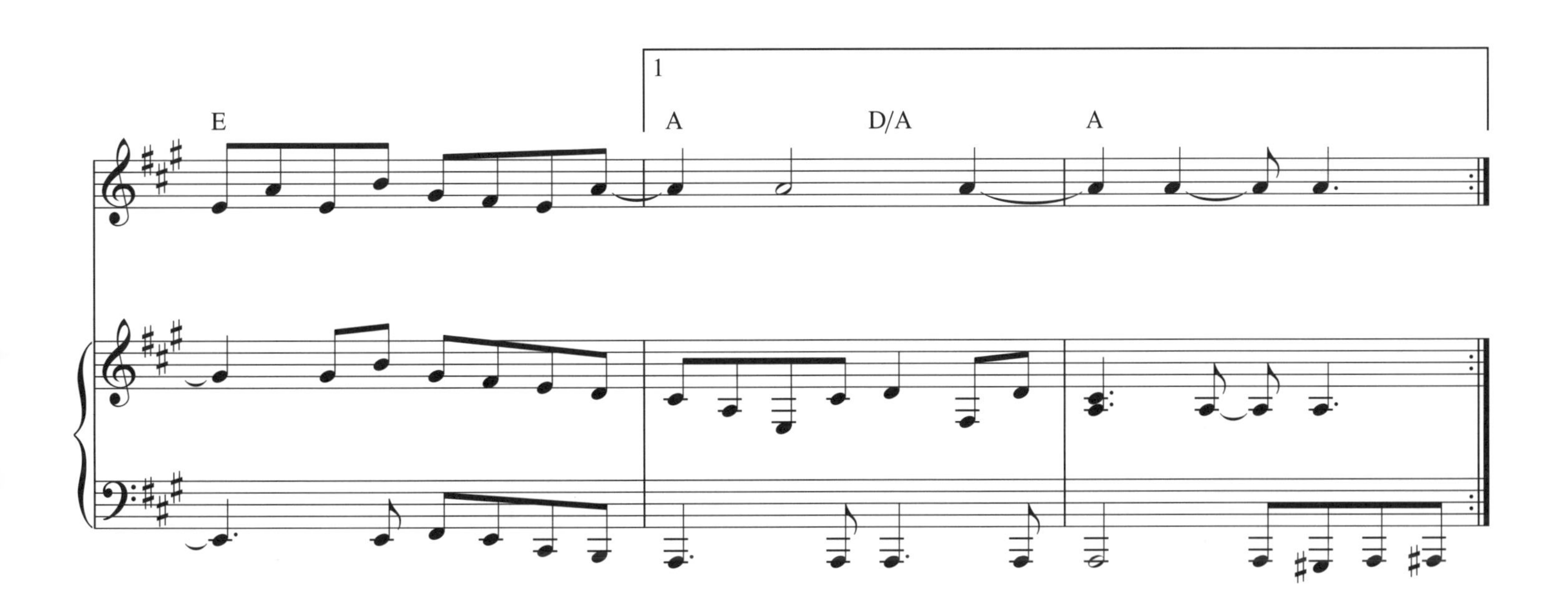
1
E
A
D/A
A

Fill 4
Guitar
Piano
Bass &
Piano

2
D.S. al Coda
A Asus A Asus(add2) A D/A A
CODA
F♯m E D A
me. 'Cause when the lov - ing starts and the lights go down and
F♯m E A F♯m E D A
there's not an - oth - er liv - ing soul a - round, you woo me un - til the sun
F♯m E A
comes up and you say that you love me.

F♯m
E
A
F♯m
E
D
Say that you love me.
Say that you love

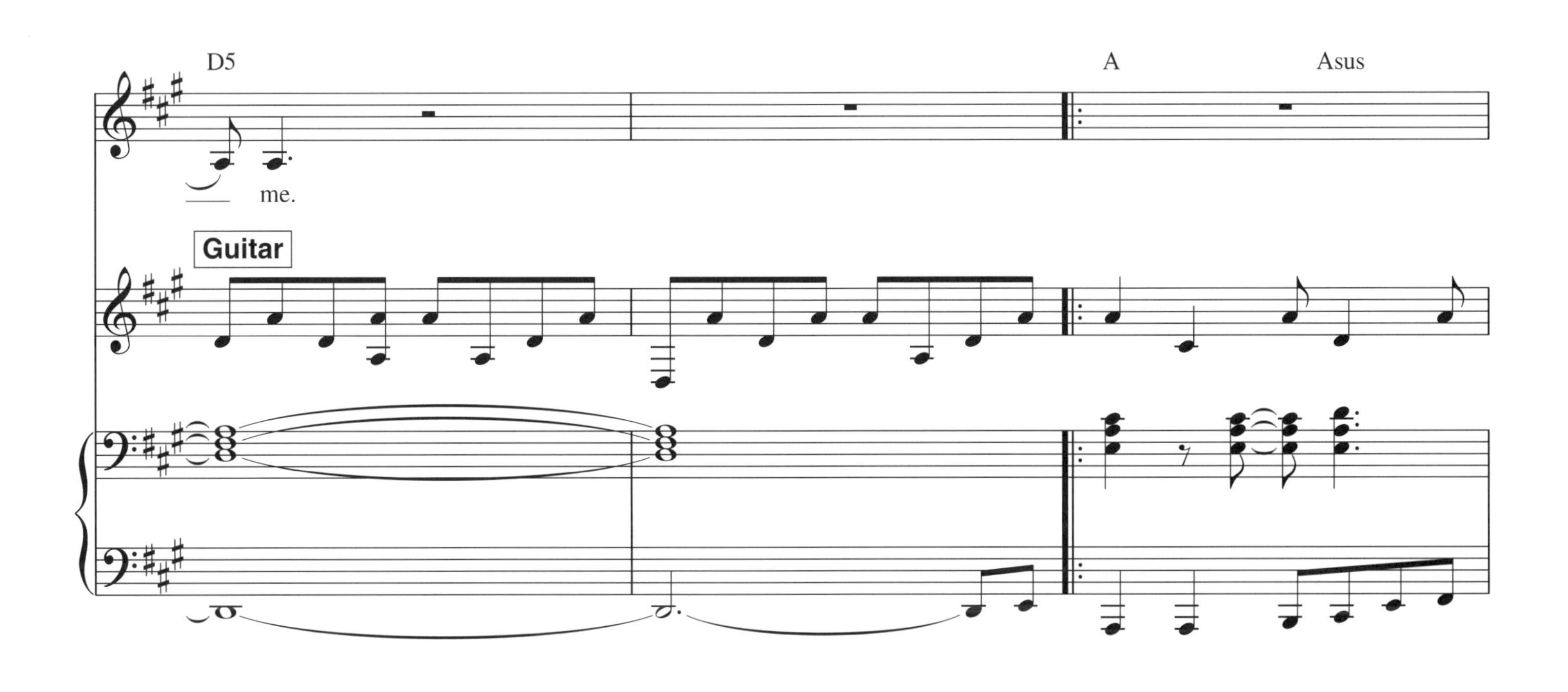
D5
A
Asus
me.
Guitar

Repeat and Fade
Optional Ending
A
Asus
A
F♯m
E
A
Fall - ing, fall - ing, fall - ing.

Separate Ways
(Worlds Apart)

Words and Music by Steve Perry
and Jonathan Cain

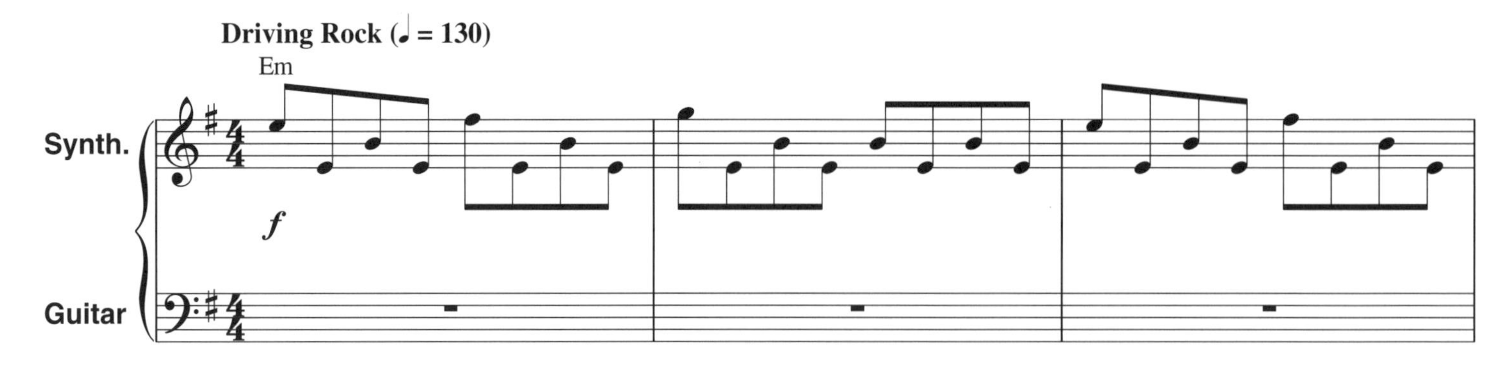

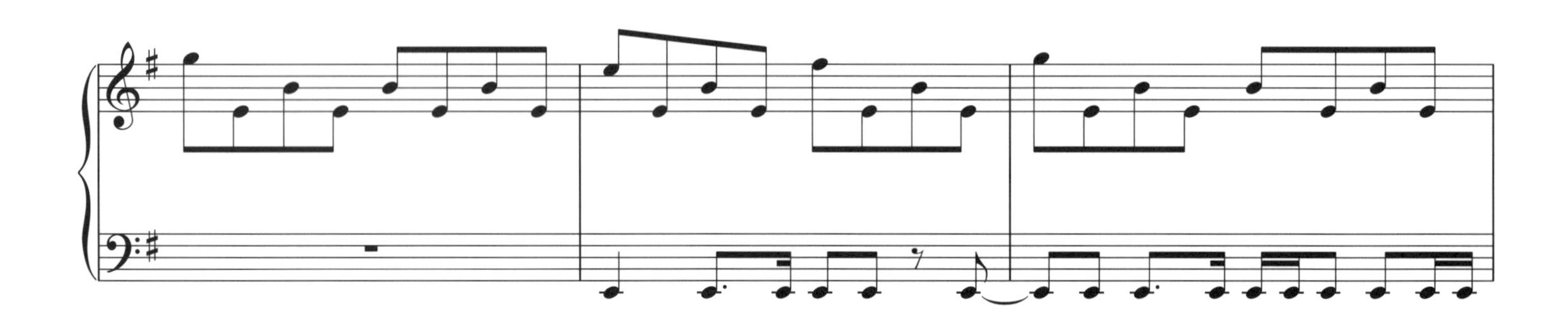

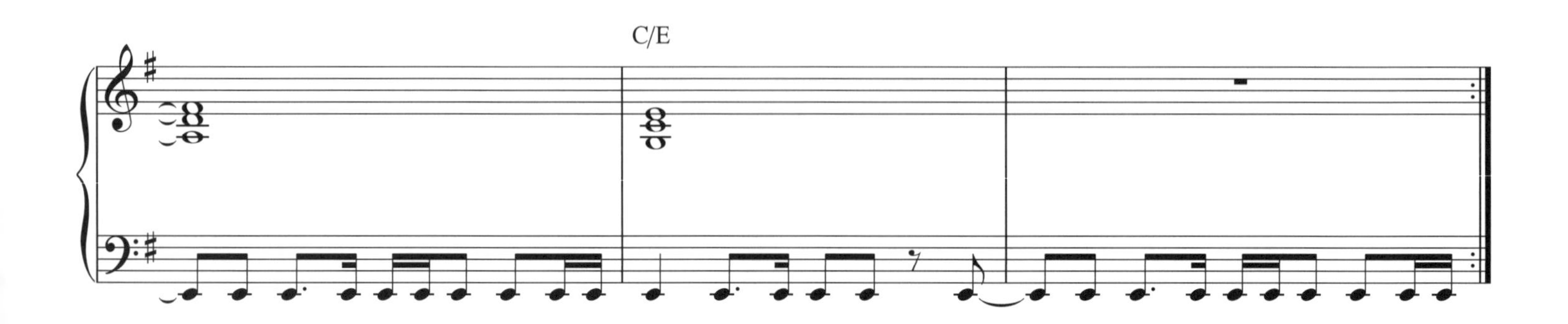

Vocal
Em D/E C/E
Here we stand, worlds a - part,
Trou - bled times, caught be - tween
hearts bro - ken in two, two,
con - fu - sion and pain, pain,
Em D/E
two.
pain.
C/E Em D/E
Sleep - less nights,
Dis - tant eyes,
C/E
los - ing ground, I'm reach - in' for
prom - is - es we made were in

Em D/E C/E
you, you, you.
vain, in vain, in vain.
Am7 Bm7 Cmaj9 D D/A
Feel - in' that it's gone can change
If you must go, I wish
Bass
Am7 Bm7 Cmaj9 D
your mind. If we can't go on,
you love. You'll nev - er walk a - lone,
D/A Am7 Bm7 Cmaj9
sur - vive the tide. Love di - vides.
take care, my love, miss you, love.

Em
Some - day love will find you.
Em/D
Break those chains that bind you.
Cmaj7
1.,2. One night will
3. One night will
Am7
D
D♯dim
re - mind you how we touched and went our sep - 'rate ways.
re - mind you.
Em
Em/D
If he ev - er hurts you, true love won't de - sert you.

To Coda
Cmaj7
Am7
You know I still love you, though we touched and went
D
D♯dim
1
Em
D/E
our sep - 'rate ways.
C/E
Em
D/E
C/E

2
Synth.
Em
Em/D
Synth.
Guitar
Cmaj7
Opt. Guitar ad lib. 2nd time
1
2
Am7
D
D♯dim
D
D♯dim

E5
G5
Bass & Guitar
Synth.
C5
1
A5
2
Bsus
Oh.

D.S. al Coda
CODA
Am7
D
D♯dim
Em
I still love you, girl.
Synth.
Guitar
Em/D
Cmaj7
I real - ly love you, girl.

Am7
D
D♯dim
Em
And if he ev - er hurts you,
Em/D
true love won't des - ert you.
Cmaj7

Synth.
Am7
D
D♯dim
Vocal
Em
No!
Bass & Guitar
No!

Sister Christian

Words and Music by
Kelly Keagy

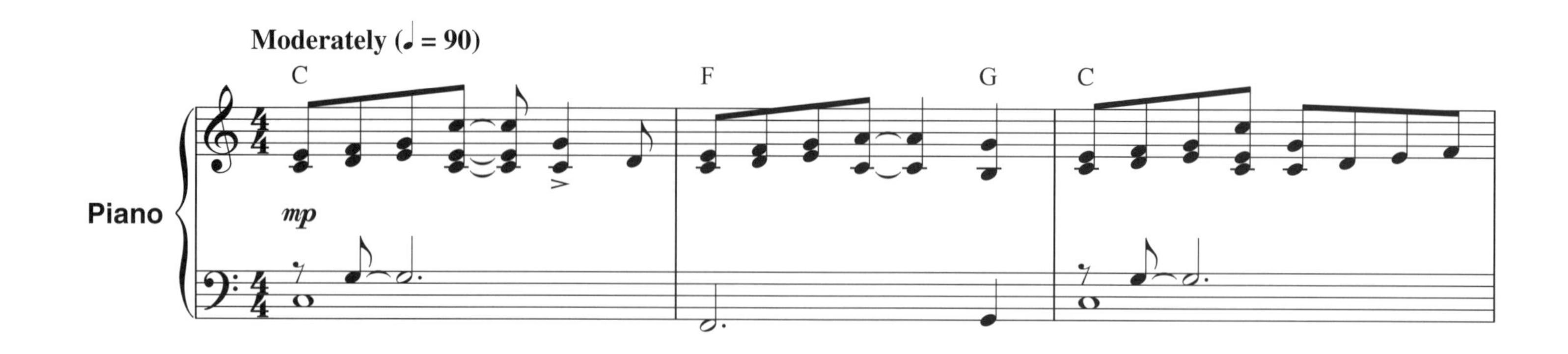

* Organ/Synth. Strings comp 1st time.

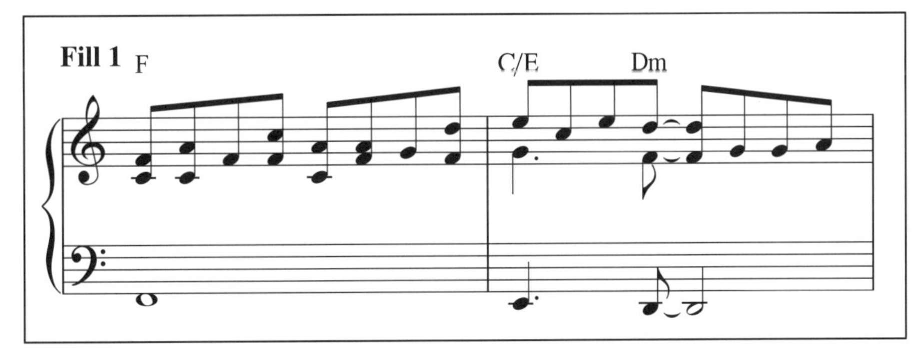

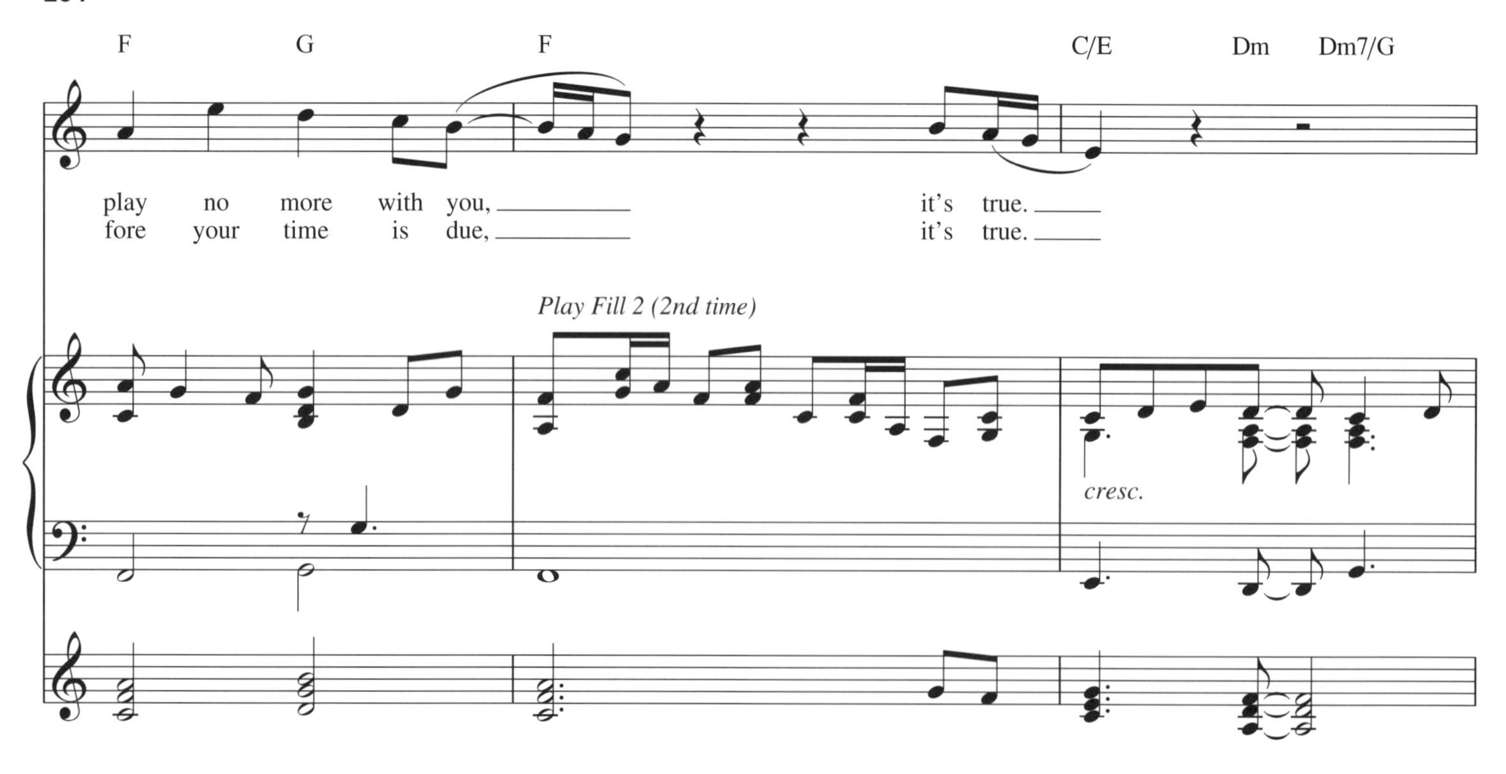
F G F C/E Dm Dm7/G
play no more with you, it's true.
fore your time is due, it's true.
Play Fill 2 (2nd time)
cresc.

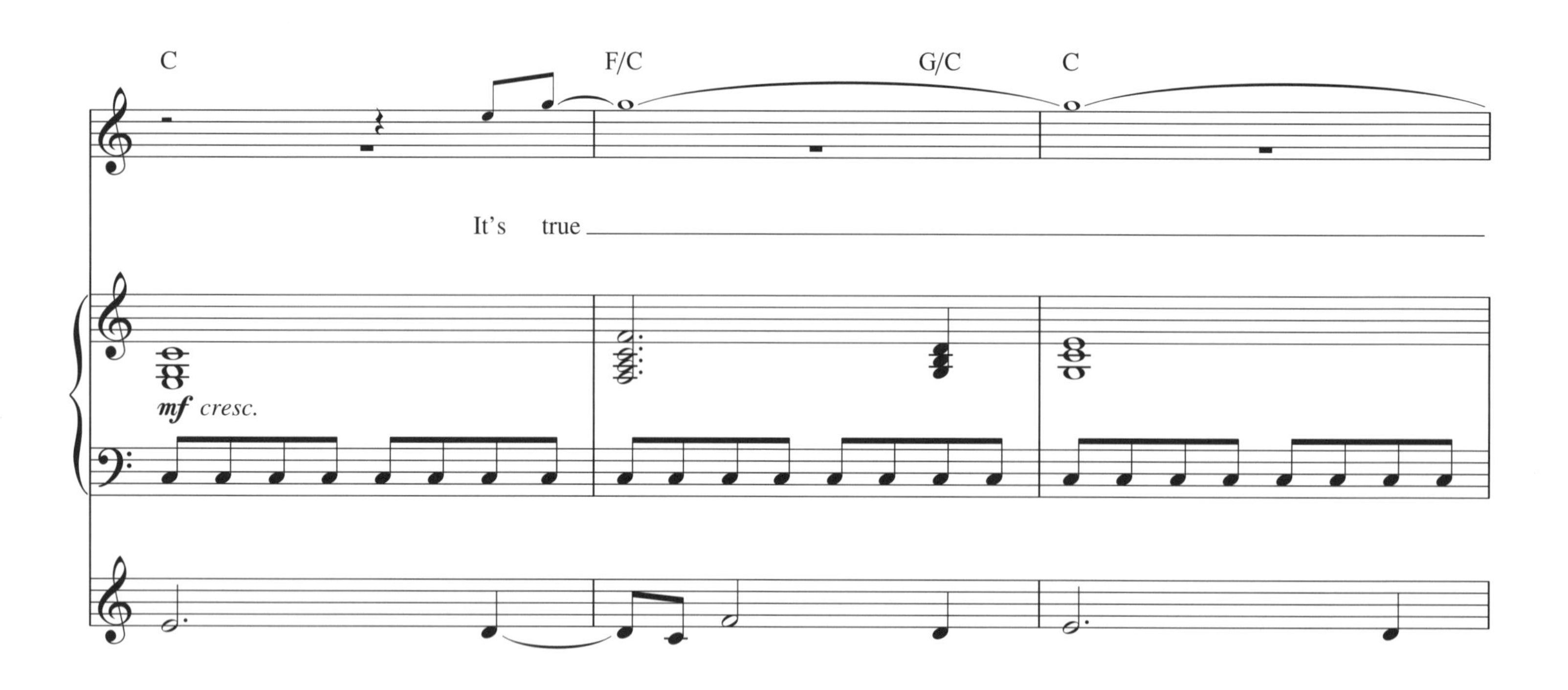
C F/C G/C C
It's true
mf cresc.

Fill 2
F

F/C
G/C
C
F
You're mo - tor - ing. What's your price for flight
yeah. Mo - tor - ing. What's your price for flight?
Guitar
Bass
C
F
B♭
C
in find - ing mis - ter right? You'll
You've got him in your sight. You're
F
1
B♭
F/A
G
be all right to - night.
driv - ing through the night.
Guitar & Piano
decresc.

2
B♭
F/A B♭ F/A B♭ F/A B♭
C
Mo - tor - ing.
F
C
F
B♭
What's your price for flight in find - ing mis - ter right?
C
F
B♭
F/A Gm
You'll be all right to - night.
Guitar & Piano
decresc.

Guitar Solo
F
G/F
F
G/F
Piano
mf
C/E
3
F/E♭
B♭/D
Dm7/G
poco a poco cresc.
G
G7
C
F
Vocal
Mo - tor - ing.
mo - tor - ing.
What's your price for flight
Guitar solo ends
f
C
F
B♭
C
in find - ing mis - ter right?
You'll

1
F
B♭
F/A
B♭
F/A
B♭
F/A
B♭
be all right to - night.
You're
2
F
B♭
F/A
G
C
be all right to - night.
Guitar & Piano
Piano
decresc.
mf
F/C
C
F/C
G/C
C
Sis - ter Chris - tian, oh, the
mp
Bass & Piano

F/C
G/D
C
F
G
time has come, and you know that you're the on - ly one to say,
Piano
F
C/E
Dm7
Dm7/G
C
"O K." But you're mo - tor -
*
poco a poco cresc.
F/C
C
F/C
ing, yeah, mo - tor -
mf
C
F/C
G
C
ing.
rit.
mp
a tempo
* Organ comps to end.

Steppin' Out

Words and Music by
Joe Jackson

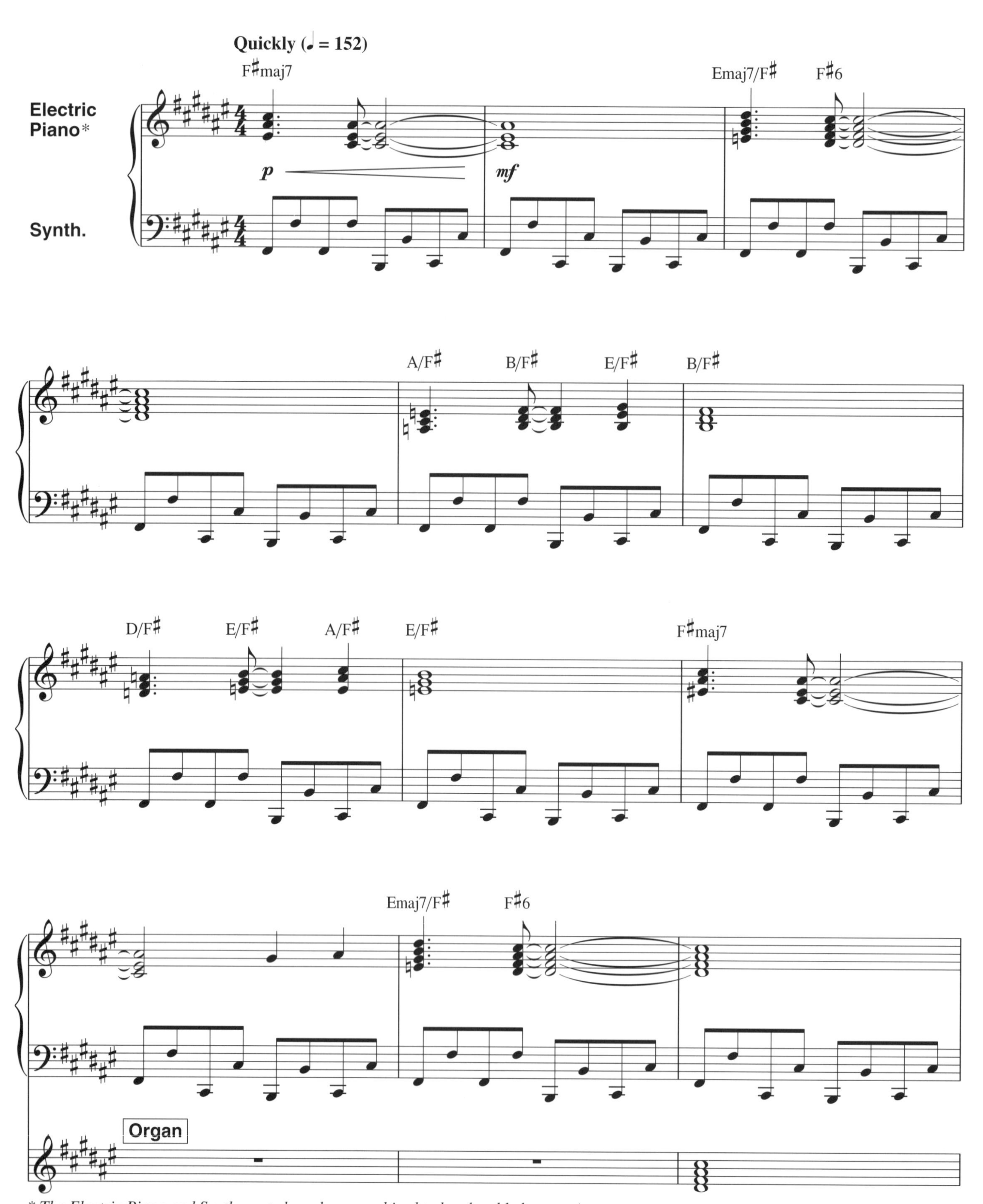

* The Electric Piano and Synth. parts have been combined to be playable by one piano.

A/F♯
B/F♯
E/F♯
B/F♯
D/F♯
E/F♯
A/F♯
E/F♯
F♯maj7
Xylophone
Emaj7/F♯
F♯6
A/F♯
B/F♯
E/F♯
B/F♯
D/F♯
E/F♯
A/F♯
E/F♯

Vocal
F♯
E/F♯
(1.) Now the mist a - cross the win - dow hides the lines,
(2.) We, so tired of all the dark - ness in our lives,
(3.) We are young but get - tin' old be - fore our time.
(4.) You can dress in pink and blue just like a child
Organ
D
E
F♯
E/F♯
D
but noth - ing hides the col -
with no more an - gry words
We'll leave the T V and
and in a yel - low tax -

E
C#m
D
- or of the lights that shine.
to say, can come a - live.
the ra - di - o be - hind.
- i turn to me and smile.
E
C#m
D
E - lec - tric - it - y so fine;
Get in - to a car and drive
Don't you won - der what we'll find,
We'll be there in just a - while
1, 3
E
F#maj7
look and dry your eyes.
to the oth - er side.
step - pin' out to - night?
if you fol - low me.
Synth. & Xylophone

Emaj7/F♯
F♯6
A/F♯
B/F♯
E/F♯
B/F♯
D/F♯
E/F♯
A/F♯
E/F♯
2, 4
F♯maj7
Emaj7/F♯
F♯6
Me, babe, step - pin' out

A/F♯
B/F♯
E/F♯
B/F♯
in - to the night,
D/F♯
E/F♯
A/F♯
E/F♯
F♯maj7
in - to the light.
You, babe,
Emaj7/F♯
F♯6
step - pin' out

A/F♯
B/F♯
E/F♯
in - to the

To Coda
B/F♯
D/F♯
E/F♯
A/F♯
E/F♯
D.S. al Coda
(with repeat)
night,
in - to the
light.

CODA
D/F♯
E/F♯
A/F♯
E/F♯
in - to the
light.

F♯maj7
Organ
Xylophone
Emaj7
F♯6
A
B
E
B
D
E
A
E

F♯maj7
Vocal
Emaj7/F♯
F♯6
Me,
You,
babe,
step - pin' out
Synth.
A/F♯
B/F♯
E/F♯
B/F♯
in - to the night,
D/F♯
E/F♯
A/F♯
E/F♯
Repeat and Fade
Optional Ending
F♯maj7
in - to the light.

Werewolves of London

Words and Music by Warren Zevon,
Robert Wachtel and LeRoy Marinel

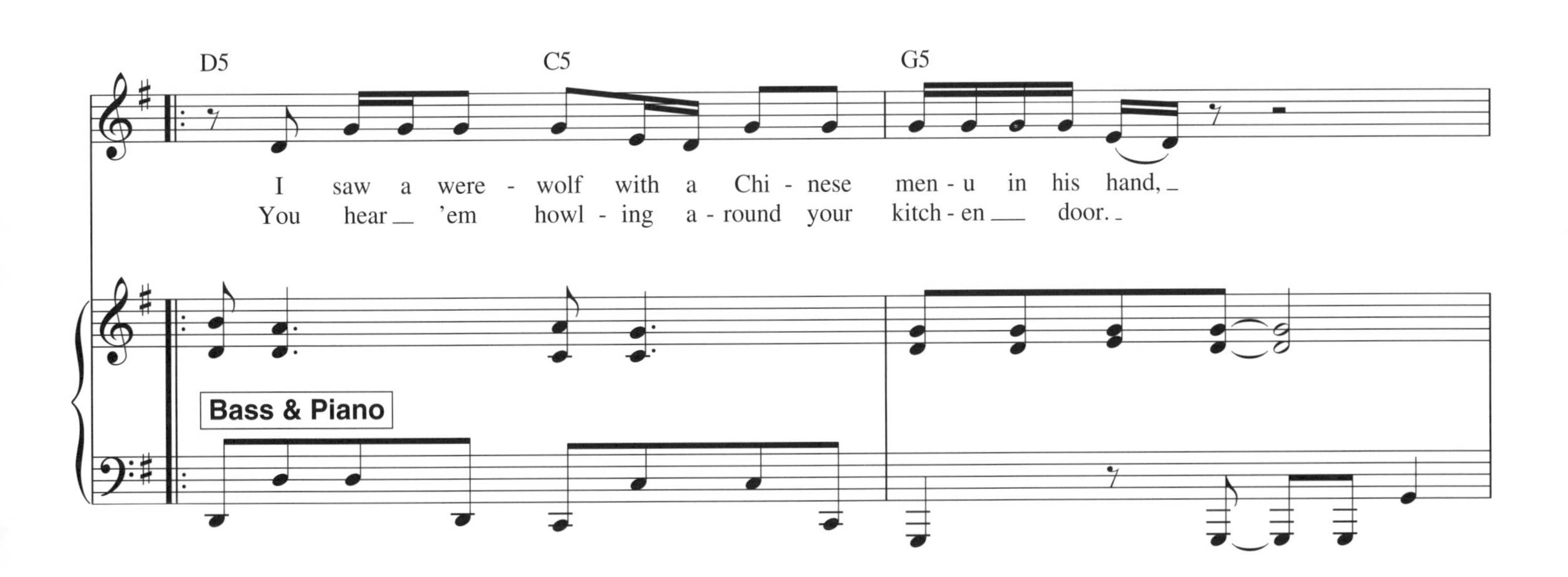

D5
C5
G5
He was look-ing for the place called Lee Ho Fook's
Lit-tle old la-dy got mu-ti-lat-ed late last night.
D5
C5
G5
D5
C5
for to get a big dish of beef chow mein.
Were-wolves of Lon-don a-gain.
Ow-ooh,
G5
D5
C5
G5
were-wolves of Lon-don.
Ow-ooh.
D5
C5
G5
D5
C5
Ow-ooh,
were-wolves of Lon-don.
Ow-ooh.

1
G5
2
G5
Guitar Solo
D5
C5
1-3
G5
4
G5
Vocal
D5
C5
Solo ends
He's the hair - y - hand-ed gent who
Well, I saw Lon Cha - ney walk-
G5
D5
C5
ran a - muck in Kent.
- ing with the queen,
Late - ly he's been o - ver - heard in May -
do - ing the were - wolves of Lon - don.
G5
D5
C5
fair.
You bet - ter stay a - way from him,
I saw Lon Chan - ey Jun - ior

G5
D5
C5
he'll rip your lungs out, Jim.
I'd like to meet his tail - or.
walk - ing with the queen,
do - ing the were - wolves of Lon - don.
To Coda
G5
D5
C5
G5
Ow - ooh,
were - wolves of Lon - don.
D5
C5
G5
D5
C5
Ow - ooh.
Ow - ooh,
G5
D5
C5
G5
D.S. al Coda
were - wolves of Lon - don.
Ow - ooh.

CODA
D5
C5
G5
I saw a were - wolf drink - ing a pi - ña co - la - da at Trad - er Vick's.
His hair was per - fect Dit.
Ow - ooh,
were - wolves of Lon - don.
Repeat and Fade
Optional Ending
Ow - ooh.

Takin' Care of Business

Words and Music by
Randy Bachman

Vocal
C7
C
B♭7
(1.,3.) They get up ev - 'ry morn - in' from the a - larm clock's warn - in', take the
(2.) eas - y as ___ fish - in', you could be a mu - si - cian if
F7
C7
eight fif - teen in - to the cit - y. There's a whis - tle up a - bove and peo - ple
you could make sounds loud or mel - low. Get a sec - ond - hand gui - tar, ___ chanc - es
B♭7
F7
C7
push - in', peo - ple shov - in' and the girls who try to look pret - ty. And if your
are you'll go ___ far ___ if you get in with the right bunch of fel - lows. Peo - ple
B♭7
F7
train's on time, you can get to work by nine, and start your slav - in' job to get your
see you hav - in' fun, just a - ly - in' in the sun, tell them that you like it this

C7
B♭7
pay. If you ev - er get an - noyed, look at me, I'm self - em - ployed, I
way. It's the work that we a - void and we're all self - em - ployed. We
F7
C7
love to work at noth - in' all day. And I've been tak - in' care of busi - ness,
love to work at noth - in' all day. And we've been
8va
B♭7
F7
ev - 'ry day. Tak - in' care of busi - ness,
(8va)
C7
B♭7
ev - 'ry way. (1.,3.) I've been tak - in' care of busi - ness, it's all mine. Tak -
(2.) We've been
8va

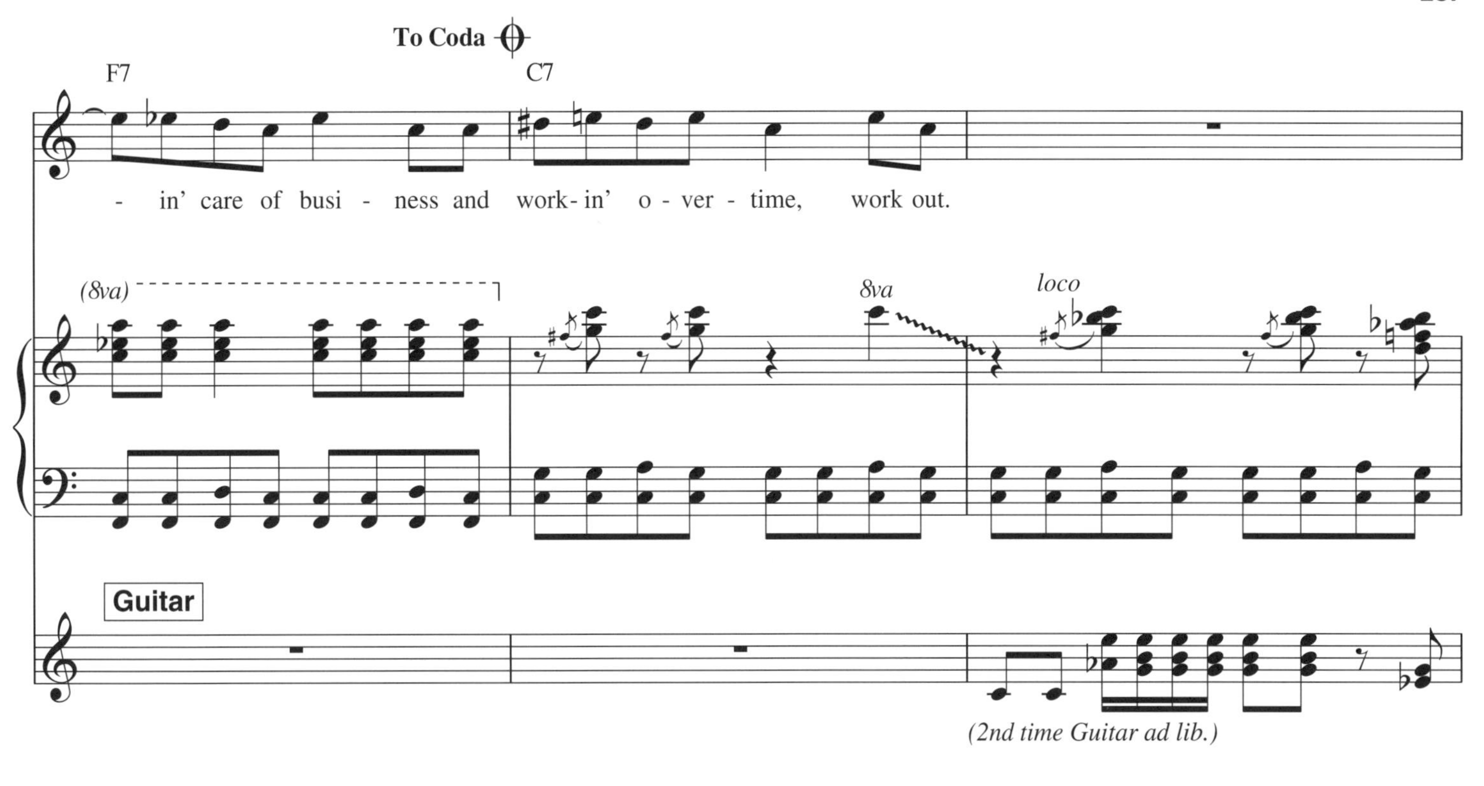
To Coda
F7
C7
- in' care of busi - ness and work-in' o - ver - time, work out.
(8va)
8va
loco
Guitar
(2nd time Guitar ad lib.)

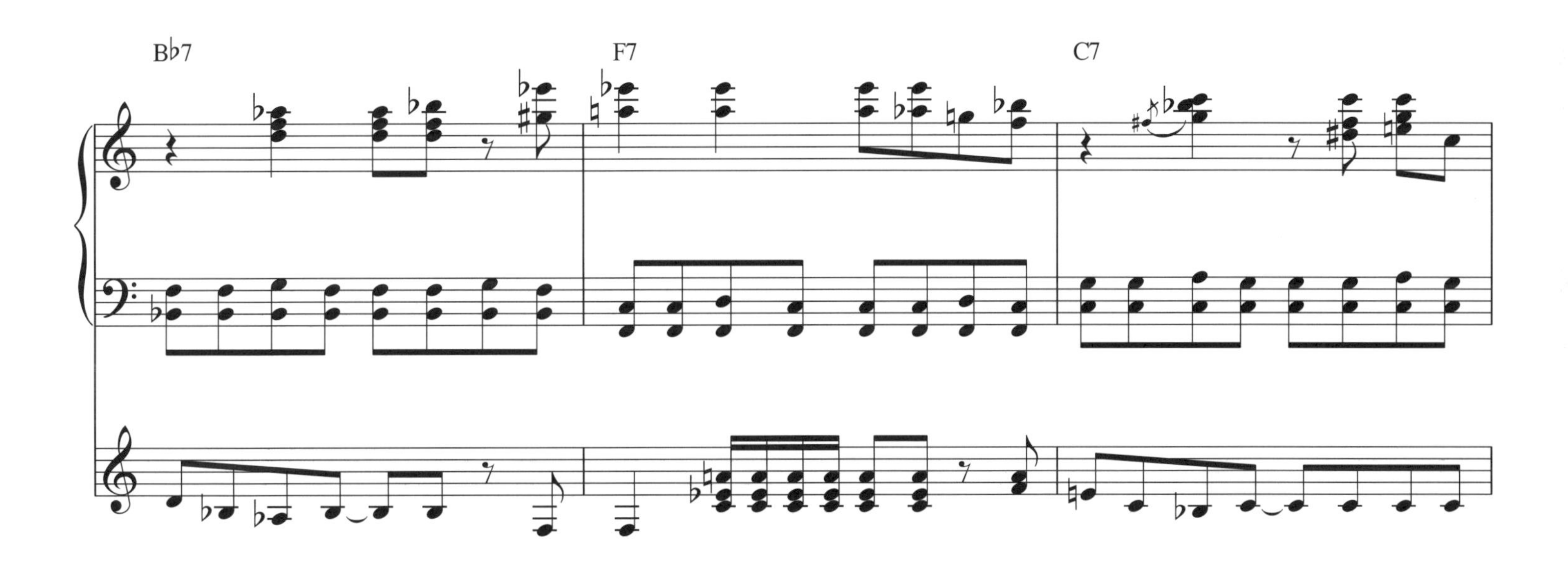
B♭7
F7
C7

B♭7

Vocal
F7
C7
(1st time only) There's work

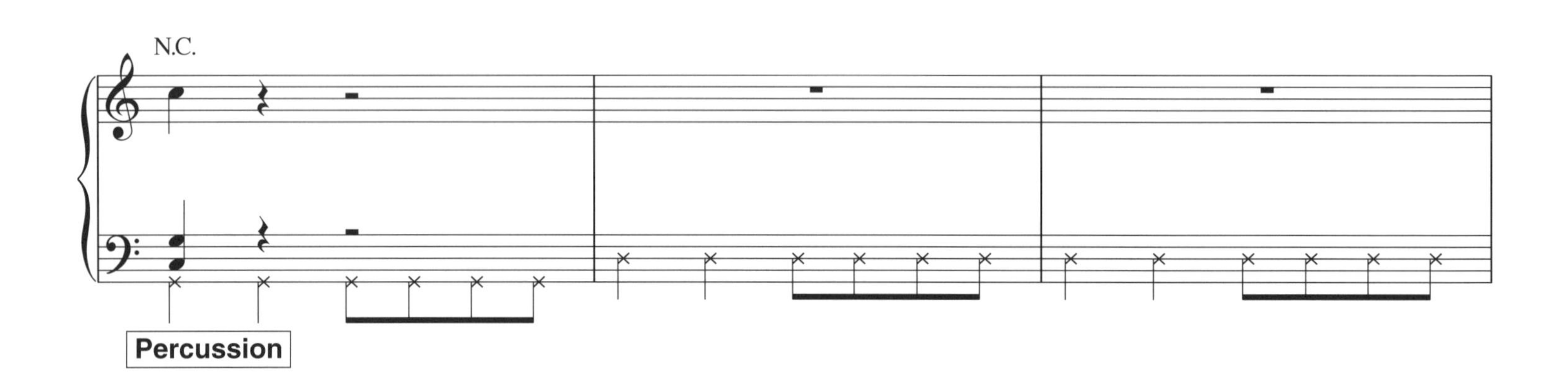
N.C.
Percussion

Guitar
C5 F5
E♭5 B♭

C5 F5
E♭5 B♭
C5 F5
Bass

8va
Piano
E♭5 B♭
C5 F5
E♭5 B♭

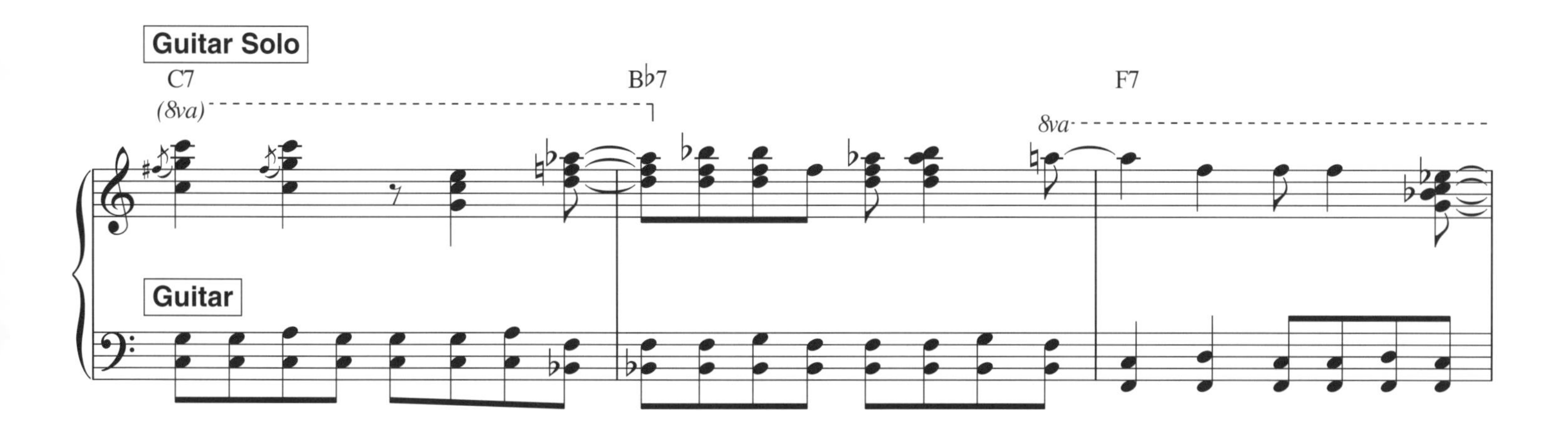
Guitar Solo
C7
(8va)
B♭7
F7
8va
Guitar

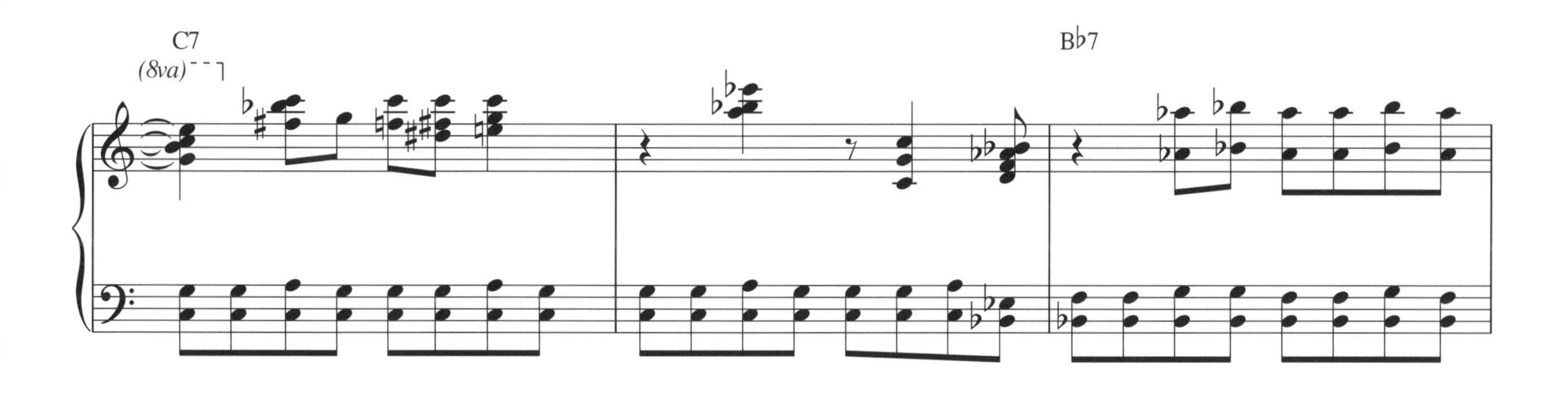
C7
(8va)
B♭7

Vocal
F7
C7
D.S. al Coda
Solo ends They

CODA
C7
work-in' o-ver-time, work out.
8va

N.C.
(8va)
Percussion
Tak - in' care of busi - ness, tak - in' care of busi - ness.
Tak - in' care of busi - ness, tak - in' care of busi - ness.
Tak -

C5
B♭5
F5
- in' care of busi - ness,
ev - 'ry day.
it's all mine.
Tak - in' care of busi - ness,
Guitar
1
C5
ev - 'ry way.
Tak -
2
C5
work - in' o - ver - time.
Piano
8va
C7
B♭7
F7
Tak - in' care of busi - ness,
- in' care of busi - ness,
tak - in' care of busi - ness.
8va
Repeat and Fade
C7
We've been tak -
Optional Ending
C7
(8va)

That's All

Words and Music by Tony Banks,
Phil Collins and Mike Rutherford

Am7 D Am7 D
and you'd say night. Tell me it's black when I know that it's white. Al-ways the same,
Am7 D E5 D
it's just a shame, and that's all. I could
G Am/G D
leave but I won't go, though my heart might tell me so. I can't
Bass
Synth.
G Gmaj7 Am/G D
feel a thing from my head down to my toes. But why does it al -

Em7 E5 D/E E5 Em7 E5 D/E E5
- ways seem to be me look-ing at you, you look-ing at me? It's al-ways the same,
Electric Piano
Em7 E5 C6/9(no3rd) D6/9(no3rd) E5
it's just a shame, that's all. Turn-ing me on,
Em7 E5 D/E E5 Em7 E5 D/E E5
turn-ing me off. Mak-ing me feel like I want too much. Liv-ing with you's
Em7 E5 C6/9(no3rd) D6/9(no3rd) E5
just a - put-ting me through it all of the time. Run-ning a - round,

Am7
D
Am7
D
staying out all night, taking it all 'stead of taking one bite. Living with you's
Bass
Synth.

Am7
D
E5
D
just a-putting me through it all of the time. But I could

G
Am/G
D
leave, but I won't go. Well, it'd be easier, I know. I can't

G
Gmaj7
Am/G
D
feel a thing from my head down to my toes.
But
So
why does it al-

Em7
E5
D/E
E5
Em7
E5
D/E
E5
-ways seem to be me look-ing at you, you, look-ing at me? It's al-ways the same,
Electric Piano

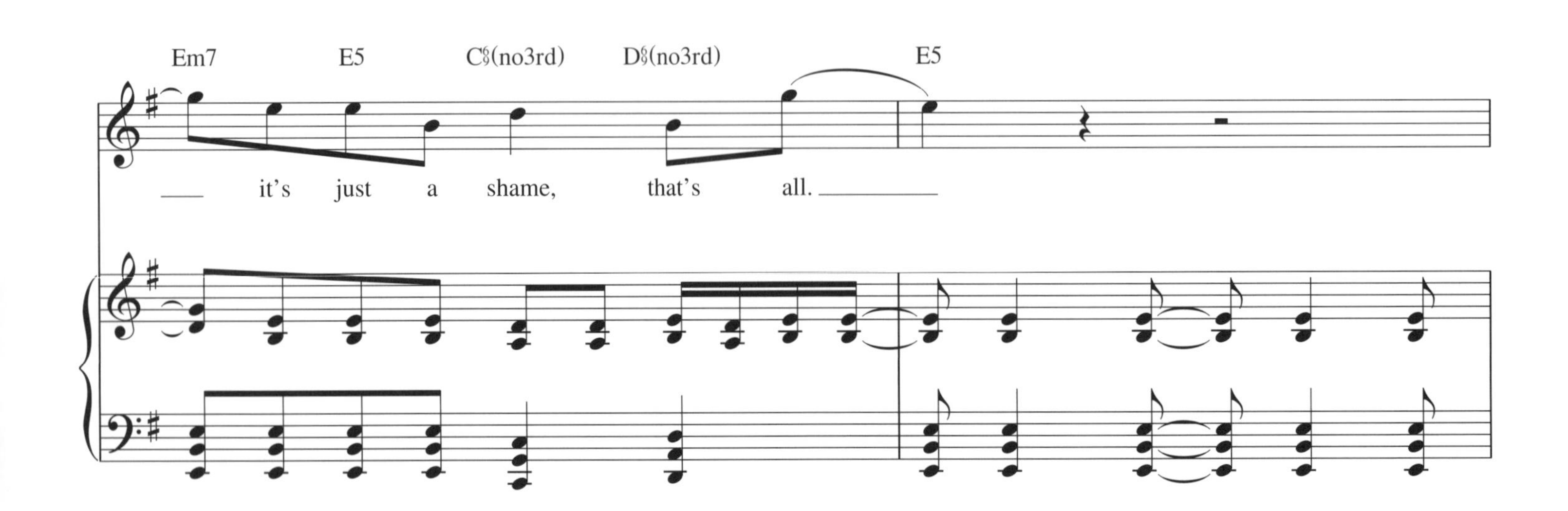
Em7
E5
C%(no3rd)
D%(no3rd)
E5
it's just a shame, that's all.

C5
Truth is,
But
I love you more than I want-ed to. There's no point in try-ing
Saxophone & Electric Piano
Bass
Organ
Em
C5
to pre-tend. There's been no one who makes me feel like you do.
To Coda
Em
Say we'll be to-geth-er till the end.
Synth.

Electric Piano
Em7
E5
D/E
E5
Em7
E5
D/E
E5
Electric Piano

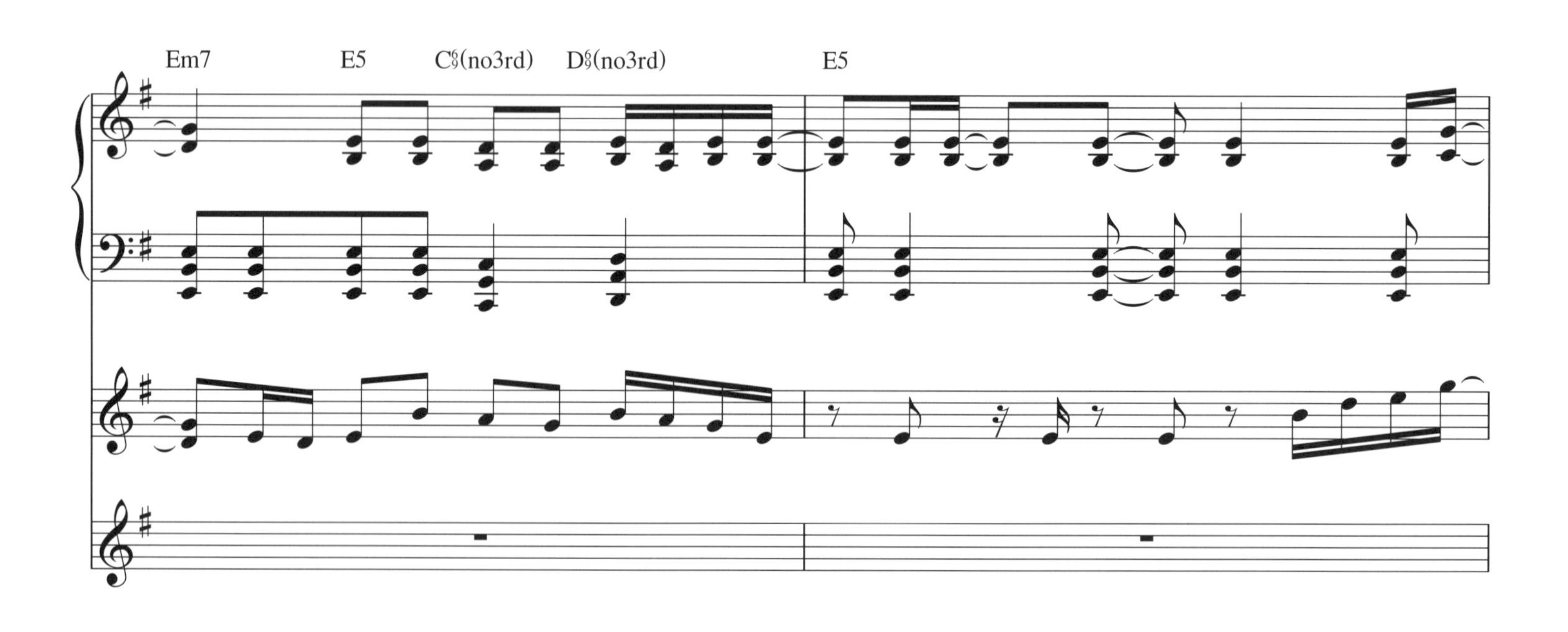
Em7
E5
C(no3rd)
D(no3rd)
E5

Am7
D
Am7
D
Bass

D.S. al Coda
Am7
D
E5
D
But I could
CODA
Em
Em7
E5
D/E
till the end. But just as I thought it was go-ing al - right, I found out I'm wrong
Electric Piano
Em7
E5
D/E
E5
Em7
E5
C𝄋(no3rd)
D𝄋(no3rd)
when I thought I was right. It's al-ways the same it's just a shame, that's all.

E5
Am7
D
Well, I could say day and you'd say night. Tell me it's black
Bass
Synth.
Am7
D
Am7
D
E5
when I know that it's white. It's al-ways the same, it's just a shame, that's all.
E5
Em7
E5
D/E
E5
Em7
E5
D/E
E5
That's all.
Electric Piano
Organ

Em7
E5
C5(no3rd)
D5(no3rd)
E5
Am7
D
Bass
Am7
D
Repeat and Fade
Am7
D
E5
Optional Ending
Am7
D
E5

A Whiter Shade of Pale

Words and Music by Keith Reid
and Gary Brooker

The Organ part has been arranged to be playable by one keyboard.
An Acoustic Piano comps throughout.

G G/F Em G/D C Em/B
I was feel - ing kind of sea - sick; the crowd called out
Am C/G F Am/E Dm F/C
for more. The room was hum-ming hard - er
G G/F Em G/D C Em/B
as the ceil - ing flew a - way, when we called out for an-
Am C/G F Am/E Dm7 G13
oth - er drink; the wait - er brought a tray. And so it
cresc.

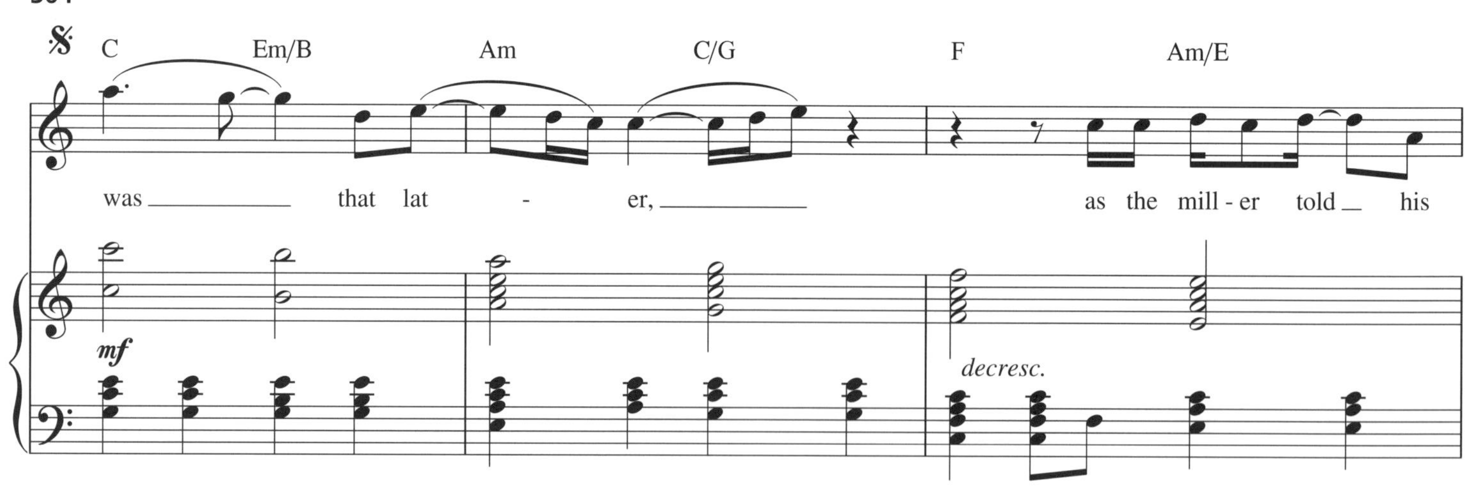

C Em/B Am C/G F Am/E
was that lat - er, as the mill - er told his
mf
decresc.

Dm F/C G G/F Em G7/D
tale, that her face, at first just ghost - ly, turned a
mp

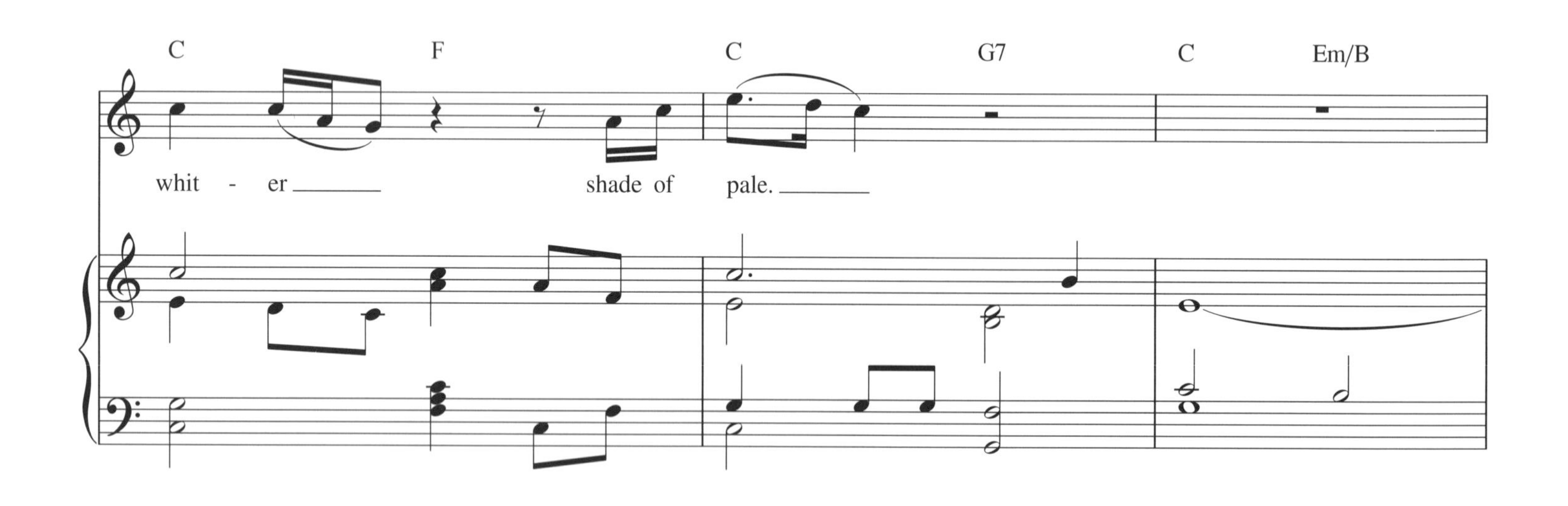

C F C G7 C Em/B
whit - er shade of pale.

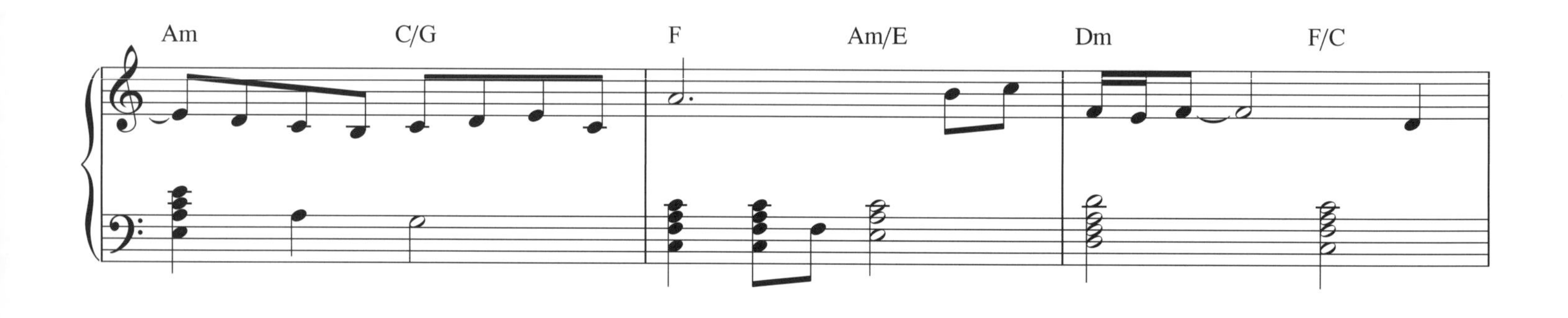

Am C/G F Am/E Dm F/C

G G/F Em G7/D C F
Vocal
G F/A G7 C Em/B Am C/G
She said, "There is no rea - son,
F Am/E Dm F/C G G/F
and the truth is plain to see."
But I wan - dered through my play -
Em G/D C Em/B Am C/G
- ing cards,
would not let her be

F Am/E Dm F/C G G/F
one of six - teen ves - tal vir - gins who were leav ing for the coast.
3
Em G/D C Em/B Am C/G
And al-though my eyes were o - pen,
F Am/E Dm7 G13 C Em/B
they might just as well been closed. And so it was lat -
3
cresc.
mf
Am C/G F Am/E Dm F/C
- er, as the mill - er told his tale,
decresc.

To Optional Coda
G
G/F
Em
G7/D
C
F
that her face, at first just ghost - ly,
turned a whit - er
shade of
mp
C
G7
C
Em/B
Am
C/G
F
Am/E
pale.
Dm
F/C
G
G/F
Em
G7/D
C
F
G
G13
D.S. and Fade
And so it
Optional Coda
C
F
C
whit - er
shade of
pale.

Woman from Tokyo

Words and Music by Ritchie Blackmore, Ian Gillan,
Roger Glover, Jon Lord and Ian Paice

(Organ)
G5 A5
G A
G A
A/E E A/E E
gliss.
A/E E A/E E
gliss.
A/E E A/E E
gliss.
Vocal
A/E E A/E E
G F/G
Fly into the ris - in' sun.
gliss.
G F/G G
Fac - es smil - in' ev - 'ry - one. Yeah, she is a
F/G G
whole new tra - di - tion. Ow! I feel it in my heart!
3
A/E E A/E E A/E E A/E E
My wo - man from To - ky - o, she makes me see.
gliss.

A/E E A/E E A/E E A/E
My wom-an from To - ky - o, she's so good
gliss.
E G F/G
to me. Talk a-bout her like a queen
G F/G G
danc - ing in an east - ern dream. Yeah, she makes me
F/G G
feel like a riv-er. Ow! That car-ries me a - way.
A/E E A/E E A/E E A/E E
My wom-an from To - ky - o, she makes me see.
A/E E A/E E A/E E A/E
My wom-an from To - ky - o, she's so good

E
A
to me.
When I'm at home and I
I just don't be - long.
Gm7
Piano
G
So far a - way from the
gar - den we love.
F
3

G
She is what moves in the soul of a
F
dove.
G
Ooh
ooh
ooh.
F
3
3

G
Soon I shall see just how
F
black was my night.
G
When we're a - lone in her cit - y of

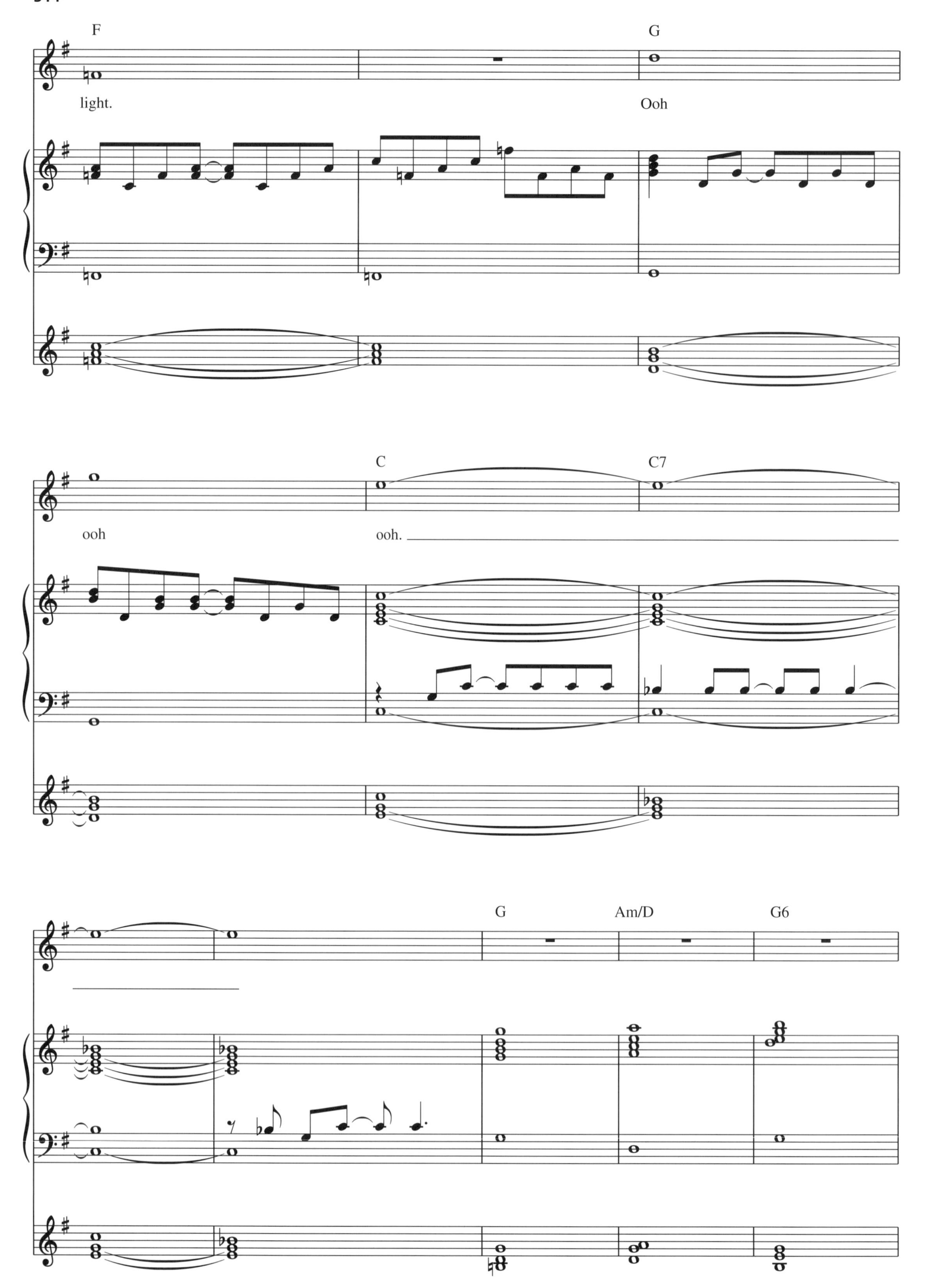
F
G
light.
Ooh
ooh
C
C7
ooh.
G
Am/D
G6

Am/E
Bm/D
C
D11
G
dim.
dim.
mp
mp
(Organ) A/E
E
A/E
E
f
gliss.
G
F/G
Ris - in' from the ne - on gloom.
Shin - in' like a cra - zy moon.
3
Yeah, she turns me on like a fire.
Ow!
I get

A/E E A/E E
high!
My wom-an from To - ky - o,
A/E E A/E E
she makes me see.
A/E E A/E E
My wom-an from To - ky - o,
A/E E A/E E
she's so good to me.
B E/B B A D/A A
(Piano)
gliss.
f
E
B E/B B E/B A D/A A
E

E
B E/B B E/B A D/A A
E
B E/B B A D/A A C
A/E E A/E
My wom - an from To -
gliss,

E
A/E
E
A/E
E
ky - o,
she makes me see.
gliss.
A/E
E
A/E
E
A/E
E
A/E
My wom - an from To - ky - o,
she's so good
E
A/E
E A/E
E
to me.
(Piano)
gliss.
A/E
E
A/E
E
My wom - an from To - ky - o.

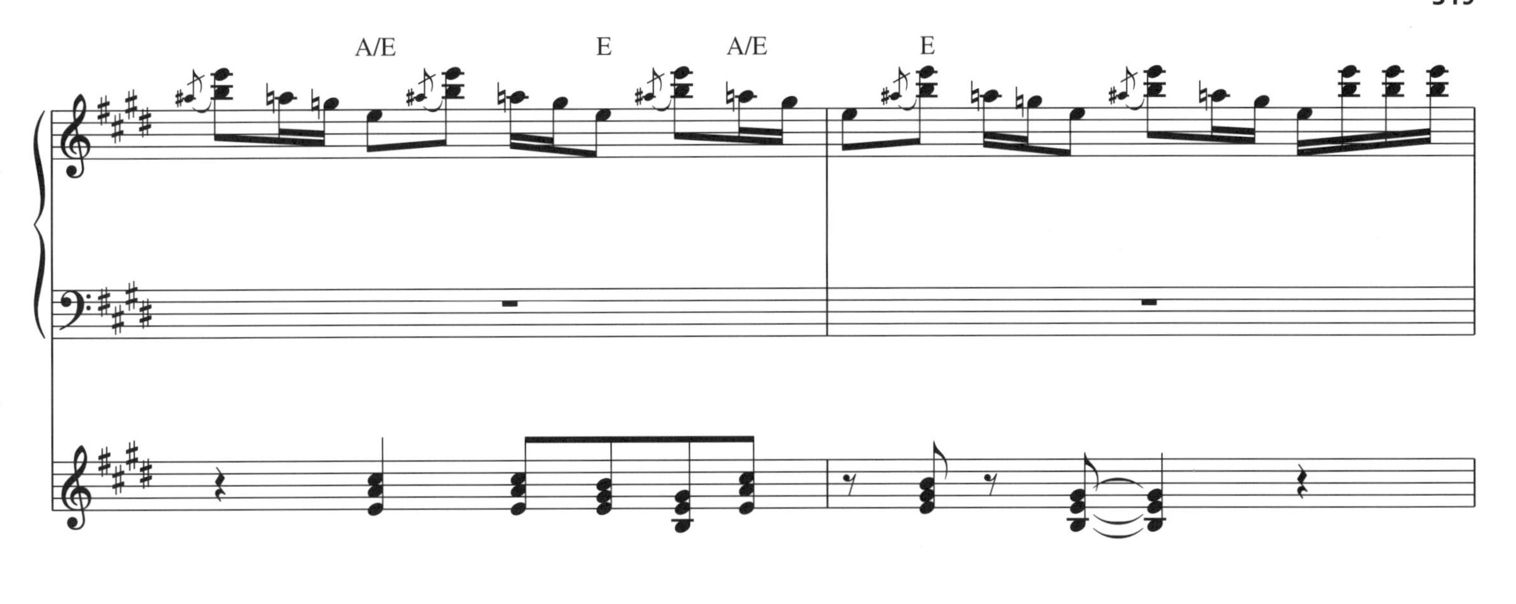
A/E
E
A/E
E

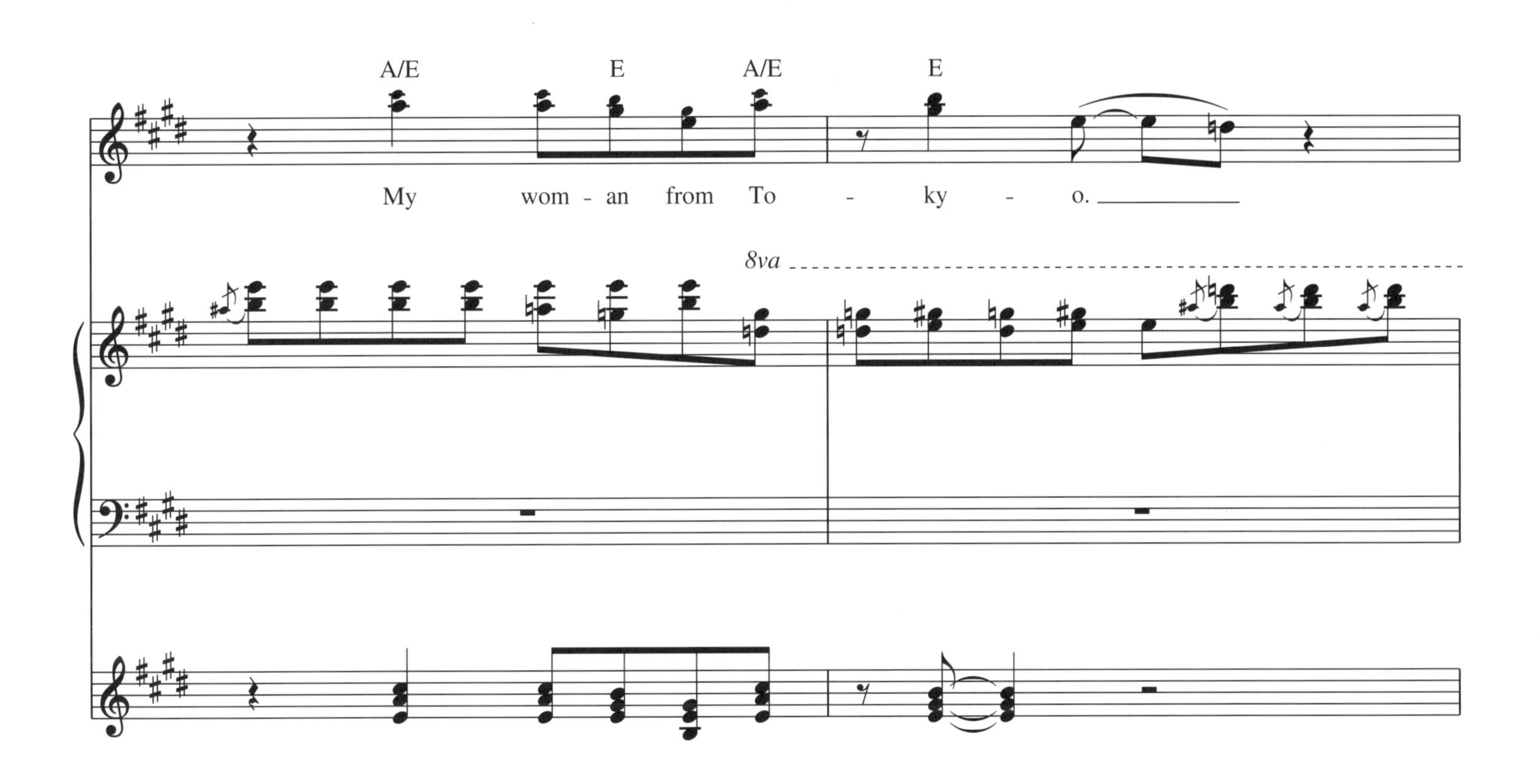
A/E
E
A/E
E
My wom - an from To - ky - o.
8va

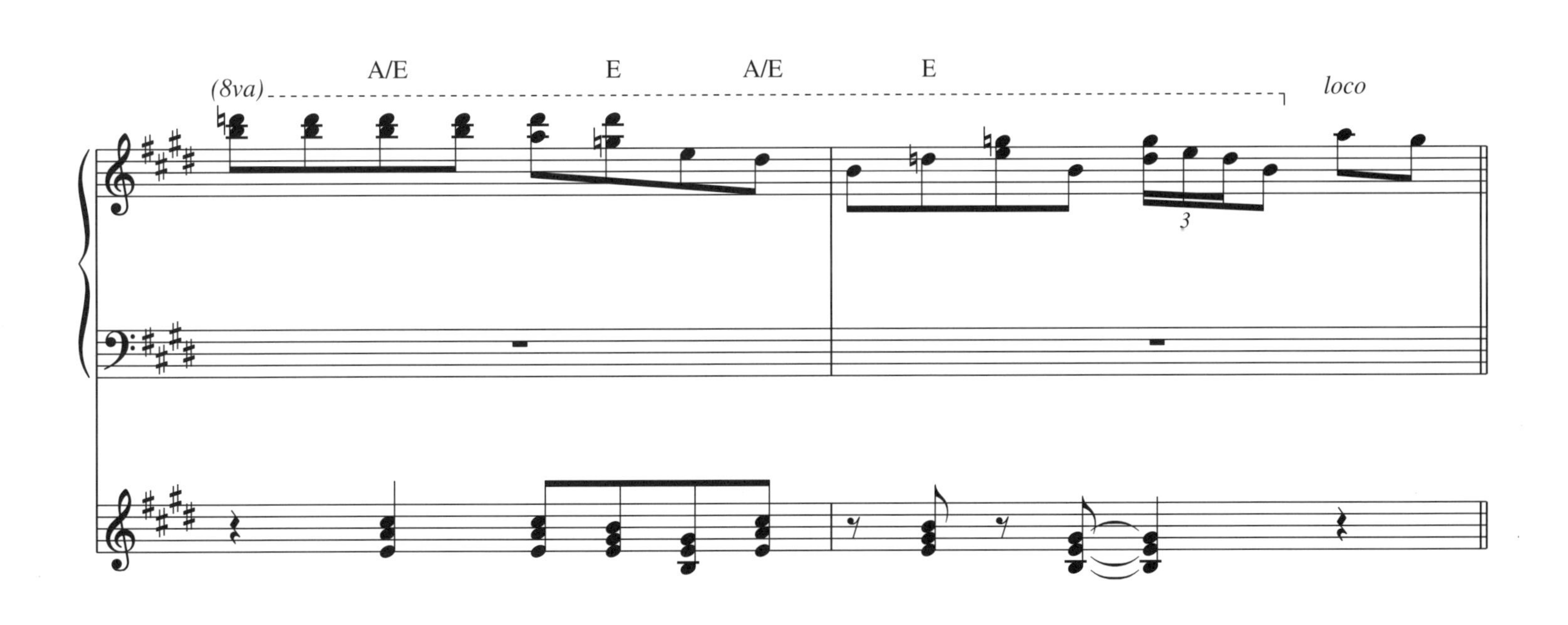
(8va)
A/E
E
A/E
E
loco
3

A/E
E
A/E
My woman from To - ky - o.
A/E
E
A/E
E
Repeat and Fade
gliss.
Optional Ending
A/E
E
A/E
E